NADAL
THE BIOGRAPHY

TOM OLDFIELD

KT-162-674

JB
JOHN BLAKE

Published by John Blake Publishing Ltd,
3 Bramber Court, 2 Bramber Road,
London W14 9PB, England

www.johnblakepublishing.co.uk

www.facebook.com/Johnblakepub facebook
twitter.com/johnblakepub twitter

First published in hardback in 2009
Published in paperback in 2010
This edition published in 2014

ISBN: 978 1 78219 909 0

British Library Cataloguing-in-Publication Data:

A catalogue record for this book is available from the British Library.

Design by www.envydesign.co.uk

Printed and bound in Great Britain by CPI Group (UK) Ltd

3 5 7 9 10 8 6 4

Papers used by John Blake Publishing are natural, recyclable products
made from wood grown in sustainable forests. The manufacturing processes
conform to the environmental regulations of the country of origin.

Every attempt has been made to contact the relevant copyright-holders,
but some were unobtainable. We would be grateful if the appropriate
people could contact us.

To my son. Looking forward to
all the family adventures ahead!

In memory of Gran and Nain.

ACKNOWLEDGEMENTS

This book could not have come about without the input and support of numerous people and I want to take this opportunity to show my appreciation for that.

I would like to thank Vicky McGeown, Allie Collins and Chris Mitchell at Blake Publishing for their hard work in making this book a reality.

I am grateful for the support from Alex Evans, Dave Supperstone, Shaun Emmerson, Matthew Caunt, Dan Ritter, Faye Bradbury, Beth Warner, Lucy Meyer, Masha Meyer-Higgins and the whole Nottingham family.

I would like to thank Patrick Kendrick, Alex Tofts, Akbar Shah, Nick Rogerson and Dave Weston for all their encouragement along the way.

I want to mention the kindness of Betty and Mike Mastrocola and family, the co-operation and good humour of my work colleagues and the generous contributions from Jeremy Bates and Richard Bloomfield.

Most important of all, I am indebted to my family and my wife, Melissa. Mum and Dad, thank you for setting me on the path to a writing career, for believing in me and providing the perfect foundation from which to chase my dreams. Matt, you're the best brother anyone could wish for - I was very lucky to grow up with a brother as sports mad as me!

And Melissa - thank you for all your love and support. Our journey together has been so special and there is so much more to come!

CONTENTS

INTRODUCTION

Rafael Nadal's arrival on the tennis scene changed the face of the sport forever. A breath of fresh air, a long-awaited rival for Roger Federer and a humble, friendly presence, Nadal seemed to be a heaven-sent gift. And it is the gift that keeps on giving.

With 13 Grand Slams under his belt before his 29th birthday, the case can be made - without exaggeration - that the Spaniard is both the greatest tennis of all-time and the greatest athlete alive today. His resume speaks for itself, including bumper seasons in 2008, 2010 and 2013 as he rose to the top of the tennis mountain, smashing countless records along the way. But it has been a rollercoaster ride of emotions, from the highs of Grand Slam victories to the lows of injury heartbreak. Backed by his close-knit family and trusted support team, Rafa has shown a remarkable ability to endure setbacks and bounce back even stronger.

Brought up in the relaxed environment of Mallorca, Nadal was a driven young man with a hunger to succeed. Early sporting flair gave indications of his potential and he was soon winning tournaments across the region.

Drilled relentlessly by his uncle Toni, his lifelong coach, Rafa began his relentless march towards a career as a professional tennis player and hours of practice paid dividends as he entered the ATP tour, aged just 15.

He has never looked back since. Adapting to the jet-setting life of a modern day sportsman, Nadal learnt many lessons during his first year among the world's best as he came to terms with the rigorous schedule and ever-changing surroundings.

His game was honed on the clay courts of Mallorca and this was the surface on which he announced himself. In 2005, Rafa shot into the media spotlight by winning the French Open at the first attempt. And this was just the beginning. He went on to make Roland Garros his own patch, winning there in 2013 to make it eight French Open titles in nine years.

Billed as a clay court specialist, Rafa endeavoured to ditch this tag, seeking improved performances on grass and hard court. This meant more hours of intense training. A Wimbledon final appearance in 2006 showed that the practice was paying off. Federer was too strong that day but Nadal was back for a second attempt the following year, only for the Swiss to reign supreme again.

The pair had soon developed one of the greatest rivalries in sports history. Clearly, they have great respect for each other but out on the court they are programmed to win. Federer held the edge on grass, Nadal was untouchable on clay.

The Swiss was beaten by Rafa in the French Open finals of

2006, 2007 and 2008. Nadal, though, managed to break Federer's stranglehold on the Wimbledon title with the greatest performance of his career in 2008. An epic five-set marathon saw the Spaniard prevail in what will go down in history as one of the finest tennis matches ever played.

Two Grand Slams out of three meant Rafa's year was going exceptionally well thus far. But he had another trick up his sleeve as he headed to the Olympics in Beijing and returned with the gold medal, fulfilling a childhood dream.

Furthermore, Nadal's brilliant run of results saw him close in on Federer and overtake the Swiss after the Olympics to become world number one. A disappointing end to 2008, in part due to a troublesome knee injury, could not detract from some staggering achievements.

Nadal then overcame his injury layoff and heroically added the 2009 Australian Open to his trophy cabinet in another spectacular final with Federer, inching ever closer to a complete set of Grand Slams.

But 2009 will be remembered more for Nadal's injury and off-court woes than his on-court efforts. Robin Soderling pulled off a stunning upset over Rafa in the French Open – the Spaniard's first ever loss there – before knee problems sidelined Nadal for Wimbledon. Rafa's return just before the US Open was a relief for tennis fans but he looked short of his best and ended the year with a string of losses in London. His parents' separation that year hit Nadal hard and his struggle to come to terms with the news played a large part in his disappointing results.

Yet one of Nadal's greatest strengths is his ability to endure adversity and hit back harder. He shrugged off the injury doubts to retain his French Open crown in 2010 and finally conquer the US Open, completing a career Grand Slam at the age of 24. This remarkable achievement puts him in elite company.

With Novak Djokovic emerging as the new threat to Nadal's supremacy, Rafa had to settle for another Roland Garros triumph in 2011 before more knee problems derailed his 2012 season, snatching away his Olympic dream in the process.

True to form, these setbacks inspired Rafa to reach another level in 2013, capturing the French Open and US Open to take his Grand Slam haul to 13.

While health issues continue to be the dark cloud hanging over Nadal's future in tennis, the Spaniard is still a couple of years away from his 30th birthday and has Federer's record of 17 Grand Slam titles in his sights.

2014 promises to be another special year for Rafa as he adds to his trophy cabinet and inches closer to cementing the Greatest of All-time tag.

CHAPTER 1

TAKING THE FIRST STEPS TO THE TOP

Rafael Nadal's journey to becoming the best tennis player on the planet and Mallorca's favourite son has been a story of hard graft and indestructible confidence, dating back to his earliest days.

He was born on June 3, 1986 in Manacor, Mallorca to parents Sebastian Nadal and Ana Maria Parera and grew up in the town with his parents and younger sister Maria Isabel. The family unit, with the Nadals all living in close proximity in Mallorca, was always special for Rafa and being part of such a tight-knit group was an important aspect of his childhood.

His parents worked hard to provide a happy environment – Sebastian in charge of a glass factory, (and later a range of entrepreneurial efforts) Ana Maria as a beautician before raising the children. They nurtured their son's talents but always kept him grounded. This approach has ensured that Nadal is as popular for his modest, friendly demeanour as he is for his outstanding displays on the court.

It was immediately clear that Rafa was a natural sportsman as he began playing tennis aged three. And it came as little surprise considering the sporting prowess of his family. His uncle Miguel Angel Nadal, played football for Real Mallorca, Barcelona and Spain, earning the nickname 'The Beast of Barcelona' for the intensity and physicality of his playing style. Meanwhile, another of his uncles, Toni, quickly became involved as Rafa's tennis coach.

The story behind Nadal's decision to become a left-handed player has frequently been attributed to Toni's insistence that this approach would bring greater benefit for the youngster's prospects. But the Spaniard dispelled that myth in his autobiography, Rafa, explaining: 'The truth is that I began playing when I was very small, and because I wasn't strong enough to hit the ball over the net, I'd hold the racquet with both hands, on the forehand as well as the backhand. Then one day my uncle said, "There are no professional players who play with two hands and we're not going to be the first ones, so you've got to change.' So I did, and what came naturally to me was to play left-handed.

Rafa recalled one of his uncle's early lectures – on not throwing his racquet in dismay – when speaking to *Sport Magazine*: 'My uncle told me when I was a child that if I did it, he would stop coaching me. He said that, if I make a bad shot, it is not the racquet's fault – it is mine. Therefore, I should not take my failings out on the racquet.'

As is so often the case with future sporting stars, Nadal threw himself into every challenge as a youngster, across a range of sports. His will to win was evident to all and he had a seemingly endless supply of energy. By the age of five he was having tennis practices several times a week. And, aged just eight, he bagged the regional tennis championships for under 12s. He was on a roll. Before long, his day was totally dedicated to sport. As Alison Kervin explained in the *Sunday Times*, by the time he was 13 he played tennis every day. He went to school from 9am until noon, then played tennis, had lunch and returned for afternoon classes. Rafa usually then found time for another two hours of tennis in the evenings to complete an active yet exhausting day.

Rafa showed particular ability at football as well as tennis as a boy and he probably had the talent to pursue either career professionally as he excelled at both, attracting attention from scouts. But Sebastian and Ana Maria ensured that Rafa remained level-headed. Ana Maria told the *Daily Express*: 'I can see how a boy in Rafa's position could let things go to his head. But from an early age we taught him he wasn't that important. He's good at tennis but being a tennis player is a job like any other.' His coach, Toni, was also charged with keeping to this family line. Ana Maria added: 'The first thing he did when Rafa won his first national championship as an 11-year-old was to congratulate him. The second thing was to sit him down with a list of the previous 20 or so champions in that age category and ask him how many he knew. Rafa only knew two or three.'

His parents hammered home the message that plenty of equally talented young players had thrown away their potential to be stars. They did not want to see their son waste his obvious ability when a career as a professional tennis player was opening up for him. Still playing tennis and football seriously, the time came at the age of 12 to make a choice and focus solely on one sport. His father, Sebastian, made it clear that Rafa needed to cut down on his extracurricular activities in order that his academic studies did not suffer. Nadal opted for tennis, turning his back on football but never losing his passion for the sport.

The opportunity soon arose for him to move to Barcelona to further his chances of making the grade in the tennis world. But his parents felt his education would suffer and, with other family members adding their support to the idea of Rafa remaining in Manacor, the decision was made. The only downside to rejecting the switch to Barcelona was that Nadal would now receive less support from the Spanish tennis federation. Life was good for Rafa. He was extremely popular, making friends easily at school, and he has kept up many of these friendships to this day. When he is able to return home, he likes nothing more than to catch up with friends.

He was very happy in Manacor. To some, a switch to Barcelona might have been a chance of a lifetime but Rafa was in no rush to leave Mallorca. Manacor, the second largest town in Mallorca after the capital Palma, is famous for its artificial pearl industry as well as local sweets and a wide range of arts and crafts. But it would soon be adding tennis at the top of that list. The island boasts a huge selection of beaches – over 70 of them – and offered perfect spots for relaxing in between tennis practice. The laid back way of life suited the young Nadal and made him an easy-going person. Looking back on the joys of the island where he grew up, he told the press: 'Majorca is my favourite place in the world, as I have my family and my friends there, and that's where I grew up. I am still close to the friends I went to school with on the island.

'Some of them are studying now, one is a tennis coach, another is a painter – he paints houses, not pictures. I feel like a normal person. I go fishing with my friends and go to play golf. I go out with friends to parties.'

As he won more and more youth trophies, the profile of tennis grew in Mallorca – and it shot off the charts thanks to Nadal's 2008 exploits. The opportunities to play tennis there are readily available. Many hotels have their own courts while there are numerous tennis centres where lessons are offered.

While he had closed the door on a potential career in football, it did not mean Rafa lost his passion for the sport. He loved Real Mallorca and Real Madrid and, of course, followed the Spanish national team fanatically. His keen interest in football often left him frustrated when tennis commitments meant he missed out on watching key games. In this regard, he had that boyish obsession with sport. It comes as a surprise to many that he does not support Barcelona – the team that his uncle Miguel played for. But Rafa set the record straight when speaking to the *Daily Mail*. He said: 'Before my uncle played for Barcelona my whole family was for Real Madrid, but when he was at Barca, we supported them. After my uncle left, we were all Real again.'

Rumour has it that Rafa was furious that rain delays pushed back one of his matches at Wimbledon in 2008 to the evening, making him miss one of Spain's Euro 2008 games. Like he has always said, behind the aura of invincibility on the court lurks a very normal person. As he later told the *Daily Telegraph*: 'My ambition is to be a very, very normal guy. A very humble guy.

To play tennis, which I love and I want to be the best. And, when I'm done, I just want to be at home with my friends.'

With Toni providing tireless coaching and tough love (to the point where there were some concerns from other family members), Rafa continued on his path towards professional tennis. There would inevitably be plenty of ups and downs along the way but Nadal could not have been better placed to have a crack at the big time. He was already becoming a force on clay courts but he had limited opportunities to hone his skills on grass courts. And with only one of the Grand Slams played on clay, Rafa knew he would have to be capable of adapting to different challenges. Going on to make his mark away from the French Open has given Rafa a lot of pleasure because his early years were not spent on a mixture of surfaces like some aspiring players.

Back in his formative years, he told the *Independent*: 'I want to do well on grass because it is a very special surface, so different to all the others. Not many players from Spain have done well there, so that is an extra motivation for me.'

He has possessed this fierce determination since his first steps on the road to tennis fame. His game continued to develop and his understanding of the tactical side of the sport improved too. As he repeatedly told the press in years to come, he did not model his game on any particular player, though he was a keen tennis fan. Instead, he developed his own style.

Nadal spoke to *Sports Illustrated* about this topic, explaining: 'People ask, "Who did you model your game after?" I never thought like that. I just played the way I was comfortable playing.'

Aged 14, Nadal gained his first chance to impress as he

faced Pat Cash, a former Wimbledon champion, in an exhibition match in Majorca. Cash was a big name and it was a great chance for Rafa to test himself against a man who had played at the very highest level. In some respects, though, he was playing without too much pressure – he was clearly the underdog and few were expecting him to last the pace. The Spaniard stepped in at the last minute after Cash's original opponent Boris Becker pulled out. It proved to be a humbling experience for Cash as Rafa produced an excellent display of clean hitting to win the match and start grabbing the nation's attention.

Nadal worked hard to balance his studies with his progress on the court. Inevitably, it was difficult to give his school work his full attention with tennis forever on his mind but he knew that having some qualifications to fall back on would be important for the years ahead. By now, Rafa was being picked out by experts as a star for the future. His family were immensely proud while his uncle took great satisfaction in the achievements of his nephew. This, though, was just the beginning. The victory over Cash, along with Nadal's domination of the youth circuit, indicated that his future was extremely bright.

Dealing with the media was something wholly new for him. But he was always courteous and generous with his time – just as he was with the autograph hunters who wanted a signature from the next big thing in tennis. Rafa grew in confidence when it came to answering questions from the press and charmed many reporters with his shy smile and his sense of humour. Those closest to him knew it would not be long before Rafa would be competing on the main circuit, taking on the best in the world. It would mean huge changes in Nadal's life and would involve sacrifices. However, the youngster clearly lived for tennis and his potential demanded that he dedicate every ounce of effort to pursuing his dream. So many youngsters would have given anything to be where he was and he was not about to let the opportunity slip through his fingers.

Rafa's prowess on the tennis court forced him to make sacrifices off it. He could not enjoy the usual teenage experiences. As is usually the case with most young athletes all over the world, Nadal had commitments and was determined to cash in on his opportunities on the court. The Spaniard had to turn his back on drinking and late night partying as he threw all his energies into making it as a professional tennis player.

His physique continued to develop, too, which aided his hard-hitting style. As well as his time on the clay courts with Toni, Nadal spent two summers at Nick Bollettieri's tennis camp in Florida. Rafa was presented with a different language and lifestyle but he got his head down and put everything into his tennis. He refined certain areas of his game and began to look forward to joining the professional circuit. Bollettieri has followed Nadal's career with great interest ever since, taking great pride in his former pupil's successes. He recalls Rafa's desire as a youngster to conquer the tennis world and the sheer brutality of his hitting. In June 2007, he heaped praise on Rafa in an article in the *Independent*. He wrote: 'Rafael Nadal is the best clay court player in the world and on course to be among the best two or three ever on that surface. But he doesn't want to be labelled that. He wants to work his ass off to win on any surface, be among the greats, period. That's what you need to remember here: he's hugely motivated to prove himself.'

And the motivation that has defined Nadal's career to date paid dividends in 2002 as he entered the ATP tour. It was a very emotional and exciting moment for Rafa and came as a real reward for all the hard work so far. He had made it this far. Now, could he make a name for himself against some of the sport's biggest stars? The young Spaniard was understandably nervous but he has never doubted his own ability on the tennis court. It was not long before he had recorded his first ATP victory, beating Ramon Delgado in Mallorca while still just 15 years of age.

This success put Rafa among rather elite company – he was only the ninth player to win an ATP match before his 16th birthday. He was becoming the talk of the tour as his progress attracted the attention of players and pundits alike. But it was still early days and Toni sought to keep his nephew's feet on the ground. There were so many pitfalls for young athletes to fall into and it was vital that Rafa did not stray from the right path.

Many young tennis players had possessed great ability yet had fallen short due to their attitude or temperament. Nadal did not want to add his name to that list. There was no doubt that, so long as he kept his focus, he could dominate the sport for years to come. For such a young player, Rafa's body was incredibly muscular, aided by his work at Bollettieri's camp. The size of his biceps, in particular the left one, were astounding and allowed him to hit with unbelievable power. Opting to wear a vest rather than a shirt, his strength was there for all to see and was a dispiriting sight for opponents. The vest also allowed him more freedom with his strokes and of course his sponsors were only too happy to promote it as a fashion item.

During 2003, Nadal moved into the top 100 in the men's singles rankings. Suddenly, he was listed alongside some players he had been watching on television just a few years earlier. He could look up the list and see the likes of Roger Federer, Andre Agassi and company. He had some way to go, of course, before he was at their level but there was a lot of encouragement in seeing these rankings. It brought home the reality of his progress but also made him more determined to continue his rise to the top. And it certainly did not unnerve him because he would finish the 2003 season in the top 50 of the rankings. Nadal was loving every minute of his purple patch and hoped to extend it into the upcoming tournaments. While he missed home, the adrenalin rush of success was very much to his liking and there was no limit to his ambition. He had jumped from the top 100 to the top 50 in no time and some of the sport's big guns were now looking over their shoulders nervously.

Being away from his family was difficult for Rafa and equally tough for Ana Maria. She told the *Daily Express*: 'Family is very important to Rafa and the support he's had from us, his grandparents and aunts and uncles have been decisive in helping him become the person he is today.' It had been a real family effort. His mother revealed how regularly Nadal was and is in contact with his family. Far from being influenced by the success he was having, Rafa supposedly even continued to ask Ana Maria's permission before buying a new pair of trousers! She also explained how the family unit operates: 'We all have our own homes and our separate lives but in winter we live together on one estate and in summer we move on to another by the coast. Rafa rings me every night wherever he is in the world and we chat for 10 to 15 minutes.'

Despite the occasional bout of homesickness, Nadal continued to blaze away on the tour, winning over new fans with strong showings in Cherbourg and Hamburg. Of course, there were still weaknesses in Rafa's game – his serve being one of them in the eyes of some pundits – but his all-round talent was incredible for a 17-year-old. Not only was he physically strong but his work with Toni had given him a real mental edge. He did not crack under pressure. He did not falter on key points or become flustered when things were not going his way.

The mental side of the game is often undervalued. Handling the ups and downs of a match was vital and Nadal had quickly learned how to cope with it. He never doubted himself on the court and, while some players went out more in hope than expectation of victory, the Spaniard was far more positive. He knew he could beat anyone.

Rafa played in his first Wimbledon tournament in 2003, still aged just 17. It was a stunning moment for him. He knew all about the history of the competition and had watched plenty of matches on television, but actually arriving at the event and walking around the courts was overwhelming. He realised that it was impossible to understand the full grandeur of the place without visiting and sampling the unique atmosphere at SW19. Playing on grass courts was something that Nadal was far from comfortable with but he threw all his efforts into making the necessary improvements. He had little experience on the surface but managed to put a few wins together, showing potential and learning valuable lessons that would prove helpful on future visits. Being part of Wimbledon was a huge honour and it really gave the Spaniard a taste for success on grass.

In the first round, the Spaniard squared off against another promising young player, Mario Ancic of Croatia. All four sets were tight but Rafa did enough to secure a 6-3, 6-4, 4-6, 6-4 victory. A first win at Wimbledon was a moment to cherish and Nadal was even surprising himself with the speed of his adjustments to the faster grass courts. Rafa then ended the dreams of Brit Lee Childs in the second round. Facing an intimidating atmosphere, the Spaniard relished the pressure of trying to silence the home supporters. It quickly became clear that there was a gulf in class between the two players as Nadal cantered to a straight-sets win – 6-2, 6-4, 6-3. He was not getting ahead of himself but was delighted to be proving people wrong with his displays so far at SW19.

However, the third round turned out to be a step too far. Facing the number 12 seed Paradorn Srichaphan, Rafa found himself trailing for the first time in the tournament and he was unable to hurt his Thai opponent, falling to a 6-4, 6-4, 6-2 defeat. The Spaniard was visibly disappointed to crash out after two solid wins.

With Federer looking dominant, Nadal knew he had a long way to go before he could be as competitive as he wanted to be at Wimbledon. Gaining experience was the most important aspect at this stage. If he learned from his mistakes and kept fine-tuning his game, Rafa felt he could be a serious contender on grass. This was the target he set himself.

An unfortunate ankle injury, picked up at the Estoril Open, slowed Rafa as the 2004 clay season began. It was the first setback of his career and he was careful not to rush back too soon. Sadly for Nadal, though, this cautious recovery came at the expense of the entire clay season. It was his specialist surface and he would have fancied his chances of bagging a number of titles. Instead, he had to endure the frustration of resting. He could not even go to practise as often as he would have liked.

He had been particularly keen to be part of the French Open, played on clay in Paris. It looked like the Grand Slam most suited to Rafa's game but he would have to wait another year before he could sample the atmosphere at Roland Garros. It would be worth the wait, though, as it would soon become a second home for Nadal.

Equally disappointing was missing out on a trip to the Olympics in Athens. The injury continued to niggle away at him and he had to accept that he would be nothing more than a spectator for this Games. It was a huge blow as he had always taken a keen interest in the Olympics and was desperate to perform on the big stage. There would, though, be other chances in the future. Rafa told Spanish newspaper *Marca*: 'It [the Olympics] was one of my main targets this year. I had it within my reach, but it won't happen and it hurts me especially to miss it.' However, Spanish Tennis Federation spokesman Pedro Hernandez revealed that Nadal could yet make a comeback in time for the 2004 Wimbledon tournament.

Remarkably, Rafa refused to treat this period as a spell for total rest. His active nature simply would not allow this and he found other ways to keep himself in shape in yet another example of his unquenchable desire to succeed. He sat on a table in the centre of a practice court and returned balls fired at him by Toni and the rest of his coaching team. As Nadal told the *Daily Telegraph*: 'I did not want to lose the feeling of playing.' Unfortunately, though, he still lost his race to make it to Wimbledon.

On the positive side, his injury allowed him to take stock and to assess his rise to fame. He was able to analyse his own game and watch plenty of tennis, looking for opponents' strengths and weaknesses. The signs were already there that Rafa would be around at the top of the tennis mountain for years to come, even if he did not see them yet. His tireless style and ability to win seemingly impossible points and games made him a fearsome opponent. The tour was a difficult and challenging place to be. With tennis being such a solitary sport and players fighting each other for spots in the rankings, it was not always possible to make friends easily. With so many different cultures and languages, there was bound to be tension and a degree of isolation. Rivalries were a natural part of any competitive sport and it was unrealistic to think that all the players would get on well with each other.

Being a part of the circuit was a wonderful experience, but also a tough environment for a young player to enter. Nadal was happy to have Toni to turn to at these times. Out on the court, he was alone and he thrived on the challenge of being in control of his own destiny. But the rest of the time it was important to be surrounded by familiar faces. Jeremy Bates, a mixed doubles winner at Wimbledon and the Australian Open during his career, agreed that young players often took time to come to terms with the locker room set-up. He explained:

'Youngsters can be intimidated by the best players. You are travelling around the world, meeting different races, cultures and languages. It takes a while to make your mark on the tour. You have to earn your place before you can get to the point where you are conversing with the top players.'

As Rafa admitted in an interview with *The Sunday Times*, Toni was a key figure throughout his progress into a professional tennis player. He said: 'I think that having my uncle and coach with me has been the best for me. He is uncle first and coach second. It is a nicer life to travel round with your uncle there. My family can't come to all matches, but I always have my family there in my uncle. I realise how lucky I am. We are a team – my uncle, me and my physical trainer. We work together.'

While other leading players including Lleyton Hewitt, Andy Roddick and Roger Federer would see coaches come and go, Rafa gained great stability from his uncle always being in his corner. Toni would be a huge factor as his nephew took on the world's best. Fortunately, Nadal's success meant that he usually had a next match to think about and plan for. Rafa worked on the idea that he should not stray from his own game and should instead let his opponent worry about handling his own weapons. However, he also liked to leave no stone unturned in his preparation.

Toni taught him that he could take positives from his performances, even in defeat. Rafa was gradually taking this on board and he told *The Sunday Times*: 'My uncle keeps saying that losing is important in this game. If you play tennis, you lose, that's how it is. Only one person can win every game in a tournament. No one man can win every tournament. The best players lose; everybody loses some time. I am learning that lesson, but I do feel much more nervous when I come out to play after having lost. Every week is a different place, a different tournament. You learn that losing is part of this game. But winning – ah, winning is so much nicer.'

Even though there were a number of other Spaniards on the tour such as Carlos Moya and David Ferrer, it was easy to feel lonely on tour and Rafa had to learn quickly how to stay occupied while travelling from city to city. Yes, he was seeing the sights of some of the most amazing places but he was constantly on the move and was living out of a suitcase. It was impossible to feel settled. But he soon struck up a friendship with Moya, who played a vital role in taking Rafa under his wing as the youngster began life on the tour. The pair often met for dinner and Nadal would usually phone his fellow Spaniard before finalising his travel arrangements for whichever tournament appeared next on the schedule. Rafa much preferred to travel with friends and sought to do so whenever possible.

He told *The Sunday Times*: 'It's more fun always to have friends and family around, isn't it? I like to have lots of people around – for eating, for flying. Always.' At this stage, Rafa still struggled with the English language, though he worked hard to improve. He added: 'Sorry my English not so good. I only speak quarter of English. Maybe quarter of a quarter. Not good.' It was easy to see why fans worldwide were besotted with the young star when he possessed this modesty and charm.

Toni's English was no better but he managed to tell *The Sunday Times* that Rafa was a good boy who worked hard and looked after people. This was exactly what his parents had hoped for when they took a tough stance to ensure he kept his feet on the ground. Nadal had matured into a humble, well-rounded young man and he was making his family proud with his achievements on and off the court. It all justified the decision to snub the move to Barcelona.

Rafa kept his focus firmly on his tennis. Such an approach led fellow Spaniard Pau Gasol, an NBA basketball player with the Los Angeles Lakers, to say: 'Rafael is so intense when he plays but really, he's just a laid-back kid having a great time.' Gasol, formerly of the Memphis Grizzlies, was playing in LA alongside talisman Kobe Bryant, who Nadal would see first hand at the Olympics further down the line.

But while he gave every ounce of energy when he was on the court, Rafa tried to make good use of his time off, picking out golf and fishing as two of his favourite hobbies. He told the *Daily Telegraph*: 'It's a funny thing, you think, that I go fishing? Yes, but I love to wake up early, take the boat to the middle of the sea, see the sunrise, be there calm and quiet.'

Nadal never really got caught up in the celebrity trap. He was well aware that he was a tennis player first and foremost and he shrugged off the idea of being a fashion icon when speaking to the *Daily Telegraph*, saying: 'No, no I don't believe in anything like that. That is not my style. In the bathroom, in the morning, I take very, very little time.'

His reputation in his homeland was soaring and the nation watched on expectantly as Rafa looked to add more singles success. But Davis Cup tennis was also drawing Nadal's attention. He was proud to represent his country and even prouder to help Spain clinch a famous victory over the United

States. Despite his fine performances thus far in his short career, his inclusion in the team for the 2004 final was certainly not expected and many supporters were taken by surprise. Rafa was not yet tried and tested on the big stage but the selectors had little hesitation in throwing him into the lion's den of Davis Cup tennis.

And Nadal did not let them down. His youthful energy lifted those around him as Spain completed a brilliant victory, silencing those who had questioned his inclusion in the side. The highlight for Rafa was a brilliant performance against American star Andy Roddick. He had been preferred to popular figure Juan Carlos Ferrero for this clash and this controversial selection made plenty of headlines. Nadal was currently world number 51 seed – could he handle the pressure?

The 18-year-old might have been playing in his first ever Davis Cup but nobody would have known it from the maturity and composure he displayed. The fact that the tie was being played in Spain made life a little easier for Rafa as he was cheered on by the passionate home crowd in Seville. He desperately needed to show his self-belief after dropping the first set in a tie-break and his response was emphatic. Roddick's serve was ranked among the best in the world yet Nadal climbed all over it in the second set with some blistering groundstrokes. He pummelled the American from the back of the court and levelled the match by sealing the set 6-2.

The Spaniard had the momentum and refused to relinquish control, outlasting Roddick in the third set tie-break to move a step closer to giving Spain breathing space in the tie. Carlos Moya had won his match against Mardy Fish to put his country 1-0 up and Nadal was on course to double the advantage. The fourth set was another Rafa masterclass as he made quick work of Roddick's bullet serve. He converted his second match point and fell to the ground in delight, clinching a 6-7, 6-2, 7-6, 6-2 victory in three hours and 38 minutes.

Rafa had made a big splash with the win over Roddick and he told the media: 'This is so important for me because it has been a long time since I played at this level. Everything went so well, just great.'

Spain captain Jordi Arrese told the press: 'I don't understand why people were so surprised when we decided to play Rafa. He is an excellent player, and truly a Davis Cup player.'

Arrese had seen enough of Nadal to go even further and make predictions on how far his compatriot might go. The Spanish Davis Cup captain added: 'I would not be surprised if he ends up doing it [winning a Grand Slam]. I have said since he was 14 years old. Nowadays, it's impossible to beat Federer because he's by far the best player in the world. Rafa has a lot to learn and a lot to improve, and he will get there. I would not rule out that he ends up winning Roland Garros.'

Roddick offered his thoughts too. Speaking in a dignified manner despite the loss, the American told the press: 'There's a guy right now that's a pretty good No. 1 player in the world. I think he [Nadal] could become possibly one of the best clay-courters in the world. It's no secret that he has a very, very bright future. Every once in a while people come along and they're big match players. He is a big match player.'

The 2002 French Open champion Albert Costa had shown his quality on clay throughout his career and he was as good a judge as anyone when it came to assessing Nadal's progress and future prospects. Costa told *Sports Illustrated*: 'Rafa has everything he needs to win four, five, six Grand Slam events. He is just an unbelievably complete player.'

Compatriot Moya proudly announced that Rafa was the best he had ever seen and picked him out as a future top ten player. Typically modest, Nadal was flattered by the praise that he was receiving but did not let it go to his head.

He was catching the eye of tennis pundits all over the world. American John McEnroe told the press: 'That kid is just fearless.' The Spaniard was winning friends with every passing match and his physique was so impressive that few worried about him being outhit by some of the bigger names on the tour.

But the Davis Cup final was not over yet. First, Rafa was due to join forces with Tommy Robredo to take on the Bryan twins, Mike and Bob. But after the ecstasy of the win over Roddick, Arrese opted to rest Rafa and draft in Ferrero. It is easy to ponder such decisions with hindsight but the Spaniards seemed to miss a trick by not unleashing Nadal again and they paid the price.

The Bryans dominated from start to finish to keep the tie alive going into the final day's play. The Americans sealed a straight-sets 6-0, 6-3, 6-2 victory and, more worryingly, there seemed to be a little unrest in the Spanish camp. Ferrero admitted his disappointment at being left out for the Roddick match and questioned the decision to put him into the doubles match, considering he rarely played doubles.

All in all, it was America's day and set up a tense finale. But Moya held his nerve and his 6-2, 7-6, 7-6 win over Roddick earned Spain an insurmountable 3-1 lead in the best-of-five tie. Nadal was delighted to see the victory secured but was disappointed not to gain more match action. Arrese picked Robredo for the final match of the tie against Fish and, while Rafa could start his celebrations, he was understandably sad not to be basking in the glory out on the court.

Robredo had a second disappointing day as Fish made the scoreline more respectable with a solid win. But it was irrelevant. Nadal and Spain were the champions. Winning the title in front of his home supporters was a tremendous moment for Rafa and the partisan crowd certainly played their part in urging the hosts to victory. Nadal would always remember these frenzied few days which gave him an early taste of life at the top.

After savouring the moment, Rafa returned to the solitude of the singles circuit. On the positive side, he developed plenty of new skills as he sought to adjust to his life on tour. One of these was cooking. He understood the importance of looking after his body and eating the right food in the build up to matches. Talking about his Wimbledon regime, Nadal admitted to the *Independent*: 'I like to cook seafood and pasta there. But I don't think my friends would say that I'm a good cook.' The Spaniard is also said to dislike cheese, tomato and ham, making for a somewhat unusual diet

He was truly living the dream. Reflecting on the satisfaction that pursuing a career in tennis brought him, Nadal told *Sport Magazine*: 'I love everything about being a professional tennis player: practising, training, the tension before a match, the emotions when you are out on court and, of course, the battle to win. I love every moment of it – and, if you win the tournament, then it is even more satisfying.'

It was a real purple patch for Spanish tennis and Rafa was delighted to see that a number of other players were coming through the ranks to join him on the tour. He told the media that the next generation seemed to be proving more versatile when it came to playing on different surfaces. The Davis Cup team appeared to have a bright future. He said: 'I think it's changing right now because Spanish players are starting to get good results on these kinds of surfaces. You can see that especially from the young players coming up that have the interest to play on these surfaces and develop their games, and I think that's good for tennis.'

The 2005 season saw Nadal really take his game to the next level. There had been plenty of media attention over the past few years, covering Rafa's rapid improvements, but now this intensified. He and Toni were well aware that making a big impact at one of the Grand Slam tournaments would help Rafa to make his mark. It was at these competitions that reputations were made and he was desperate to reach a Grand Slam final.

Nadal headed to the Southern Hemisphere at the start of the season to compete in the Australian Open. It was a chance for him to further his experience of playing on different surfaces, having spent so much of his brief career to date on clay courts. The Australian Open did not bring him that Grand Slam final he craved but he put in a respectable performance, reaching the fourth round before losing in five sets to home favourite Lleyton Hewitt. Going toe-to-toe with Hewitt confirmed Rafa's rise in the world of tennis but the Spaniard was not satisfied, despite his solid showing. Of course, he was not expected to set the world alight immediately but he had very high standards.

He then reached the final of the Miami Masters but lost out again in five sets, losing to Roger Federer. It was a painful defeat as Nadal stormed into a two-set lead yet could not hold off Federer's fierce comeback. Rafa was still only 18 and sampling the pressure of such an occasion stood him in good stead for the future. He would remember the agony of seeing the prize slip from his grasp and it was bound to be a character-building loss. It was a rare occasion when the moment got the better of him.

As he entered the clay court season, he appeared determined to make up for having to sit out the events the previous year. This was his forte. He won ATP Masters tournaments in Monte Carlo and Rome as the hours of practice time on the clay surface paid dividends. He was truly at home on the clay and had the stamina to outlast his opponents. Having only just climbed into the top 100, Nadal used this hot streak to shoot up the rankings to number 5 by May 2005, using a 24-match winning run to gain momentum. This was a record for a teenager in the open era and Rafa was looking every inch a future Grand Slam winner.

As the French Open grew ever closer, Nadal prepared for his biggest test and also his best opportunity to win a Grand Slam. There were few players on the circuit who looked as comfortable on the clay. Commentators had certainly taken notice of his brilliant form – they frequently put him among the favourites for the tournament.

Nadal's tireless running and ferocious hitting ensured that he made a strong start to the French Open. It was easy to forget that this was his first ever appearance at Roland Garros. With each round he found himself facing more experienced players yet he brushed them aside. Frenchman Sebastien Grosjean, a talented clay court player, fell to Rafa's unstoppable momentum. Highly-rated Richard Gasquet, also of France, saw his tournament hopes ended by Nadal. He was fighting off all the home favourites and relishing the chance to play party-pooper.

Suddenly, Nadal found himself in the semi-final. His opponent would be none other than Roger Federer, who was seeking to add a French Open triumph to his string of Wimbledon successes. This would be just the first in a series of Nadal-Federer clashes at Roland Garros.

It was a huge occasion for Rafa but he did not wilt under the pressure. He handled everything that Federer could throw at him and came back for more. He successfully chased down seemingly impossible balls and struck brutal returns from behind the baseline. The crowd were stunned as the Swiss struggled to keep up with the ferocious pace.

Federer had no reply and Nadal rejoiced as he completed a staggering 6-3, 4-6, 6-4, 6-3 victory. He would now move into his first Grand Slam final. Having reached the French Open final at the first attempt, he had every reason to be ecstatic after the match. All that stood between Nadal and the trophy was unseeded Argentine Mariano Puerta, who had enjoyed a phenomenal run himself. Could Puerta handle Rafa that afternoon? It seemed to be Nadal's destiny to lift the trophy.

Stepping onto the court for his first Grand Slam final, Rafa was naturally nervous. It was a massive occasion for someone so young and inexperienced. But once the match began, Nadal settled and made a superb start with a break in the first game with some frantic defence.

After receiving treatment for a thigh injury, Puerta recovered to break back in the sixth game but Nadal's nerves were holding up well and he pumped his fists as he kept his composure to level again at 5-5. The set headed into a thrilling tie-break which could have gone either way before the Argentine sealed it 8-6. Rafa had led at 5-4 but had been marginally outgunned on the big points.

It was a big blow for Nadal after putting together a solid set but he tried to stay positive. The non-stop pace of the match favoured the Spaniard and he cashed in on the quick tempo to break for a 3-1 lead in the second set. He was covering so much ground at the back of the court and Puerta was struggling to find winners. Rafa looked the fresher of the two players, with the Argentine looking a little jaded from his five-set marathon in the semi-final with Nikolay Davydenko.

As Nadal's forehand continued to find its mark, he edged closer to levelling the match. Puerta closed to 5-3 but a vicious backhand set up the decisive point in the following game as Rafa took the set 6-3 and made it one set all.

It had become a gripping final and Nadal upped the aggression again to make a flying start to the third set. He was now dominating Puerta's serve, quickly moving 2-0 up. Another brutal forehand gave Rafa a double break and a 4-1 lead as his opponent began to run out of steam.

Ruthlessly, Nadal pounced on the opportunity to clinch the lead. Puerta surrendered his serve for the third time in the set and a 6-1 scoreline meant that all the momentum was with the Spaniard. He had recovered brilliantly from the agonising first set tie-break and was steamrollering his way towards the finishing line.

The question was: did Puerta have anything left in the tank?

He started the fourth set as if he knew it was now or never. He broke Rafa in the opening game but the Spaniard showed courage to break back immediately. A love service game from the Argentine made it 4-4 and meant the set had stayed on serve since the early breaks, though Rafa had been forced to fight off three break points in the seventh game.

Puerta then opened the door with some sublime work at the net and he earned a break when Nadal went long. But he could not hold off the Spaniard as the pressure of serving for the set got to him. Puerta crafted three set points but Rafa's stubborn defence denied him and then Nadal showed his own ability at the net to break back for 5-5. The disappointment of throwing away three set points stung Puerta and, while he dwelt on what might have been, Nadal made the most of his reprieve. Things looked a little shaky at 40-30 but the Argentine fired long and Rafa was now 6-5 up.

More pulsating rallies followed in the next game as Puerta served to stay in the match. Nadal moved 30-15 up with a sizzling forehand but the Argentine answered by putting away a short ball. Thriving on the pressure, Rafa cranked up the aggression again and an elegant backhand brought up match point.

The tension was unbearable: his first visit to the French Open, his first Grand Slam final. Now he was a point away from a momentous victory. And with all the emotions flying through Rafa's head, he was grateful to see Puerta fluff his lines and hand him the French Open title. Nadal sunk to his knees, overcome by the moment. The 6-7, 6-3, 6-1, 7-5 victory was the icing on the cake for the Spaniard's perfect fortnight. Could it get any better than this?

The last point of the match was one Rafa would never forget. Nor would he ever forget the feeling of walking up to collect the trophy with the crowd showing their appreciation. Nadal had toiled hard to be ready for Roland Garros and now he was receiving the reward for that effort.

He basked in the glory of the moment and, as would become his trademark, bit the trophy! This is an act that he has continued throughout his career. The trophy-biting routine would soon catch on with the media and it was not long before reporters questioned him about it. Why did he put the trophies in his mouth after each tournament triumph? Rafa explained it in *TIME* magazine, saying: 'I started doing it one day when I won my first tournament. I continued. I don't know, I just prefer that to kissing the trophies. It's one of my trademarks.'

He hoped it would be a habit that spectators would witness many more times in the future. He was the first teenager to win a Grand Slam singles tournament since Pete Sampras in 1990 and the first player since Mats Wilander in 1982 to win at Roland Garros at the first attempt. A beaming Rafa told the media: 'It's incredible to win at Roland Garros. It's a dream come true to win on my first appearance here. Mariano was my toughest opponent in the two weeks. It was a great final.

'I thought I was going to lose after he won the first set, I really thought he could win. But I fight for every ball. When I have problems in the match, I fight, I fight, I fight every game. For the first time, I cried after winning a match. It has never happened to me before.' It had been an occasion to remember.

Looking back on that day, the Spaniard added: 'There's nothing I can say. You spend your whole life thinking about, talking about, how to win a Grand Slam. Suddenly you find you've won it. What can I say? I just have to be very thankful. Everybody now pays attention to what I do.'

It would be unfair to say that Nadal's focus was diminished after this triumph but his form seemed to dip at the remaining Grand Slams, despite solid performances at ATP events. His swashbuckling run to French Open glory had taken its toll on him and it led to something of a slump.

Heading to Wimbledon later in the summer, Rafa crashed out in the second round, failing to come to terms with the change of surface. It was a concern for him because he wanted to be regarded as a great all-round player, not simply a clay court specialist. Speaking to reporters, the Spaniard acknowledged the differences in playing on grass. He said: 'There are a lot of things that have to change for grass. First thing is the mentality. Then I have to improve my serve and my volley. But I'm still young and I have time to learn. I will try to improve my game and win Wimbledon one day. I love it. It would be a dream.'

But at the same time, he was honest enough to admit that he had not expected to make a big impression at SW19. It would take several years before he felt capable of handling the grass courts, which were still very alien to him after his clay court upbringing.

Prior to Wimbledon, he had been asked about the possibility of adding another Grand Slam and outdueling Federer. He replied: 'I have no chance. No. I am realistic. He's an unbelievable player. Roger is on another level.' Federer did indeed go on to bag another Wimbledon title.

It was a similar story for Rafa at the US Open, where he was eliminated in the third round by American James Blake. Nadal had been one of the top seeds going into the tournament but did not live up to his billing on this occasion. There would, however, be plenty more trips to the US Open to look forward to. Federer completed another majestic year by adding a victory at Flushing Meadows to his two other Slams, setting the bar high for the likes of Rafa.

Nadal's season then came to a somewhat premature end when, after victory at the Madrid Masters, he suffered a foot injury. It wiped out his chances of playing at the Masters Cup and left him a frustrated spectator as the year drew to a close. Even after such an impressive season, he hated missing tournaments and chances to add more trophies to his collection – but he understood that he needed to be patient and let the injury heal.

All this meant that the season ended slightly more disappointingly than Nadal would have liked. Nonetheless, he had established himself among the top players in the world, winning 79 matches during the season and matching Federer's record of 11 ATP titles and four Masters Series successes.

There was plenty to be happy and optimistic about for Rafa as he reflected on the season. After all, he was just 19 and had already captured his first Grand Slam title. He hoped it would not be long before he improved his results away from the clay courts too.

He had proved himself unflappable at the French Open as he silenced crowds of around 15,000 cheering for Frenchmen Gasquet and Grosjean. Now he had the rewards – almost £1 million in the bank already! It was easy to see how young players went off the rails after early career success. Fortunately,

Rafa had the right people around him to make sure he stayed on the straight and narrow.

Naturally very modest from the outset of his career, Nadal dedicated time to signing autographs and posing for photos with supporters. But he did not think of himself as a big celebrity. However, even he could not resist a hint of cockiness after his first Grand Slam title. He told the media: 'Playing against me is probably not so easy. Luckily, I'll never have to do it.' This was the type of confidence that had ensured the Spaniard enjoyed an impressive year and it would serve him well in the challenges ahead.

He had shown no fear throughout some testing times but when questioned about this, Rafa denied that he was immune to such an emotion. He said: 'No, I am afraid of lots of things. A dog. I could be scared of a dog that's upset, for example. And on the tennis court, maybe on the outside I look fearless, but on the inside I'm scared. There's not one player in the world who isn't nervous before matches – especially important matches.' In Nadal's autobiography, his mother also confirms his discomfort with thunder, lightning and sleeping in the dark.

In his *Times* blog during the 2009 Australian Open, the Spaniard revealed more. He wrote: 'I hate spiders. Not sure if it is frightened but *agggggg*. Thank God I have not seeing any here. We are in Melbourne so no creepy creatures where we are.' But Nadal had quickly established ways to handle the nerves. He explained: 'Before the French final I sat in the locker room warming up and listening to music on my headphones. It didn't matter what music. I don't have something special. I just listen to be only thinking about myself. To concentrate and think about what I have to do. This is an hour before the match. Ten minutes before the match I am already jumping.'

Federer was still comfortably the top player in the world of tennis, appearing head and shoulders above the rest on the grass and hard courts. But he had a target on his back and Nadal was determined to be among the pack hunting down the Swiss number one.

CHAPTER 2

BUILDING ON HIS EARLY SUCCESS

The new season began as frustratingly as the previous one had ended for Nadal. His foot injury was still causing him distress, making it impossible to train and prepare for tournaments early in the year.

He had targeted an appearance at the Chennai Open in January but, after consulting doctors, Rafa decided to withdraw from the event in order to gain more time to recover from the injury. This was a very testing time for the Spaniard as he was unable to get out onto the court for practice. The Spaniard told the media: 'Both my medical team and I have been working very hard during the last few weeks so that I could participate at Chennai. But my doctor has now recommended that I don't play and it's my misfortune that I can't make it.'

Having managed a double figure title haul in 2005, Nadal had hoped to go from strength to strength in this new season. But the setback forced him to rethink his plans. He saw the Chennai tournament as a good way to kick off the year so it was a serious blow. Also, it was a place close to Nadal's heart and he has since donated $25,000 to a relief fund for tsunami victims.

Despite resting his body, the foot injury continued to impede Rafa and the Spaniard revealed in his autobiography that the injury to his tarsal scaphoid bone was a rare disease of the foot and that there were major concerns over his future in the game. It was taking longer than expected to heal and it was a nightmare, particularly with his active nature. He just wanted to get back out onto the court but was spending much of his time resting and receiving treatment. Worse was his enforced absence from the Australian Open. He hated missing any events but to miss out on a Grand Slam was especially disappointing. Federer once again crushed everyone in his path on the way to yet another title. For Rafa, it was all very painful. He was yet to make any impact in the event and had seen this as his year to put together a good run.

Still, the season was just a matter of weeks old and the Spaniard would get plenty of chances to make up for lost time. He was still young and it was important not to rush back from niggling injuries – he had to think about his long-term future in the sport rather than the urge to win trophies in the short term.

He was soon back out on the court and he put together a solid run of results at Indian Wells before losing out in the semi-finals. He fared less well in Miami where he was eliminated in the second round. Still, after a lengthy layoff, he was bound to need time to get back to his sharpest and these tournaments gave him the match practice he required before he headed onto the clay.

When the clay court season began, something immediately clicked for Nadal. He was so prolific on this surface and he was quick to make his mark. At the Monte Carlo Masters, Rafa shone throughout on his way to the final and his coaching team were delighted to see him moving around the court with ease after the foot problems. His displays were mature and dominant, leaving his opponents flummoxed.

Alison Kervin, of *The Sunday Times*, studied Nadal's closely during the tournament and left Monaco an even bigger admirer of the Spaniard's considerable talent. Viewing one of Rafa's practice sessions, she wrote: 'Standing on court while the world No. 2 plies his trade is a rare treat. The colossal speed of the ball and the unnerving accuracy of every shot are there in all their glory. Their impact is exacerbated by proximity. It is all breathtaking.'

Such workouts with Toni always attracted hoards of noisy fans, eager to catch a glimpse of the Spaniard. Nadal was happy to accommodate the requests of his supporters but he managed to keep his mind on the task in hand, preparing for his next match with typical vigour and displaying the mental fortitude that has become one of his trademarks. There are some players on the tour who clearly do not enjoy practice, only managing to find their best form when faced with the pressure of a match situation. But Rafa is not one of them.

The Spaniard went on to topple Federer in the final 6-2, 6-7, 6-3, 7-6. It was a tremendous boost for Nadal to produce such a fine start to the clay court season and he continued in the same vein at the Rome Masters, blazing his way through the early rounds. Again he faced Federer in the final and again he came out on top. It was an absolute thriller for the Italian crowd as the match went the distance before Nadal claimed the fifth set tie-break to win 6-7, 7-6, 6-4, 2-6, 7-6 in more than five hours of pulsating tennis. Federer had appeared on course for victory but Rafa never gave up and the Spaniard gained his reward. The Swiss continued to be bamboozled by his rival on this surface.

There was no doubt that Nadal held a slight mental edge over Federer on clay, even at this early stage. The Swiss simply did not seem to have the same belief that he exhibited against every other player on the circuit and it let him down tellingly at key moments in matches against the Spaniard. He could not figure out a way to win on the slower surface against Nadal's deadly cocktail of backspin, topspin and relentless defence, and it was incredible to see the world number one struggle so much when supporters were used to seeing him decimate all before him with a stylish swagger. Federer would need to rediscover his composure if he wanted to have any chance of dethroning Rafa at the French Open.

Both players then withdrew from the Hamburg Masters in order to prepare their bodies for the arduous contests that lay ahead at the French Open, ensuring that there could be no excuses over tiredness. Federer was still searching for his first title at Roland Garros and Nadal was determined to deny him.

There was plenty of pressure on Rafa heading into the event. As defending champion, much would be expected of him and everyone would be raising their game when facing him. However, the Spaniard had looked in top form in the recent tournaments and it would take a brave man to bet against Nadal on clay. With the Grand Slam just around the corner, he felt ready. And, in a strange way, he would benefit from sitting out the early stages of the season because he was entering the event a lot fresher than many of his fiercest rivals.

As Nadal returned for a second taste of the French Open atmosphere, he had one goal in mind – retaining his crown. He had fallen in love with the tournament after his glorious triumph last year and was keen to build on his King of Clay nickname.

Nadal showed little sign of the pressure as he joked with the media and focused on his rigorous training routines. The draw paired him with Sweden's Robin Soderling in the first round. Soderling could be a tricky opponent on his day, as he would prove to Nadal four years later, and Toni made sure his nephew watched plenty of footage in the build-up. But the Swede failed to produce the quality to hurt Rafa and the Spaniard eased into the second round. Nadal broke twice in the first set, punishing Soderling's stuttering start and taking the match by the scruff of the neck.

After clinching the set 6-2 in less than 30 minutes, it seemed like more one-way traffic lay ahead but the Swede rallied. Soderling enjoyed a purple patch to force a break and move 4-2 ahead in the second set. But it just seemed to fire up Nadal who tore into the Swede's serve again.

He broke back immediately with some crunching returns and, in no time, had powered his way into a 5-4 lead. Soderling broke back for 5-5 but Nadal would not be denied, snatching a third successive break and then bagging the set 7-5.

This sudden turnaround knocked the fight out of Soderling,

who lost all confidence in his serve, and Rafa, moving with the confidence and grace of a matador, made all the right decisions. He earned an early break and raced away, completing an emphatic 6-2, 7-5, 6-1 victory in front of a Parisian crowd that had taken him to their hearts.

While Nadal had preferred to focus on the match all week, the media had made no secret of the fact that Rafa would break Guillermo Vilas' record for consecutive clay court wins if he overcame Soderling. This was the Spaniard's 54th straight success on his favourite surface and it etched his name into the history books again. Nadal, who would turn 20 on the Monday of the second week of the tournament, said: 'I'm very happy. It's a special moment. It's important to win and important to be part of history.'

His reward for the thumping victory over Soderling was a clash with Lucky Loser American Kevin Kim. Few gave Kim a chance of overturning the formbook, especially as Rafa would be desperate to extend his winning streak on clay. In truth, Nadal barely had to move out of first gear as he cruised through. He fizzed shots to all corners of the court and left Kim bewildered with the power of his hitting. Grateful to see that the previous day's rain had cleared, Rafa wasted no time in sealing the first set 6-2. This was a sign of things to come as the Spaniard rushed to get through the contest.

The second set was even more one-sided as Kim's serve continued to suffer. Nadal's intensity left the American shattered and he moved quickly to a 6-1 scoreline. He was looking more invincible than ever on the clay – a worrying sign for his fellow title contenders.

The biggest worry of the match came when Nadal called for

the trainer in the third set. He had not appeared to be hobbling and a hush fell over the crowd as the Spaniard took off his shoe. However, all fears proved unnecessary as Rafa simply wanted help in adjusting the tape on his right foot. It was not, as he stressed after the match, the same ankle he had injured back in 2004 when he missed three months of action. The way he was playing, picking up an injury seemed to be the only way that the Spaniard would be denied at Roland Garros.

Nadal went on to complete a dominant 6-2, 6-1, 6-4 victory and could reflect on some impressive tennis. However, he still had several more gears to push into if necessary and had not been stretched in either of his wins. In many ways, he hoped to face a stiffer test in the next round to ensure that his competitive juices were flowing in advance of the later rounds. He told the press that the record streak was pleasing but that being the last man standing at Roland Garros was the only target he cared about. He would be able to enjoy the record after he had secured a second consecutive French Open title. The Spaniard added: 'I was especially nervous in the first round and the second round for Roland Garros. I'm playing a difficult tournament.' Undoubtedly, the stakes were high.

He was certainly hiding the nerves very well so far because he had looked cool, calm and collected on court and had offered few signs of weakness to cheer his rivals. Missing out on the 2004 French Open seemed to have worked in his favour as he may not have been ready for the pressure two years ago. Instead, he had taken the tournament by storm a year later and had never looked back. With a fourth round slot on the line, Nadal walked onto the court on his 20th birthday and took on Frenchman Paul-Henri Mathieu, the number 29 seed.

It was billed as potentially the first test of Nadal's title credentials and it was definitely true that Mathieu possessed more weapons than either Soderling or Kim. But on the day, he did not have the firepower to eliminate Rafa. Mathieu made a superb start, though, and was cheered on by the home fans. On first impressions, it looked as if Nadal would have a birthday to forget. Mathieu, playing with freedom, pulled out some big shots on the key points to take the first set 7-5. He had saved nine break points in a single service game to keep Nadal at bay and looked delighted to bag a 93-minute opening set.

Nadal's 9-0 record at the French Open suddenly seemed under threat and he had to rely on all his positive memories from Roland Garros in 2005. He had not played badly in the first set and hoped that Mathieu would tire as the match progressed.

Errors did indeed begin to creep into the Frenchman's game as Rafa refused to be down-hearted after the first set. He mishit returns and lacked some of his early spark as Nadal found enough opportunities to graft his way back into the match with a large dose of mental toughness. The Spaniard edged ahead in the second set and never relinquished his grip, taking it 6-4.

The third set was a similar story. Mathieu continued to blast winners but Rafa was able to weather the storm and pick his moments to attack. The Frenchman, who went on to rack up 60 winners in the contest, faltered as Nadal secured the all-important break. It was not often that players managed so many winners yet found themselves heading for defeat.

Bizarrely, play was halted when Rafa, serving for the third

set, almost choked on a banana and needed time to compose himself. He shrugged this off, though, and went on to snare the third set 6-4 as his opponent visibly began to tire. Winning the final two sets always looked beyond Mathieu and Nadal was in no mood for charity. He served well and relied on his opponent's growing number of unforced errors, keeping his nose in front. Rafa was certainly not at his best but was showing once again that he had the mental strength and physical stamina to grind out wins.

The end came after nearly five hours of gripping tennis as the Spaniard completed a 5-7, 6-4, 6-4, 6-4 victory. Rafa was into the fourth round but this had been an epic match and he would need to rest sensibly before the next test.

Referring to the banana scare, Nadal told reporters: 'I started being a little frightened. I didn't want to stop in the middle of the game – I didn't think it would look very good.' Mathieu seemed unimpressed by the incident post-match but praised Rafa's immense ability on clay. The Spaniard's winning streak on the surface was now at 56 and he seemed to be in irresistible form.

The quarter-finals saw Nadal face Australian Lleyton Hewitt. Hewitt had disposed of Dominik Hrbaty in the fourth round 7-6, 6-2, 6-2, producing an excellent display of serving and well-placed groundstrokes. With the Australian's never-say-die attitude it promised to be a war of attrition as he stepped out to face Nadal. Both players were tireless competitors and spectators settled in, expecting some very lengthy rallies.

Hewitt had won their three previous matches, though none of them were on clay. Pundits tended to lean in the

Spaniard's favour and Rafa made a brilliant start as Hewitt was simply blown away in the first set. Nadal was everywhere, racing to reach groundstrokes and pouncing on any short balls. He dominated Hewitt's serve and took the opening set 6-2. It looked ominous for the former world number one. Rafa was in the zone and finding a better rhythm than he had managed against Mathieu in the previous round. However, Hewitt had been on the circuit long enough to know not to panic and he fought his way back into the match through sheer determination.

The defence on show from the pair was top class as both had to find extra shots to earn points. They pounded around the court, stretching and straining every muscle to keep rallies alive. Nadal earned a break early in the second set but the Australian hit back. Hewitt grabbed a break of his own to even things up and then struck the killer blow with another break to snatch the second set 7-5, levelling the match.

It was clearly a setback for Nadal but he refused to be rattled. The third set was also tight but, at 4-4, Rafa pulled away. A clever drop shot led to a break in the ninth game and he did not waste this advantage, serving out to win the set 6-4. Now Hewitt had a mountain to climb again.

The Aussie hung around in the contest, though. Nadal broke his serve but Hewitt did likewise to Rafa. Just as it looked like another tense set lay ahead, the Spaniard cut loose and punished his opponent's wavering serve. In the end, Nadal just had too much power for Hewitt and he wrapped up a 6-2, 5-7, 6-4, 6-2 victory in three hours and 17 minutes.

Rafa was thrilled to extend his run but, more importantly, he could look ahead to a quarter-final clash with unseeded young Serb Novak Djokovic. After demolishing Hewitt, there was plenty of reason to believe that Nadal could repeat last year's heroics in Paris. He said: 'Today I probably played my best match of the tournament so far. I was feeling the ball very well and even in the second set I felt like I was controlling the match.' Hewitt, who was beginning to become accustomed to being outhit by the game's biggest guns, added: 'At the start, he was smoking it, hitting heavy balls and I couldn't dictate.' In truth, the Australian had never looked like taking the match the distance.

Nadal's fine performance was an encouraging sign. The very best players managed to find peak form as they headed into the latter stages and Rafa always stepped up his game at the business end of tournaments. Apart from a few lapses of concentration in the second set, he had looked very commanding.

Djokovic had impressed many with his progress during the tournament and had brushed aside number 23 seed Tommy Haas and number nine seed Fernando Gonzalez along the way. He was playing without pressure and had the attributes to make Nadal toil. However, the Serb was bound to be nervous and Nadal's aggressive start showed his intention to capitalise on his opponent's serve. He broke Djokovic in the opening game of the first set, lost his serve immediately but broke again in the third game with a fine volley. It was proving to be another fast and furious start.

Rafa became the first man to hold serve in game four, bagging a 3-1 lead. And this was enough to keep Djokovic on the back foot. The Spaniard went close to another break at 5-3 but, having missed out, he was immaculate on serve to clinch the first set 6-4 with a trademark crunching forehand.

Djokovic had plenty to think about as he returned to his chair. He began shakily again in the second set, though, as Rafa showed his ruthless side. Nadal found a peach of a drop shot to seal an early break and moved 3-0 up with more classy winners.

The Serb seemed to lose his stomach for the fight and, to make matters worse, was struggling with injury. He called the trainer out, received treatment and then promptly broke Rafa's serve. It briefly roused those spectators that remained but Nadal silenced them again with yet another break as Djokovic's movement appeared restricted.

The end was clearly nigh but the Spaniard seemed to take his eye off the ball and, with his concentration wavering, his opponent managed a second successive break. The serving in this contest had been far from impressive but such was Rafa's dominance that it was hardly surprising that he began coasting. Djokovic closed the deficit to 4-3 with some positive tennis and finally asked Nadal the questions that the media had predicted he would. Rafa responded admirably with a love service game and then, serving at 5-4, produced the big shots for a two-set lead.

There seemed no way back for Djokovic, especially as he continued to be hampered by injury. The Serb agreed, choosing to retire from the match and sending Rafa into the semi-finals. It had not been the classic contest that many had predicted but it was still a shame for it to end in such a manner. Nadal was delighted, though, to advance into the last four. He was one step closer to retaining his title but Federer was looming large in the other half of the draw. While Djokovic tried to claim he could have won if he had not been restricted by his injury, the gulf in quality had been clear and Nadal preferred to look ahead to a semi-final with fourth seed Croat Ivan Ljubicic.

Rafa told the press: 'I'm playing better and better. Maybe I'm arriving in the semi-finals with my best level in the last two weeks. That's the most important thing.' Would Ljubicic have the weapons to become the first man to defeat Rafa here? It was the first time since 1985 that the top four seeds had contested the French Open semi-finals and Nadal knew he would have to beat the best to relive his Roland Garros glory of 2005.

In the heat of the Paris afternoon, Rafa walked out for his second Grand Slam semi-final. This time, though, he was the clear favourite. Ljubicic had enjoyed a relatively easy run and would face a different proposition as he squared off against Nadal. The Spaniard calmed his nerves with an early break and, leading 3-1, looked comfortable already. He was hitting the lines with his shots and forcing errors from Ljubicic, such as the mis-hit forehand that presented the Spaniard with his break.

That became 4-1 as Rafa broke again, capping off a game of graft with a clinical passing shot. Though the Croat broke straight back determinedly, he had left himself too much to do. Ljubicic saved a break point at 5-3 but Nadal refused to falter and the Spaniard bagged the first set 6-4 with another solid service game.

After another solid start, the Croat then fell away in the second set and Rafa found himself enjoying a 4-1 lead again. He was tireless in defence and had the killer instinct when he crafted break points. He consolidated his double break to go

5-1 up. Nadal had won five games in a row and was within touching distance of an overwhelming lead.

Ljubicic just about clung onto his serve in the next game but was powerless to stop Rafa winning the set 6-2. The final was moving into view for the world number two. Nadal had turned up the heat and the Croat was wilting badly. Pundits were already looking ahead to the final.

With defeat now likely, Ljubicic took more chances and finally applied some pressure on Rafa. He attacked the net more often and rediscovered some confidence in his serve. The Croat was a very dangerous server and Nadal was grateful that he had been off target in the opening two sets. The Spaniard's own serve had been highlighted by some pundits as a weakness but it was looking imperious against Ljubicic as he levelled at 3-3.

As Rafa's intensity dropped off a little, his opponent managed to keep up with the pace. Ljubicic delivered an excellent service game to go 6-5 ahead but, serving to stay in the set, Nadal made no mistake to force a tie-break. The Spaniard's body language during the tie-break suggested he was keen to finish the job here rather than risk a fourth set. However, it was Ljubicic who stormed into the lead. At the changeover, he led 4-2. But Nadal hit back, helped by a double fault from the Croat, and set up match point with a big ace. Ljubicic survived it. Moments later Nadal had a second chance but was again denied. However, it was third time lucky for the world number two as the Croat fired wide to hand Rafa the win.

Nadal could not hide the ecstasy of the moment as he celebrated the 6-4, 6-2, 7-6 victory. He had reached another

French Open final and, while he and his team are not typically advocates for dwelling on successes, he wanted to savour the achievement before he focused on the big one. He would face rival Federer who was desperate to complete his set of Grand Slam successes. A beaming Nadal told the media: 'A lot of people want me to win, I'm very relaxed and I'm playing well.'

However, Ljubicic had little praise to put in Rafa's direction when he addressed reporters after his defeat. He said: 'It's ridiculous how much time he [Nadal] takes between points. I think the umpire should be more aggressive on that.' And looking ahead to the final, the Croat firmly nailed his colours to the mast. He admitted: 'I would love to see Roger winning. Everyone in the locker room would.' It all sounded rather like sour grapes.

Nadal was angered by these remarks and felt the need to reply. He told the press: 'You've got to learn to control yourself after you lose a match, you can't go just go about saying anything. I've been on the circuit for many years, and I've never had any problems with anybody.'

So tennis fans all over the world now had the French Open final that they had been dreaming about – the reigning champion Nadal against the world number one Federer. For weeks, spectators and pundits had debated the match-up and speculated as to who would come out on top. Now, the waiting was over and everyone would get a definitive answer.

Rafa had his eyes on the prize and knew there was the added bonus of extending his winning streak to 60 matches on clay. Federer was bound to be his biggest test yet but Nadal felt as though the Swiss was stepping into his backyard, especially after recent superb victories over the world number one on clay.

The early signs, though, were that Federer was very much at home. The Spaniard had won five of their six meetings to date but the world number one wasted no time in taking control of the first set. The great Pete Sampras had dominated Wimbledon – just as Federer was currently – but had never won the French Open. The Swiss seemed determined not to go the same way. Federer showed poise to hold serve in the first game and then took his chances expertly on Nadal's serve. The Spaniard had no answers to his opponent's fine start but was encouraged to be creating several breaking opportunities on the Swiss' serve – he just could not take them.

Rafa quickly found himself staring embarrassment in the face as Federer stormed into a 5-0 lead. This was supposed to be Nadal's big day again but the Swiss had not read the script as he took the opening set 6-1. Nobody could have predicted a start like this. It might have knocked the stuffing out of less confident, less talented players but Nadal composed himself and kept in mind the fact that this was a best-of-five-sets contest. There was still plenty of tennis ahead but he needed to make a statement in the second set.

His failure to capitalise on break points had cost him dearly in the first set but he made amends in the second. Nadal cashed in on his seventh chance of the match to open up an early 2-0 lead. Now it was Federer's turn to crumble as mistakes flew from his racquet. He looked bewildered as the Spaniard gave him a taste of his own first set medicine. Rafa clinched the second set 6-1 to level the match with a flourish. They had played two very one-sided sets and were no nearer to deciding on a winner. But while Nadal had put his woes behind him, Federer appeared incapable of doing so as he dwelt on the 16 unforced errors he had made in the second set. Nadal relentlessly kept up the pace, forcing the world number one into more and more mistakes. After the Swiss missed out on break points in the fourth game, Rafa clinched the vital break and served out for a 6-4 scoreline. He was playing the big points better than Federer and was now a set away from a second successive French Open crown.

So far the final had not lived up to its billing. Instead of seeing the top two players in world tennis fighting out a match of brilliant rallies, viewers were left with a sense of anticlimax. Federer had gone down without much of a fight in the last two sets and his stunning start suddenly seemed a distant memory.

Nadal upped the tempo, searching for a quick start in the fourth. He got his reward to leave the Swiss cursing. But Federer came again, rediscovering the form and tactics that had allowed him to begin so smoothly. Rafa kept him at bay until, leading 5-4, he was serving for the title. He faltered and his opponent needed no second invitation to break back. After two solid holds, the duo headed for a tie-break of huge significance and the crowd willed on Federer as they prayed for the match to go the distance. But it was Nadal who came up trumps under pressure, winning four straight points to keep his nose in front.

Match point arrived for the Spaniard and he grabbed it with both hands, punching home a forehand to seal the title. As his spectacular achievement sunk in, Rafa was overcome by waves of emotion. He had done it again, just as he had set out to do. Nadal really was the King of Clay and his stunning string of wins stood at an outstanding 60. An ecstatic Rafa told reporters: 'This is a fantastic victory and an incredible moment in my career as a tennis player. Federer is the best player in history – no other player has ever had such quality.' Such modesty and respect in victory helped make Nadal a popular figure.

Federer had promised to get things right at Roland Garros this year but, despite an excellent tournament, he had been added to the list of Rafa's big name victims. The Swiss told the press: 'I really want to congratulate Rafael. He is so strong on clay and played a really good match. He is so hard to beat on this surface. He truly deserves to win.' He would have to wait until next year to prove that he could handle Nadal on clay. It was hugely frustrating for Federer as he bid to complete his set of Grand Slam titles. With age firmly on Rafa's side, had Federer's best chances of victory in Paris passed him by?

Roland Garros had quickly become Nadal's home away from home. He had passed the biggest tests of his career on these courts in Paris and now had two Grand Slam titles under his belt. His family watched on proudly and, as always, Rafa viewed his victory as a victory for them too.

The next target was to win a Grand Slam elsewhere. He did not want to be known simply as a clay court specialist. With Wimbledon just around the corner, there was no reason why Nadal could not aim high. As many experts pointed out, he had reduced Federer to a stuttering wreck in Paris, why not in London too? It was a big ask considering the world number one's higher level of comfort on grass court. Federer was at his best on the grass and had the motivation of being defending champion again. It would take something very special for Rafa to rain on the Swiss' parade.

Nadal was keen to give himself the best possible chance of Wimbledon glory and so he headed to Queen's for some valuable match practice on grass. He put together a couple of wins before missing out in the quarter-finals against Hewitt, injuring his shoulder in the process. It proved to be just a minor problem and he was disappointed that it had hindered him out on the court. But, most importantly, he was finding his feet on the grass. Whether he could crank things up enough to match Federer remained to be seen. Winning again at Roland Garros was a tremendous feeling but putting in a solid display at Wimbledon was now the only thing on Rafa's mind. This was the next step on the road to being considered a true great and lifting the gold cup was a lifelong dream.

He managed to put his shoulder problem to one side as he began his Wimbledon run. His mindset was never anything but positive. Rafa refused to enter any tournament with pessimism. What was the point? Though he had never been beyond the third round at Wimbledon, he felt that he was ready to make a big impact.

The atmosphere at SW19 was a treat for any tennis player and Nadal loved it. His English was improving all the time and he generously made himself available to the media whenever he was asked. But when match day arrived, Rafa would find his zone. His focus would be spot on and all the laughter would stop. Tennis was a serious business and the Spaniard liked to treat it as such.

Nadal faced British player Alex Bogdanovic in the first round and had to overcome a partisan home crowd. Bogdanovic impressed neutrals with a stubborn performance but Rafa found openings and took them ruthlessly. If anyone had doubts over the Spaniard's desire to progress at Wimbledon, he set the record straight with his opening performance. At 4-4 in the first set, Nadal made the vital break before serving out the set. He began well in the second set too, breaking Bogdanovic early on, but the home favourite broke back to force a tie-break. The Spaniard would not be denied, and he snatched the tie-break 7-3. The home fans were desperate for Bogdanovic to prevail in the tie-break and the noisy support mellowed after Rafa bagged the second set. The third set was again hard work for Nadal but he found a way past Bogdanovic, clinching the match 6-4, 7-6, 6-4. He had not produced his best tennis but he was still far too good for the Brit, who himself had put together one of his better displays. The home supporters craved a British champion but Bogdanovic simply did not have the weapons to go any further in the tournament.

After the victory, Rafa admitted he was not entirely happy with his forehand but added: 'It was important to win the first match, it is never easy.' On a more positive note, his shoulder held up to the strain of the match and he claimed he experienced no problems. Bogdanovic was dignified in defeat, telling the media that he thought Nadal was getting more and more comfortable on grass. He said: 'I think he's getting used to grass now. He's got a title in the future and it could be this year. He's adapted to grass really well, it shows what a great player he is.'

Nadal spent just over two and a half hours on the court and was then able to rest his body for the next round. Little did he know at this stage how priceless this recuperation would be. He understood that he would not find his best grass court form instantly and that it would take time to settle in on the different surface but the signs were encouraging.

In the second round, Rafa faced American Robert Kendrick in what proved to be an epic contest. Nadal was subdued early by Kendrick's aggressive game plan as the world number 237 won the first set tie-break 7-4 with five straight points. The crowd was stunned. But this was just the beginning as Kendrick broke Nadal in the second set to move 2-0 ahead. Suddenly, all the hopes that Rafa had had going into Wimbledon were in jeopardy. He knew he needed to respond but Kendrick made few mistakes, serving 28 aces in the match. The third set went to a tie-break and this time Nadal came out on top, keeping the contest alive. But there was still a lot of work to do. Luckily, his intense training with Toni had conditioned him to fight through tough tests and he needed every bit of resolve to prevent the panic from setting in.

As the world of tennis waited anxiously to see whether they were about to witness the first big shock of the tournament so far, the Spaniard battled on. He won the fourth set 7-5, despite nervous moments at 30-30 and 5-4 down. Kendrick was within two points of the upset but when this chance came and went there was only going to be one winner. The fifth set was gripping but Rafa had the all-important momentum. He showed great spirit as he broke Kendrick's serve in the fifth game and hung on for the grittiest of victories. As he won the final point, clinching a 6-7, 3-6, 7-6, 7-5, 6-4 triumph, he sunk to his knees in a mixture of celebration and relief as if he had won the Wimbledon title itself. This victory was a huge moment in his development as a grass court player.

Nadal told the media: 'I was worried. It was very tough. He played a very good match. I had chances to break but he came up with a good serve every time. He served unbelievable. It made me think that I couldn't afford any mistakes. It was important to come through. I think I played a good match overall.'

Rafa's strong mentality and physique had seen him through but he knew he needed to raise his game. Andre Agassi, playing in his final Wimbledon tournament, awaited Nadal in the third round. The adrenalin rush from winning the last point against Kendrick kept Nadal on his toes and provided a useful experience on which to draw during future difficulties. His support team worked tirelessly to prepare his body physically after the five-set marathon, trying to heal the Spaniard's aching muscles. Agassi, who won the tournament in 1992, presented a different challenge for Rafa. The American was 16 years older than Nadal and had an abundance of experience at Grand Slam events. It was sure to be an emotional day as a legend of the past met a star of the future at SW19. It was billed as one of the matches of the round.

In the end, though, it proved to be an easier contest than Nadal could have possibly expected. After the Spaniard won a tight first set tie-break 7-5, he powered past Agassi with an array of brutal groundstrokes. The American's older body was exposed to Rafa's ruthless streak as he scampered around, desperately striving to keep up with the frantic pace of the rallies. Agassi had led 5-2 in the tie-break before Rafa showed why some had tipped him to oust Federer this year. He clawed his way back to 5-5 and then struck a stunning cross-court winner before closing out the tie-break with an ace. This was as close as the former champion would come to troubling the Spaniard, who had admired Agassi as a boy not so long ago.

Nadal completed a 7-6, 6-4, 6-2 win in two hours and 14 minutes, sparking a standing ovation for Agassi as he stood on a court at Wimbledon for the last time. He had been a tremendous competitor for so many years and the American would be sorely missed. Rafa told the media: 'He's one of the best players in history and I want to congratulate Andre on his career – he's unbelievable. This was my best result on grass. I'm improving so I'm very happy for that. This Centre Court is the best.'

Agassi had fought hard but Nadal was not in a charitable mood – the American failed to earn a single break point. Rafa could reflect on an excellent all-round performance as he prepared to enter the second week of Wimbledon for the first time. He was growing in confidence and his energy levels were showing no signs of fatigue.

Nadal, seemingly determined to avoid the type of five-set nail-biter he played against Kendrick, wasted little time in beating Irakli in the fourth round. Again, Rafa did not give up a single break point as he triumphed 6-3, 7-6, 6-3. Things were starting to look really good for the Spaniard. He remained totally focused after this impressive win, telling the press: 'It's very important for me to be in the quarter-finals. I wasn't thinking that before the tournament. I am playing a very, very good tournament.'

It was 40 years since a Spaniard had won the Wimbledon men's title but the media speculated that the barren spell might be about to come to an end. Rafa's fans just hoped that the exertions at the French Open would not hinder his chances. The statistics were not in his favour – it was 26 years since anyone won the French Open and Wimbledon back-to-back.

Suddenly, a lot of people were taking notes on Nadal's grass court performances. While it should not have been a surprise to see the world number two excelling, the speed of his development was the particularly intriguing aspect. Federer suggested it would still be a surprise to many if Rafa reached the final. But former champion Hewitt thought otherwise. 'The guy's a class player,' the Australian explained. 'It was never going to take him long before he won some matches on grass and then started beating good players like Andre Agassi and these kind of guys on the surface. So it doesn't surprise me that he's still in the tournament.'

Nadal, still just 20, handled the growing attention well and just focused on his tennis. Back on the court against Finnish player Jarkko Nieminen in the quarter-finals, Rafa motored on. The match had been postponed by a day due to rain and Nadal seemed to have handled the delay better - as he admits, rain delays are part of the game and it is critical not to let the frustration mount. He looked relaxed and focused while Nieminen self-destructed. As the Finn struggled with his serve, Nadal pounced on any loose balls. The Spaniard clinched the first set 6-3, breaking Nieminen in the fourth game, and overcame some sloppy moments to win the second set 6-4.

By this point, Rafa was in complete control and his opponent did not possess the spirit or the quality to mount a comeback. Nadal earned a straight-sets victory, taking the third set 6-4 to book his place in the semi-finals. It had been a routine afternoon. He could barely contain his delight as he shook hands with the Finn and soaked up the applause of the crowd. Previously, he had not progressed beyond the third round. Now, he was one match away from the final. Nadal, with a huge smile, told the media: 'I'm very happy about reaching the semi-finals. Just a month ago I was playing on clay but I'm trying and I'm getting good on grass.' Nieminen was despondent after the defeat. He said: 'He's a tough opponent but at the same time I'm disappointed how I played. I think this was my worst match here.'

The number two seed roared on into the semi-final, where he met Marcos Baghdatis of Cyprus. Baghdatis had stunned Hewitt in their quarter-final and was coming in with almost as much momentum as Nadal.

Rafa had not always begun sharply in the tournament but against Baghdatis he found his rhythm immediately, making the Cypriot toil. Since his stirring comeback against Kendrick, the Spaniard had barely put a foot wrong. It was a hugely one-sided first set and Nadal took advantage, breaking him in the first, fifth and seventh games and claiming the set 6-1. The Spaniard went into the semi-final having spent almost 13 hours on court during the tournament, largely due to his marathon match with Kendrick. Baghdatis was not far behind with more than 11 and a half hours on court. Nonetheless, both players produced thrilling tennis in the second set.

Baghdatis looked a totally different player after his poor start and he caused plenty of problems for Nadal with a barrage of fearsome groundstrokes. But Rafa refused to buckle and held his nerve to win key points, leaving the Cypriot frustrated. Nadal missed out on two set points at 5-4 but made amends two games later to take the set 7-5. Though

Baghdatis never gave up, coming back from two sets down against Rafa was near impossible. Nadal broke his opponent's serve in the fourth game of the third set and showed few nerves as he completed a fine performance to win 6-1, 7-5, 6-3 and move into the Wimbledon final.

It was a massive moment for him. The crowd were on their feet, aware that they were in the presence of a future champion. Federer had beaten Bjorkman in the other semi-final and so he and Nadal would fight it out again for a Grand Slam title. Federer's place in the final had been expected but the same could not be said for Nadal. People had questioned his serve. Was it fast enough? Could it be effective on grass? They had questioned his volleying and his positioning at the back of the court. Rafa had answered them all in the best way possible. Now, he had a final to look forward to.

The Wimbledon men's final 2006 was an occasion that Nadal would never forget, even though he admittedly entered the match thinking that he had little chance of winning. The feeling of walking out onto the court and the atmosphere generated by the crowd were sensational. All eyes were on him as he took further strides towards ditching the clay court specialist tag.

Whether it was Federer's brilliance or Rafa's nerves, the match began terribly for the Spaniard. Nadal was immediately on the back foot and the champion refused to let him settle. Federer battered him, winning the first set 6-0. Rafa had lost his serve just twice in the competition before the final, yet suddenly he had been broken three times in less than half an hour. It made for painful viewing. Lesser competitors would have crumbled at this point but Nadal collected himself and made rapid improvements. He took the game to Federer in some hard-hitting rallies and broke the champion's serve. Sadly for the Spaniard, he stuttered when serving for the second set and Federer was able to force a tie-break. Nadal, unfazed, took a 3-1 lead in the tie-break but Federer was just too strong, fighting back to win 7-5 and take a two-set lead. The Swiss had a phenomenal knack of producing a big ace or a roaring forehand when it mattered most and he silenced the Spaniard's supporters inside Centre Court. Could Rafa come back again? He had stunned Kendrick with his resilience, but could he do the same to Federer?

He gave it his best shot. The third set went with serve throughout, despite some brilliant shots from the Spaniard, and another tie-break was required to separate the two players. This time, Nadal made no mistake. He seized the initiative straightaway and won it 7-2. The crowd cheered. Game on. Federer, though, would not wilt as Kendrick did. As if angered by losing the tie-break, the Swiss raised his game another notch and picked apart Nadal's serve. Rafa was broken twice and, despite some desperate attempts to save the fourth set, he succumbed to the champion. Federer saluted the crowd after a well-deserved 6-0, 7-6, 6-7, 6-3 victory. The world number one had put together another masterclass at SW19.

Nadal's face told the whole story. He was bitterly disappointed but put a positive spin on the day and the past two weeks. The Spaniard told the media: 'I want to congratulate Federer, he played unbelievable. This is a difficult surface but I played my best tournament of the year here and that's unbelievable. I hope to come back to this final and win.' Federer was modest as he spoke with the press, praising the quality of his opponent. He revealed: 'I want to say it was a great tournament for Rafael, I honestly didn't think he was going to play the finals here this week.'

As Nadal packed his bags and left England, he could reflect on a remarkable fortnight in which he produced some breathtaking grass court tennis. Prior to the tournament, his record on grass stood at three wins and three losses – he had played just six matches. The experience of reaching the final had enabled him to prove his critics wrong but also prove to himself that he could compete for titles on all surfaces. Federer had been too good on this occasion but would the Swiss be able to hold off an ever-improving Nadal in a year's time or two years' time?

In the meantime, there was plenty more tennis to concentrate on. Now his goal was to put together a strong run at the US Open. Again, this was a tournament in which Rafa had failed to match his French Open success but he had shown at Wimbledon that he was taking his play to the next level and getting better with every match.

He knew that he had the ability to go deep in the tournament but the question marks remained over his fitness. Nadal could not possibly be in peak condition after progressing to the final at the French Open and Wimbledon, and he had been troubled by a shoulder injury prior to the latter event. Could he find the energy to trouble some of the experienced hard court players in the draw? With all his success, it was easy to forget that Rafa was still a youngster and that burning out was a real possibility if he did not take care of his body. It seemed like he had been on the scene for many years yet he had only entered the top 100 in 2003. Some pundits worried that all his successes were coming at a price and that his career at the top might be limited by injuries further down the line.

The battle between Nadal and Federer was a hot topic of discussion in the build-up to the tournament. It was undoubtedly a healthy rivalry, based on mutual respect, and comparisons had been drawn to previous examples such as Pete Sampras–Andre Agassi and Bjorn Borg–John McEnroe–Jimmy Connors.

Rafa was not as vocal as McEnroe and Connors, nor did he have the trophy collection of Sampras or Borg, but he had shown himself to be among the best clay court players in the history of tennis and he was only going to keep improving. With the rest of the circuit trailing in the wake of Nadal and Federer, the top two seeds found themselves squaring off in more and more events on a range of surfaces, building the notion of an intense rivalry.

It had been a special year so far for the Mallorcan but now was not the time for reflection. There were plenty more tournaments on the horizon and he was soon packing his bags ready to chase more silverware. The tour really was non-stop for the top players, allowing them few opportunities to recharge their batteries. Seemingly paying the price for all his recent success, Nadal struggled to recreate the form that had seen him star at the French Open and at Wimbledon. He travelled to Toronto for the Rogers Cup, having won the title in Montreal in 2005, but fell in the third round to Tomas Berdych in disappointing fashion, 6-1, 3-6, 6-2. It was a similarly disheartening story in Cincinnati where Rafa seemed to be putting together a good run but then came unstuck in the quarter-finals against compatriot Juan Carlos Ferrero. With the US Open just around the corner, Nadal had hoped to take better form to Flushing Meadows.

Nadal remained confident, though, as he headed for New York and the US Open. It was another big event and Rafa had a taste for the big stage. He had adapted excellently to the grass at Wimbledon and hoped to adjust equally well to the hard court. His recent results had not been spectacular but he backed himself to turn it on when it really mattered. Visiting New York was always an exciting experience for a young player and Rafa was no different. Seeing sights such as The Empire State Building, Madison Square Garden and The Statue of Liberty was an added bonus and gave the Spaniard inspiration going into the Grand Slam, though as his fame grew, it became harder and harder to venture outside without attracting a swarm of attention. If a player could not get excited about performing in New York, they were in the wrong job.

In the first round of the US Open, Nadal faced Australian wildcard Mark Philippoussis. The Aussie was in the twilight years of his career but still presented a threat with his experience and powerful serve, giving Rafa a tricky start. Nadal would need to begin boldly and return serve well to advance to the second round. It proved to be a tight contest as Philippoussis cashed in on the freedom of having nothing to lose as the underdog in the contest.

But Rafa dug deep and managed to snatch a break of serve in each of the three sets, earning a 6-4, 6-4, 6-4 victory. It had not been easy and the Spaniard would have to raise his level of play as the tournament progressed. However, mentally he had held his nerve and worked out a way to win. This was a positive sign for the challenges ahead and his coaching team appeared pleased with most elements of the performance.

In the next round, Nadal took on Peruvian Luis Horna and was again forced to grind out a victory. Horna, ranked 61 in the world, showed no fear and stubbornly stayed in some brutal rallies against the Spaniard. Rafa edged the opening set 6-4 as he found his best form on the big points but the Peruvian refused to back down and some fine hitting saw Horna win the second set 6-4. It came as a shock to most viewers as Nadal had been expected to breeze through. Now the Spaniard had to buckle down and dig deep. He did so successfully, gradually wearing Horna down and seizing the upper hand on the Peruvian's serve to take the third set 6-4. Then Rafa was able to open up a bit. Horna's resistance began to crumble and the fourth set became a formality as Nadal raced to a 6-4, 4-6, 6-4, 6-2 victory and reached the third round. However, his displays were hardly striking fear into the hearts of Federer and the other top seeds. Rafa told the press: 'He was beginning to hit the ball harder in the second set and I had some problems so I had to play more aggressive.'

South African Wesley Moodie awaited Rafa in the third round. Once again, Nadal was made to toil against an unseeded player as Moodie proved to be full of confidence after claiming the scalp of number 27 seed Gael Monfils in the previous round. Rafa still had too much for Moodie to handle but the South African refused to roll over. Nadal grabbed the all-important break to claim the first set 6-4 but then required two tie-breaks to get the job done in three sets. He won the first 7-2 and the second 7-4 to book his place in the fourth round. It was not the most convincing performance again, though, and a few pundits questioned whether he was capable physically of hanging in there with fresher top seeds. It seemed as if he would come up short against superior talents than Moodie. Nadal's next match was against Slovakian Jiri Novak and he was hoping to up the tempo.

The opening set showed Rafa at his finest, pummelling winners from the back of the court and serving solidly. He ripped into Novak's serve and quickly sealed the set 6-1. It seemed like it would be plain sailing from then on for the Spaniard but he took his foot off the gas, as he is prone to do at times, just as Novak appeared to be on the ropes. Rafa still claimed the second set but was forced into a tie-break to win it. The Spaniard rose to the challenge and sealed a two-set lead, taking the breaker 7-3. This hit the Slovakian hard and he never looked capable of mounting a fightback. Going two sets down to Rafa is never good news and few ever recover from it. Nadal made sure, though, dominating the third set and completing a 6-1, 7-6, 6-4 victory. This was an improved display and talk began again of Rafa and Federer meeting in a third straight Grand Slam final after their exploits at Roland Garros and Wimbledon.

In the quarter-finals, Rafa took on Russian Mikhail Youzhny, who would become a nemesis for Nadal. The Spaniard was well aware of the quality left in the tournament. Federer was looking imperious as usual while Roddick, Blake and Davydenko were in impressive form too. But Nadal simply focused on Youzhny. The Russian was unseeded but few doubted that he was a star in the making. At 24, he had plenty of years to work on his game and move up the rankings. He had made his mark in New York with brilliant victories over Rafa's compatriots

David Ferrer and Tommy Robredo. The demolition of Robredo had been especially eye-catching and Youzhny was now seeking a third Spanish scalp.

He began confidently against Nadal. Considering it was the Russian's first ever Grand Slam quarter-final, he appeared very calm and outgunned Rafa in the early exchanges before coolly sealing the first set 6-3. He had been clinical and murmurs of surprise spread around the stadium. Was Nadal going to be punished for his patchy form? This was arguably Nadal's first big challenge in the tournament and he responded well, upping the aggression and eventually making inroads into Youzhny's serve. The Spaniard levelled the contest as he clinched the second set 7-5. Now, he had the momentum but the Russian continued to impress, matching Nadal shot for shot.

Rafa was still slightly in the ascendancy, though, and he crafted three set points in the third set. But Youzhny answered back with some fine decision-making under pressure and, having taken Nadal to a tie-break, the Russian cashed in to bag the breaker 7-5. The Spaniard's failure to clinch the set points seemed to have affected his concentration and now he had it all to do.

Unfortunately for Rafa, Youzhny was not in a charitable mood. The Russian was flawless in the fourth set, drilling winners and forcing a string of errors from Nadal. The Spaniard dropped his serve and Youzhny motored on to complete a stunning 6-3, 5-7, 7-6, 6-1 victory. It was a very disappointing end to Rafa's US Open run but he remained positive when speaking to the media. If he had capitalised on those set points, he knew it could have been a different story but he could not fault the excellent display from Youzhny. He would now rest his aching body and switch his attention to the next challenge. Nadal said: 'Maybe I played my best match in New York here today. I am happy with my tennis, but I was not playing with my best calm in the important moments.' It was a tough loss but, like he told the press, he had plenty more chances to win in New York. He was still in the formative years of his career and few doubted that he would be celebrating with the trophy in the future. It was important, though, that he learned from these moments and stayed calmer under pressure. It was unlike him to dwell on missed opportunities.

It was easy to forget just how young Nadal was at times and understandably all the pressure and wear and tear caught up with the Spaniard towards the end of the season. His style of play had left his body aching and all the travelling was another factor in his exhaustion. But there was no obvious break in his schedule. In the end, Rafa decided to take the sensible, cautious option. He chose to play just three tournaments in the final months of the season. He hoped that this would help his chances of beginning next season relatively fresh. The Spaniard arrived in Sweden for the Stockholm Open but was soon heading home as the world number 609 Joachim Johansson dealt him a humbling straight sets defeat.

Nadal seemed to have nothing left in the tank as he crashed out of the Madrid Masters in the quarter-finals and it was particularly upsetting not to be able to put on a show for the Spanish fans. The end of the season just could not come quickly enough as Rafa's stunning first half of the year caught up with him.

Nadal rounded off a below-par few months with a semi-final defeat to Federer in the end-of-year Tennis Masters Cup. In the tournament's round robin stage, Nadal conquered Davydenko and Robredo but lost to Blake. This had been enough to send him through to the semi-finals where Federer dispatched him 6-4, 7-5. He openly admitted that tiredness had played a key part in his failure to emulate his early season form. With experience, the youngster would learn ways to keep himself fresh for the full season and give himself every chance of bagging more trophies. He told the media: 'I had a lot of matches in the first half of the season and my muscles were very tired. Mentally, too, it was a big effort.'

He had not gone beyond the semi-finals of a tournament since reaching the Wimbledon final but backed himself to bounce back for the challenges that lay ahead in 2007.

Rafa would never forget the achievements of 2006 but he also saw plenty of areas to improve upon. His form at Wimbledon had pleased him greatly but he was desperate to win there in the years ahead. Similarly, he had his eye on better finishes in the Australian Open and the US Open. But it was hard to be too disappointed considering he had reached two Grand Slam finals that year and was still just 20 years old.

CHAPTER 3

HOT ON THE HEELS OF FEDERER

A new season meant more trophies to fight for. Rafa had enjoyed a break from tennis but was raring to go as he kicked off his 2007 season in India at the Chennai Open, preparing for the Australian Open later in the month. He certainly found his groove, easing through the tournament with some solid tennis before falling to Belgian Xavier Malisse 6-4, 7-6. Malisse went on to win the tournament.

The Spaniard also made solid progress in the doubles – something he rarely competed in but always relished. He teamed up with compatriot Bartolomé Salva Vidal and the pair surged into the doubles final in Chennai before Rafa came unstuck against Malisse again. Malisse and Dick Norman claimed a hard-fought final 7-6, 7-6. Nadal's strong performances gave him plenty of confidence as he looked ahead to the big events of the year but his preparation was hit by a groin injury he picked up in Sydney prior to the

Australian Open. He had to pull out of his match with Chris Guccione and began a nail-biting race against time to be fit for the Grand Slam.

Fortunately, Rafa's natural fitness allowed him to recover quickly and, after testing out the groin in practice, he felt ready to make a big impact as the tournament began. He had not participated in the 2006 Australian Open and so was desperate to make an impact this time. Missing out two years in a row would have been devastating.

His first match saw him face Kendrick, the American who had thrillingly taken him to five sets at Wimbledon in 2006 in one of the most significant matches of the Spaniard's career. Kendrick again threatened to be a thorn in Nadal's side, starting well and dominating a number of the rallies. The first set went to a tie-break and the Spaniard had a sense of déjà vu as Kendrick refused to be overawed. Rafa finally found the answer in the tie-break, winning it 8-6. It was proving a real struggle, though, as the American once more showed an appetite for the big occasion. But this time the Spaniard denied Kendrick a fast start.

From then on, Nadal was in command. He broke Kendrick's serve to win the second set 6-3 and then outclassed the American completely in the third set to clinch a 7-6, 6-3, 6-2 victory. After a slow start, Rafa had recovered his poise and was looking comfortable on hard court surface. It was just a case of eliminating the slow starts.

Nadal met German Philipp Kohlschreiber in the second round. Despite appearing to be free of the injury that he had suffered in Sydney, Rafa struggled at times against the German. This was the problem with having a style of play that was founded on an ability to cover incredible ground along the baseline. He needed to be totally mobile to succeed. The match began well. He roared into an early lead, easily breaking serve in the fourth game. But a wobble in the ninth game, an unforced error and a double fault, allowed Kohlschreiber to break back. Nadal stayed calm at 5-5 as the German earned a couple of break points but wasted them. Soon after, the Spaniard earned three set points on Kohlschreiber's serve. He, too, failed to cash in but, after missing a fourth chance, Nadal clinched the opening set 7-5 when a fifth arrived.

It had been hard work for Rafa and, despite his supreme fitness levels, he was feeling the effects of a tricky start. The second set was also tight for the majority, with Nadal and Kohlschreiber exchanging baseline shots. The German upset Rafa by aiming a shot directly at him and then trying to hit him again while he was grounded.

This was a very bad move. Nadal used his anger in the most dangerous way to break Kohlschreiber's serve in the eighth game for a 5-3 lead and then held his serve to move two sets ahead. The German had been gritty but he now had a mountain to climb if he wanted to reach the third round.

Nobody had told Kohlschreiber this, though. Far from being disheartened by his predicament, he came out fighting and took control of the third set as he forced Nadal into errors. In the sixth game, Rafa struck a forehand wide to give the German the crucial break. But from this moment on in the third set, neither player managed to hold their serve as anxiety kicked in. Kohlschreiber immediately allowed Nadal to break back before re-establishing his lead when the Spaniard double faulted. The German eventually took the set 6-4 as Rafa's serve deserted him. Would this be the start of a remarkable comeback for Kohlschreiber?

The answer from Nadal was an emphatic 'no'. Seemingly angered by his poor third set display, Rafa powered into the lead in the fourth set. After breaking the German's serve in a 15-minute opening game, Nadal burst into a 4-0 lead as his forehand cut Kohlschreiber to shreds. The German, ranked number 61 in the world, remained stubborn but Rafa was at his clinical best as he completed a 7-5, 6-3, 4-6, 6-2 victory.

He was extremely relieved to get through the match but knew that the sloppy errors had to be eradicated. He prided himself on forcing mistakes from opponents and so making in excess of 25 errors was a frustrating statistic. On the plus side, his groin injury had not flared up and he was feeling more comfortable with every passing day.

A third round clash with Swiss Stanislas Wawrinka was Nadal's reward for overcoming Kohlschreiber. Wawrinka, the world number 40, was unable to provide the same resistance, though, as Rafa upped his game. It was a particularly one-sided contest and the Swiss received no opportunities to impose himself. Ferocious baseline hitting saw Nadal grab the first set 6-2 and things got no better for Wawrinka, who struggled to hold his own serve throughout the match. Rafa took the second set by the same scoreline before dominating the third to win 6-2, 6-2, 6-2 and saunter into the last 16. This type of form gave him a great chance of going all the way to the Australian Open final and confidence was high.

Nadal was buoyant after his win over Wawrinka, telling the media: 'I played my best today for sure. I feel very comfortable with my forehand, with my serve, with my backhand too. Today I played a very complete match. I am very happy because if I keep playing like this, I have a chance for a win.'

Murray was the next man blocking Rafa's path to the final. The Scot had cruised past Juan Ignacio Chela in straight sets and was playing with plenty of confidence. It promised to be an entertaining encounter between two of the top young players in world tennis. Both seemed destined to be around on the world stage for many years to come. And they certainly lived up to this billing. A gripping first set stayed with serve throughout with Nadal looking particularly comfortable. But despite putting pressure on Murray, the Spaniard could not find the break of serve that he needed to wrap up the set. The Scot gifted Nadal a break point at 6-5 but it came and went and the opening set headed into a tie-break.

Murray, relieved to have saved his final service game of the set, had the momentum and began to force errors from Nadal. Rafa clawed back to 3-3 but then the Scot took charge again, winning the next four points to win the tie-break 7-3. A combination of fine serving from Murray and poor execution from Nadal had settled things in the Scot's favour. It was clear at this stage that the two were very well-matched and that the contest could go the distance. Both players had an abundance of energy and it took fine shot-making for either to hit a winner. Neither was likely to tire any time soon and the crowd settled in for a long match. Everyone knew that Murray had the quality to trouble some of the world's best and this was his chance to prove he had the mental strength to find results when he needed them most. So far, he had more than matched Rafa but question marks remained over the

Scot's temperament and his ability to bury opponents when he saw them faltering.

So much of tennis – and any professional sport for that matter – is dependent on a player's mentality. Those who could put the high stakes or disappointments to one side quickest tended to be the most successful. Often, this is what separates the youngsters from the seasoned professionals and it is a skill that only comes with a number of seasons on the tour. How a player responds to going 30-0 down on their own serve or earning a break point, for instance, will often decide the outcome of a match. It is in areas like this - and in the mental side of the game in general - that Rafa believes he has a true advantage.

Nadal, having served so well in the first set, struggled to match that standard in the second. After saving his opening service game from 0-40 down, Rafa should have had some momentum but Murray refused to let him settle. The Scot had been defensive early on but was now dominating the rallies and he broke Nadal on the way to a 4-1 lead.

Things looked bleak but Rafa held his serve to cut the gap to 4-2 and then broke back, finally finding his groove to smash two sensational winners. His forehand was beginning to make inroads into Murray's approach play and Nadal was building momentum. As his fist pumps became more frequent, the second set began to drift his way. After holding his serve for 4-4, Rafa hammered more baseline bullets and Murray was unable to handle them, losing his serve again with a double fault.

The Spaniard pounced on the opportunity to serve out the set with Murray struggling with a side injury. From 4-1 down, Nadal had won five games in a row and the match was level at one set all. It was hard to take for Murray who had been in the ascendancy during many of the rallies. The contrasting body language at the end of the second set suggested that Rafa would ease in the quarter-finals. Murray looked down and out, worrying about his injury and letting his frustrations get the better of him. He opted not to call for the trainer, choosing to fight on alone.

The Scot was flustered and let his disappointment carry on into the third set while Rafa began brightly. The Spaniard had learnt to seize upon such moments of indecision from his opponent and took it as a positive sign when he saw despondency across the net. It was simply a case of maintaining his intensity. Nadal took a 3-1 lead in the third set, breaking in the third game as Murray served up two double faults. But the Scot seemed to find a second wind, breaking back in the sixth game and regaining his poise on serve to go 5-4 up. Rafa had lost four of the past five games and was suddenly serving to stay in the set. He had created break points but had failed to capitalise. The Spaniard paid the price as Murray crafted two break points of his own with some gutsy attacking tennis and took the second of them to go 2-1 up. It was a hammer blow for Rafa.

The match had swung one way then the other and the momentum was currently with Murray. If Nadal wanted a spot in the quarter-finals, he would have to win in five sets. He would have preferred to get the job done more easily but the Spaniard was ready to do whatever it took to win. He certainly had sufficiently good fitness levels for the task.

The fourth set stayed with serve initially, despite Rafa's best efforts to force break points. Nadal was at full stretch in the fourth game, saving five break points to make it 2-2. By contrast, Murray held to love for 3-2 and was looking rock solid. Rafa needed to start making inroads as soon as possible or else the match would slip out of his grasp. But the Scot's suspect temperament handed Nadal a way back into the match. When things started to go wrong, Murray quickly grew frustrated rather than keeping his cool. As a result, he began to play looser shots and the unforced errors count quickly increased. Rafa got the all-important break and powered on to take the set 6-3. Murray had led 3-2 but once the Spaniard got his break, it was plain-sailing and the Scot's double faults had returned.

A fifth set seemed to favour Nadal rather than Murray, though both appeared to be weary as the match dragged on into the early hours in Melbourne. Rafa's opening service game presented his opponent with two break points but Murray missed out on both occasions. The Scot was furious with himself. He had created 14 breaking points in the match but had taken just three – again the mental side of the game was rearing its ugly head. He could not get away with surrendering rallies so limply against a player of Rafa's quality.

After that disappointment, Murray was left floundering. Nadal struck a stinging cross-court forehand to earn a break for 2-0 and then staved off three break points to go three games in front. Rafa moved to within touching distance of the win as he broke Murray for a second time, leaving the Scot shouting at himself. Murray finally got on the scoreboard at 5-1 but Nadal clinched a quarter-final spot as he won his next service game.

The match had lasted almost four hours and the crowd

rightly applauded both players' efforts in putting on a fine spectacle of tennis. Once again, Nadal had shown that even when he was not in peak form, he could find a way to win. His consistent hitting and tireless running had allowed him to edge past Murray, who had performed excellently himself. It was for matches like this that Nadal gave the extra 10% in every practice session. Rafa told the media: 'It was very, very tough and he's a great player, he's playing at an unbelievable level. It was a very important match for me, I need one match like this against one top player so I'm very happy.'

He added that he had felt in good shape, despite the gruelling nature of the match. If ever a match was going to test Nadal's fitness, this had been it. He said: 'I felt good physically in the fifth set, so that's important in these moments. He had a lot of chances in the fifth set in the beginning. I was trying all the time my best, trying to fight every point and just like that I can win this match.'

As he headed off for some well-earned rest, Nadal's mind wandered forward to the quarter-finals, where he would face Chilean Fernando Gonzalez. Gonzalez, like Murray, would play with passion and tireless energy and, if Rafa wanted to reach the semi-finals, he would have to be ready to work as hard as he had against Murray. He had not been totally honest about his fitness as some aches and pains still plagued him. But he vowed to fight on. However, the quarter-finals proved a step too far for Nadal on this occasion as Gonzalez capitalised on opportunities that Murray had squandered. The Chilean dominated the opening set, clinching it 6-2 as Rafa failed to find a rhythm. Too often, Nadal made unforced errors as Gonzalez simply waited for the Spaniard to attempt a winning shot. The Chilean served well too and Rafa was unable to claw his way back.

The second set was a similar story, although it was tighter. Gonzalez won it 6-4 and had again been the more dominant player. His measured approach left Nadal frustrated and the Chilean roared on to complete a superb 6-2, 6-4, 6-3 win. After all the fine displays that Rafa had produced so far in 2007, Gonzalez could not have anticipated progressing in straight sets but he had deserved it on the day. Nadal admitted as much to the press, saying: 'He was playing at a very good level. It wasn't good for me.' The Spaniard also revealed that an injury he had picked up against Murray had hindered his mobility on the court against Gonzalez.

There were plenty of positives to take away from the tournament for Rafa but the disappointment of not reaching the last four pre-occupied him as he packed his bags. Then again, there was always next year. Plus, there was no shame in losing to Gonzalez, who had put together a top drawer performance.

Elsewhere, in early April, Spain were in Davis Cup action against the USA. Unfortunately for Spanish supporters, Nadal was not with the team for the clash and, boosted by his absence, Roddick and his US team-mates produced an emphatic 4-1 victory in the tie. Considering his heroics the previous year, Rafa would have been the main danger man for the Americans to worry about.

And Nadal clearly had equal respect for his American counterparts. In fact, he jumped to their defence when speaking to the press. The faltering form of Roddick brought its fair share of criticism. Why had the American not fulfilled his potential? Was it fair to say that Roddick had under-achieved in his career? And where was the country's next crop of talented tennis players?

On the topic, Nadal defended the American production line, telling *TIME* magazine: 'Roddick is No. 4, and Blake is in the Top 10. So it's not bad, no? It's not the same as when Sampras and Agassi were No. 1 and 2. But American tennis is working.' It was a fair point but many still felt that America ought to be producing more stars for the future. The nation had played such a huge part in the history of the sport, contributing many great champions, that it was surprising to see them suffering a blip.

Roddick had reached successive Wimbledon finals in the past but he was one of many players struggling to keep up with the young blood joining the circuit. The likes of Nadal and Djokovic had motored past Roddick, leaving the United States without a serious contender. Reports would follow, mentioning a nationwide search for an American Rafael Nadal, which was naturally very flattering for the Spaniard.

He headed to Dubai next, where he played in the Dubai Tennis Championships. He reached the quarter-finals but was beaten 7-6, 6-2 by Russian Youzhny, who had dumped Rafa out of the US Open last year. While every tournament was important for the Spaniard, his next big objective was the French Open. All the hard court competitions would serve as opportunities for Rafa to get into a rhythm and ensure he was in peak condition.

After Dubai, Nadal's seemingly non-stop schedule saw him in Indian Wells, California, for the Pacific Life Open. He put together a fine string of results to reach the final, avoiding an unwanted hat-trick of quarter-final exits after the Australian

Open and Dubai. He met Djokovic in the final and outplayed the Serb to win 6-2, 7-5. When it came to the best-of-three-sets tournaments, Rafa rarely seemed to go into a third set. He would either outgun his opponent easily or stumble to defeat in two sets.

This success was a big boost for Nadal. It was always nice to get a few trophies under his belt before the clay court season began and he had played consistent tennis on the way to victory at Indian Wells. Of course, he would ultimately be judged on how he fared in the Grand Slams but the smaller tournaments were very useful for building momentum. The quarter-final curse struck again, though, at the Sony Ericsson Open in Key Biscayne, Florida. Nadal progressed to the quarters with some fine tennis but lost to eventual winner Djokovic 6-3, 6-4. The Serb put in a big performance to avenge his defeat at Indian Wells and Rafa had no answer on this particular occasion. It had been an up and down start to the year for the Spaniard but he remained pleased with his progress.

The clay court season was now approaching and Rafa knew that players would be lining up to end his dominance – just as they had last year. At the same time, though, there would be few players who genuinely believed that they could hang with Nadal in a five-set clay court contest. He loved this part of the season and enjoyed the challenge of living up to the expectations being placed on his shoulders. Seemingly, the more pressure that was applied, the better he played.

The press were calling him the King of Clay and he endeavoured to live up to this billing. Prior to the big prize – the French Open – Rafa gained valuable preparation time on court as he demolished the opposition in the warm-up events. If this was a sign of what was to come, the rest of the pack might as well forget about prising the Grand Slam away from Nadal. At the Monte Carlo Masters, he powered his way to the final without even having to find his best form. He then earned psychological points with a 6-4, 6-4 win over Federer in the final. The world number one appeared to be the likeliest man to dethrone Nadal in Paris but even he was some way short of Rafa's current level.

It was the Spaniard's third straight win in Monte Carlo and he became just the second player to achieve the feat there, after Ilie Nastase. Any win over Federer was worthy of praise but Rafa was the only player on the tour who possessed the weapons to beat the Swiss on a regular basis. Nadal then returned to his native Spain, where he won the Open Seat in Barcelona for the third consecutive year, beating Guillermo Canas in the final. Just for good measure, he completed an amazing few weeks by winning his third straight Rome Masters tournament with a victory over Gonzalez, his conqueror at the Australian Open, 6-2, 6-2. With this triumph, Rafa became the first man to win three successive Rome Masters titles – yet another record.

His one blip on the road to Roland Garros came in the Hamburg Masters where Federer beat him in the final 2-6, 6-2, 6-0. Rafa had started in sublime form but the Swiss fought back impressively and finished with a flourish. The defeat ended Nadal's winning streak on clay at 81 matches – unsurprisingly, a record in the open era for consecutive wins on a single surface.

Rafa had enjoyed an almost flawless run of results yet

again on his favourite surface and could not have felt more prepared or more confident as the French Open loomed. The Spaniard even found time to score another victory over Federer in the 'Battle of the Surfaces' – an exhibition match played on a half-clay, half-grass court. Nadal won a thrilling third set tie-break to triumph 7-5, 4-6, 7-6. He was looking untouchable.

Rafa was ready to hunt down another French Open crown and his title defence began in style. The same fear factor that many players experienced when facing Federer was apparent when opponents stepped onto the clay against Nadal. Often, they did not appear to actually believe they had a chance of victory and the Spaniard preyed on such doubts ruthlessly.

He faced promising young Argentine Juan Martin Del Potro in the opening round at Roland Garros and progressed with the minimum of fuss. Del Potro was talked of as a future star and a man capable of challenging the game's elite but Nadal's power and ability to chase down every ball left him stunned. The Spaniard took a relatively tight first set 7-5 before easing away from Del Potro, clinching a 7-5, 6-3, 6-2 win. On this evidence, it was going to take something special for Rafa to lose one set, never mind three. It was hardly encouraging for the rest of the field to see the champion begin in such convincing form. As soon as the point became a lengthy rally, Nadal always seemed to be in control.

Qualifier Flavio Cipolla was the next obstacle for Nadal – though obstacle was probably the wrong word. The Italian, ranked number 227, was given little time to enjoy his big moment in the spotlight as Rafa breezed through to the third round. He was clearly in a hurry to get the match wrapped up.

Nadal took the opening set 6-2 as Cipolla tried valiantly to compete with Rafa's intensity but came up well short like so many before him.

Worse was to follow for the Italian as Nadal annihilated Cipolla's serve as he blasted his way to a 6-1 scoreline in the second set. It was all too easy for the champion. Rafa finished off his masterclass with a strong third set showing, despite Cipolla's best efforts, clinching a 6-2, 6-1, 6-4 triumph. It had been a massacre but the Spaniard would have beaten far better players with a performance like this. The champion understandably seemed pleased with his efforts when speaking to the media. Cipolla had made the most of his day too. 'I had seen him [Nadal] on TV,' the Italian remarked touchingly. 'But playing him really makes an impression.'

After two comfortable victories, there was no reason to question Rafa's French Open credentials. He seemed to be the obvious frontrunner but there was some suggestion that Nadal would have greater difficulty against fellow Spaniard Albert Montanes. However, such claims proved to be wide of the mark as Rafa was on target from the very start and looked to be in total control.

Nadal broke Montanes early in the opening set on the way to a 6-1 scoreline. His opponent has barely found his feet and already Rafa was a set up. Seemingly intent on sending a message to the other title contenders, Nadal continued to fire bullets from well behind the baseline, sending Montanes scrambling from one corner to the other, just like so many opponents before him. Rafa eased into a two-set lead, winning the second set 6-3. Montanes had earned several break points – and would go on to claim nine in total in the match – but was quickly learning that Nadal could snatch them away in the blink of an eye.

Despite Montanes' best efforts, the champion wore him down and sealed his passage into the last 16, taking the third set 6-2. This victory, combined with his 21st birthday being the next day, ensured that Nadal was all smiles when he spoke to the media. It had been a very comfortable match. 'It was the best match for me so far in the tournament,' he said. 'I didn't play my best tennis but I played better than in the first two rounds. I like having my birthday here but I wasn't thinking about it today.' His modesty played down the fact that he was cruising along and was looking more and more likely to win a third straight French Open title. As Nadal enjoyed his birthday celebrations, he looked ahead to his fourth round clash with Hewitt, knowing that the Australian was a stubborn opponent but would be unable to handle Rafa on top form.

Hewitt had been at the top of the men's rankings not so long ago, winning Wimbledon along the way. The Australian had enjoyed great success with a similar approach to Rafa's, based on speed and gritty defence, but the Spaniard had greater power and therefore could conjure more winners. When he wound up his booming forehand, few could find a response. This was the case once more as Rafa showed yet again why he was called the King of Clay.

Nadal has sometimes been accused of being hesitant in the early exchanges of matches but he made a powerful start against the Australian, storming into a 4-0 lead with two fine breaks of serve. Hewitt felt the pressure immediately as unforced errors streamed from his racquet and Rafa seemed to be connecting with every stroke. A brief fightback from the Australian saw him close the deficit to 5-3 with a break but Nadal broke straight back to win the first set. It was a relentless start and he had caught Hewitt off guard.

The Spaniard had played an almost flawless set and Hewitt was having to chase hard just to stay in rallies, even on his own serve. The power of Rafa's forehand outweighed anything that the Australian could throw at him and the ball kept coming back with interest. Hewitt was still in great shape and had plenty of experience to fall back on, but it counted for nothing with the Spaniard finding his rhythm and pummelling winners.

It made for gripping viewing. When Nadal was playing this well, it was simply mesmerising and it came as a shock when he overhit the occasional ball because the accuracy of his shots was largely spot on. The number of times he hit deep returns was not a coincidence. He worked hard on landing balls near the baseline, often making it impossible for opponents to conjure a challenging response as the ball speared in around their feet.

The confidence of 17 consecutive wins at Roland Garros was propelling Nadal towards the quarter-finals in a hurry. He broke to love to go 3-1 ahead and Hewitt wilted, allowing the champion to win the next three games and clinch the second set. Any time that the Australian felt that a door was opening into the match, Rafa slammed it shut. Hewitt finally showed his true ability in the third set as his serve improved and his ground strokes began to hurt Nadal. The Australian missed out on a break point in the second game but he was winning his own service games with ease. Never one to throw in the towel,

Hewitt displayed real spirit to force an in-form Nadal into a tie-break.

The tie-break was as tight as the set itself but the Spaniard still found a way to win. He trailed twice by a mini-break but produced killer shots when it mattered most. Racing to return a fine Hewitt forehand, Rafa managed to reach a ball that few others would have bothered chasing. The Australian put the return into the net. It summed up the match – Nadal was just quicker and stronger than Hewitt. The champion clinched the tie-break 7-5 and he had still not dropped a set yet in the tournament.

Those expecting a close contest had been left disappointed but it was impossible not to credit Nadal for battering Hewitt into submission in the opening two sets. The Australian had given everything but had come up short on this occasion. It was an ominous sign for the chasing pack. Rafa told the press: 'It's perfect to be in the quarter-finals and it's perfect play. Ten times better than the last few days. The match was tough all the way. I'm very happy with my game.' Hewitt admitted: 'He served really well and he hit his forehand up the line extremely well. He just hits the ball so differently to anyone out there. The spin he gets, it's quite amazing.'

With everyone piling praise on Rafa, it was important not to get too carried away with all the hype - and he had his family and Toni, in particular, to ensure that never happened. His opponent in the quarter-finals was fellow Mallorcan and good friend Carlos Moya and Nadal was well aware of the threat that Moya posed on clay. However, most pundits believed the champion would storm on and achieve another three-set victory.

Moya, French Open champion in 1998, had played an important role as Nadal's mentor when Rafa first arrived on the scene but there was no room for sentiment with a semi-final place at stake. Djokovic had won his quarter-final earlier in the day and was awaiting the winner. Both players struggled to hold their serve in the opening set. Nadal crafted a break point in the third game but Moya denied him an early advantage. Rafa would not be denied, though., though. Having levelled the set at 2-2, he broke Moya in the fifth game as the 30-year-old put a drop shot into the net.

But both were returning serve so well that more breaking opportunities soon arrived. Moya capitalised on an ill-advised drop shot from Nadal to break back immediately. His joy was short lived, though, as Rafa secured another break in the seventh game. The youngster was increasingly becoming a brilliant returner of serve, using his speed and anticipation to pile pressure on his opponent. Moya, who had shown such faith in Rafa years earlier at the Davis Cup, was quickly being reminded that there would be no easy games.

Nadal's power and accuracy enabled him to cling onto the lead, moving 5-3 ahead despite some ferocious forehands from Moya. The champion was forced to scamper around the court as Moya took him to 30-30 before Rafa's power overwhelmed him. Nadal kept his composure as he served for the set and Moya made life easy for Rafa with some wild returns. He won the game to love and took the opening set 6-4. Moya had wracked up 17 unforced errors in the first set and would have to improve that statistic dramatically if he wanted to get back into the contest. He did his best but Nadal was on fire from behind the baseline, using the slower speed of the clay court to lie in wait and pounce on loose balls. Moya fought off a break point in his opening service game and when his forehand was on target he troubled the champion.

Nadal just seemed able to raise his game whenever he sensed danger and produce some incredible winners. Moya was playing well yet he had no answer to some of Rafa's ruthless forehands. Nadal broke serve in the third game as his opponent double-faulted and Moya appeared to be losing self-belief by the minute. The champion was left grasping at thin air, though, as Moya fought back and cranked up the pace of his first serve. But the early break kept Nadal ahead as he defended his own serve defiantly. Trailing 30-0 in the eighth game, Rafa rattled off four quick points to effectively end Moya's hopes in the second set. He added another break to win the set 6-3.

Moya had shown in the past that he was capable of coming back from two-set deficits but BBC Sport analyst John Lloyd echoed the thoughts of many when he said: 'Moya has come back from two sets down five times in his career which must be up there as one of the best records out there. But against Nadal? On clay?' As if to re-enforce Lloyd's point, Rafa made a storming start to the third set as the nine-year age gap between the two men began to show. With Djokovic waiting, Nadal appeared determined to take care of business as soon as possible. He broke in the second game as he outgunned Moya for a 2-0 lead.

It was truly staggering to watch as Moya – one of the hardest hitters on the tour – found himself overwhelmed by the efficiency of Nadal's play. It was clear that this contest would not go beyond the third set as Rafa took a 4-0 lead, picking apart Moya's serve. As his opponent tired, Nadal marched on towards a flawless set. He was briefly troubled in the fifth game but came back with some clinical winners. Rafa then completed his compatriot's misery as he broke Moya's serve yet again to seal an emphatic 6-4, 6-3, 6-0 triumph. If Djokovic was watching, he might well have been hiding behind the sofa. It was impossible not to be troubled by what he saw. In just under two hours, Nadal had powered past Moya and now he was gunning for the Serb. Rafa explained to the media that he felt he was playing even better than last year but was well aware of Djokovic's threat. The Serb had not been on the scene for long but he was already being mentioned in the same breath as the top players in world tennis. He and Nadal had squared off in the French Open quarter-finals last year, when the Serb retired due to injury, but many expected a tighter match this time.

The Spaniard was full of respect for Djokovic, telling the media: 'He's had an amazing season. I'm not surprised he has got so far. I'll have to be at my top level.' It promised to be a real spectacle as two stars of the future squared off. Moya dished out plenty of praise for his friend after being swept away by Nadal's quality. 'If he's focused the whole match, I don't see many players who can get a set,' he explained to reporters. 'Roger Federer's one of them, and Novak Djokovic can be one of them. To beat Rafa, you need to dictate the play, to dominate. But in a best-of-five-set match, that is difficult.'

The task for Djokovic was clear but by no means easy. He would need to throw Nadal off his usual game plan yet the champion had reached the semi-finals without coming close to dropping a set. And Rafa seemed to have a plan B and C to turn to if necessary. With Federer and Nikolay Davydenko contesting the other semi-final, the smart money was on a Nadal–Federer final.

Federer did indeed book his place in the final, leaving all eyes on Rafa and Djokovic. The Serb was fearless and made a bright start, showing he could produce enough winners to hurt Nadal. But in the fifth game, the Spaniard cranked up the pace and pushed Djokovic onto the back foot. Rafa created a break point and took it ruthlessly, overpowering the Serb in a rally then smashing a forehand winner.

Both players were producing their best tennis as the crowd enjoyed arguably the most exciting set of the tournament. Nadal powered into a 5-2 lead with a second break of serve but Djokovic did not falter as others had against the champion. The Serb broke back as Rafa double-faulted on break point and won the next two games, clinching a second break for 5-5. For the first time in the tournament, Nadal was under pressure. He had failed to take set points at 5-4 and Djokovic had made the most of his reprieve with such stylish winners. Errors were creeping into Rafa's game and the Serb seemed to have the momentum. The spectators were on the edge of their seats.

But Nadal had won the past two French Open titles for a reason: he came up with decisive shots when it mattered most. He hit with more power, chased harder and piled more pressure on Djokovic. And the Serb did not take a step back either, playing his part in some glorious rallies that provided a glimpse of the future. Rafa eventually managed to induce errors from his opponent. He found another break of serve to move 6-5 ahead and then served calmly, taking his third set point with a classy forehand winner. It was vintage Nadal and he heaved a sigh of relief as he headed for his chair.

It had been a gruelling opening set and Djokovic had played exceptionally well, yet Nadal had still proved to be too good. It was a frustrating moment for the Serb. The crowd were glued to the action, watching two youngsters battling tooth and nail, and it was a great advert for tennis. The pair seemed capable of breaking each other's serve at will as they played rally after rally from the baseline.

Djokovic certainly showed the stomach for a fight. He began superbly in the second set, holding serve to love and battering Nadal's serve. But, despite crafting three break points in the second game, he just could not shake off the Spaniard. Nadal's serving improved as the set wore on and he snatched a vital break in the seventh game, sprinting to curl a forehand winner past the Serb. So often against the world's best, one break point was all an opponent could hope for in a set and, if they failed to take it, they were usually punished severely. And that proved to be the case in this semi-final as Rafa's relentless play began to leave Djokovic shell-shocked after such a promising start to the set. Against any other player, the Serb would have been on the way to victory with such a high standard of performance. Yet against Nadal, he was clinging on for dear life in the contest. He threw everything at the Spaniard to close the gap to 5-4 but Rafa once again found key shots at crucial moments.

Serving for the set he moved 40-0 ahead before Djokovic stormed back with four straight points. Suddenly facing break point, Nadal stayed composed and fired just his second ace of the day. It was perfect timing. When Djokovic overhit a forehand, his fate was sealed in the second set as Rafa clinched it 6-4.

The exhausting rallies were beginning to take their toll on both players, especially Djokovic. Nadal was able to capitalise on some weary shots from the Serb as he dominated early in the third set. After two tight sets, the Spaniard cut loose and left Djokovic trailing. Breaks of serve in the first and third games allowed Rafa to surge into a 4-0 lead and effectively end the Serb's hopes. He was finding the most amazing angles with his winners. Even at his freshest, Djokovic would have been unable to chase down some of the thunderbolts that Nadal was hitting.

An enthralling encounter ended as Rafa served out successfully to complete a fabulous 7-5, 6-4, 6-2 victory and set up everyone's dream final against Federer. Djokovic had been good but, on this particular day and this particular surface, just not good enough. Nadal acknowledged the quality of Djokovic's display and looked ahead to the final. He told the media: 'It should be a great match. Anytime you have the number one and number two in the world playing each other it is something special. He [Federer] is playing well and has dropped just the one set in the tournament so I will have to be at my very best to be able to beat Roger. I will do all I can to achieve that.'

A third French Open crown at 21 would unquestionably put Nadal among the most successful clay court players in history but Federer would be throwing everything into finally conquering Roland Garros. It promised to be a brilliant contest. Federer had dropped one set en route, Nadal had not dropped any. Both players had cruised through much of the tournament and neutrals were desperate for a great, closely-contested final. Judging by the crowd reaction as the players were introduced, the Swiss seemed to have the backing of the home fans but most just wanted to see an epic clash.

The opening five games saw the two players feeling each other out and settling in for a long afternoon. They stayed with serve, despite Federer earning two break points at 2-1. The challenger took a 3-2 lead into the sixth game and once more attacked Nadal's serve. In all, Federer crafted five break points in the game but Rafa relied heavily on his first serve to get himself out of trouble. He was increasingly becoming invincible at key moments – and this was usually Federer's speciality. And after the frustration of failing to snatch the break, Federer momentarily crumbled. A relieved Nadal stepped up a gear and forced his opponent into sloppy errors. He raced to 40-0 on the Swiss' serve and, unlike Federer, the Spaniard capitalised for a 4-3 lead and the first break of the match. A momentary lapse in concentration from his opponent was all he needed.

The Swiss looked to level things up as he made light work of Rafa's serve again. Nadal was finding it difficult to impose himself on rallies and was making too many mistakes. Federer moved to 40-0 up to earn three more chances to break. But the champion survived again through a combination of clever serving and some poorly-executed strokes from Federer, whose despair was evident as each point slipped away. Of course, Nadal had shown great fight but the challenger knew that taking none of his ten break points thus far was simply not good enough. Against someone of Rafa's quality, he had to be better than that.

To rub salt into the wounds, Rafa grabbed his second break to take the first set 6-3 with a scorching forehand. Nadal had played the big points better than Federer but had to feel a little fortunate to be a set up despite playing below his best. As BBC Sport analyst John Lloyd observed at the time: 'I don't think Nadal played a particularly good set there but Federer faded badly.'

The second set saw Federer in more clinical form but Nadal was steadily improving too. The Spaniard seemed to be more in control with his serve as he denied the Swiss break chances in the early stages. He was mixing up his serve to great effect and Federer was having more difficulty dictating play. The rallies became more intense as the power of the hitting went up another notch. Nadal held off a Federer surge to go 3-2 up but the Swiss levelled with a solid service game.

It all finally came together for Federer in the seventh game. He raced to 40-0 up on Rafa's serve and, although the champion saved one break point, the Swiss would not be denied as he moved into a 4-3 lead. Nadal earned chances to square things up in Federer's next service game but the challenger withheld the onslaught and produced a string of fine forehands to keep his advantage. Nadal closed to 5-4 but Federer had his eyes on levelling the match and produced some timely big serves to move to set point. Rafa sent a forehand long and those hoping for an epic final were all smiles as Federer made it one set all.

How would the champion recover after losing his first set of the tournament? By winning three straight games was the answer. He broke Federer's serve at the first opportunity and heaped the pressure back onto the Swiss. The set was tighter from this stage onwards but Nadal had made the all-important inroads. Federer's forehand had become somewhat erratic and he was failing to trouble Rafa's serve as he had in the opening set.

The Spaniard crafted a set point in the eighth game on Federer's serve but the challenger scrapped his way out of trouble, closing to 5-3 with an ace. Relentless attacking strokes from Nadal found the mark in the following game, though, as he wrapped up a convincing set 6-3. It was an emphatic response to losing the second set and Rafa seemed to have plenty left in the tank. But did Federer have the energy to take the match to five sets? Could he raise his game again? The early signs were not encouraging in this regard. Nadal was still full of running and the power of his shots did not seem to be fading. He troubled Federer in the opening game of the set, then broke in the third game as he clinically finished with a thundering forehand. It did not bode well for the rest of the locker room if even the world number one was unable to handle Rafa's brutal style of play.

Federer was on the ropes as Nadal held serve for a 3-1 lead. Five Live analyst Pat Cash remarked: 'The errors just keep creeping up from Federer but he's got to keep going for his shots, he can't go back to rallying with Nadal.' This was true. Any time that the two players participated in a lengthy rally, it favoured the Spaniard, who invariably found the decisive blow on his favourite surface.

Rafa gave Federer no route back into the match as he continued his unerring hitting. The Swiss managed to hold serve under intense pressure from Nadal but the champion would not falter, easing to a 5-3 lead with a comfortable service game. It was now or never for Federer as he served to stay in the contest. A big serve kept his hopes alive but Nadal seemed capable of breaking at any moment and each service game was a struggle for the world number one. Federer knew the end was nigh as Nadal served for a third successive French Open title.

The Spaniard was struggling with nerves, as he so often does when approaching the finish line, but he did not show it. He raced to 40-0 with three confidently-constructed points. Federer then sent a forehand long and that was it – Rafa had done it again.

He fell to the ground in celebration. He was the champion once more and was now 21 games unbeaten at the tournament. Rafa climbed the stands and enjoyed the moment with his family who had watched on proudly all afternoon. 'I'm sorry for Federer, he's a terrific player and a great competitor,' Nadal explained to the media. 'The first set was very important, he had a lot of break points. It's just a dream to win here and I've got to keep working to get better and better.' Federer revealed his anguish after the defeat, saying: 'It was an incredible effort from Rafa once again. Of course I am disappointed but I was playing a great player. I had so many opportunities but I couldn't take them unfortunately.'

Nadal's sensational victory brought down the curtain on another stunning clay court season. His play had been relentless and he had only lost once – to Federer in the final in Hamburg. It was a record to be proud of and led many to suggest he would finish his career as the greatest clay courter in history.

The key now was to use the momentum of this victory to improve his efforts on other surfaces. He focused his attention on returning to the final at Wimbledon and improving at the US Open, where he hoped to reach the last four for the first time. Though he would have enjoyed a rest after Roland Garros, there simply was not time. The grass court season beckoned and Nadal was determined to be well-adjusted to the surface before Wimbledon began. All eyes would be on Federer's attempt to equal Bjorn Borg's five straight titles at SW19 but the Spaniard had ambitions of his own. He hoped to sneak up on Federer under the radar and his string of recent wins over the world number one gave him plenty of belief.

A year on from his gallant defeat against Federer in the Wimbledon final, Nadal was back in London hoping to go one better and lift the trophy. Rafa had again successfully defended his French Open crown against the Swiss but was now intent on making the necessary adjustments to playing on grass. If he did not succeed in London, it would not be for the lack of effort.

Nadal arrived at Queen's prior to Wimbledon with a determined look in his eye. This early practice enabled him to get to grips with the different surface – the faster courts and lower bounce. Though Rafa was beaten in the quarter-finals 7-5, 7-6 by Frenchman Nicolas Mahut, he felt pleased with the practice and the way he was striking the ball. Still, another match or two would have been even more beneficial. Nonetheless, he was confident. The draw ensured that he could not meet Federer until the final and he felt capable of matching the previous year's achievements. And so, with his first round match against American Mardy Fish looming, Nadal was raring to go. Unfortunately, he was forced to be patient as the longevity of Tim Henman's match led to a wait in the locker room before the Spaniard could step out onto the court. He passed the time listening to music and trying to stay loose. When he did head out onto the court, he was clearly eager to avoid a lengthy match.

Fish, whose big serve can make him a tricky opponent on his day, had no answer as Rafa out-hustled him. Nadal took the first set 6-3 and never looked back on the way to a 6-3, 7-6, 6-3 victory. He loved the atmosphere of Centre Court and it seemed to bring out the best in him. His journey towards the final had begun. He summed up his day's work perfectly when he told the media: 'I played very, very good today. I felt very comfortable on court but it is my first match.' Admittedly, there was still a long way to go but he had made an excellent start.

The world number two had even fewer problems in the next round as he disposed of Austrian Werner Eschauer. In a slow start, Nadal was broken in the second game but bounced back immediately as Eschauer lost his serve in the third, fifth and seventh games. Rafa won six games in a row in the first set to take it 6-2. Being such a consistent returner of serve gave him endless opportunities to gain an advantage. It meant that even when he was trailing, he felt sure that a purple patch would arrive to pull him level.

The second set went with serve until Nadal broke Eschauer in the seventh game with a powerful winner. The Austrian otherwise played a solid set but the margins are so fine against Nadal and that single break was enough to see the Spaniard go two sets up, taking the second 6-4 with a blistering ace. Eschauer looked a beaten man as the third set began and he put up little resistance as Nadal cranked up the tempo. There was rarely much hope to cling to once Rafa had gone two sets ahead. The history books showed he was far from charitable in that regard.

The Austrian held his serve for 1-0, only to lose the next six games. Sloppy errors cost Eschauer dearly and Rafa completed a comfortable 6-2, 6-4, 6-1 victory. He had not needed to be at his best but had nonetheless played some sparkling tennis at times, showing glimpses of his all-round genius. The only concern was that he still sometimes took a few games to get into his stride and might be punished by more talented opponents in the early stages of matches.

Nadal began his third round match against Swede Robin Soderling on the Saturday but did not complete it until Wednesday as the English capital experienced heavy rain and the Spaniard failed to take his chances to progress. As a result, he had to dig himself out of a potentially disastrous situation. In a tight first set, Rafa struggled to find the timing on his passing shots and Soderling gave him limited opportunities to impose himself. However, Nadal grabbed the all-important break in game seven as Soderling opted to leave a volley that just dropped in. The Spaniard held on to take the set 6-4.

Momentum swung one way then the other in the second set as Nadal broke for 2-0 only to see Soderling pull back to 3-3. This did little to deter Rafa who managed to break again and, after a lengthy rain delay, clinch the set 6-4 as the Swede wildly fired two unforced errors. It seemed that there was no way back for Soderling but the upheaval of the rain delays appeared to distract Nadal and suddenly the Swede began to claw his way back. The third set had begun well for Rafa as he took a 3-1 lead yet he was punished for not putting the match to bed. Soderling broke him twice to go 5-3 up, only for Nadal to break back and set up a tie-break. Tension was building between the two players as the Swede in particular increased his aggression.

A dramatic tie-break saw Nadal up 4-2 then down 6-5. The Spaniard saved a set point and, at 7-7, the players were forced off the court by yet more rain. When they returned, the Swede was the quicker out of the blocks as he won two straight points to take the tie-break 9-7 and keep the match alive. Would this be a rare example of Rafa squandering a healthy advantage?

Nadal looked frustrated in the fourth set and let his emotions get the better of him. He knew that he had had plenty of chances to end the match in the third set and was dismayed by the on-off nature of the rain breaks. But he could not use this as an excuse. Soderling was fired up and broke Rafa in the seventh game. With the light quickly worsening and Nadal in disarray, the Swede delivery a solid service game under pressure to make it two sets all as this incredible match took another dramatic twist.

It was time for the winner-takes-all fifth set. There was no question that Soderling was on top but Nadal gritted his teeth and dug deep. As the animosity between the two players intensified, the Swede upset Rafa with a delay to change his racquet. Nadal responded with some delaying tactics of his own and Soderling began to imitate some of the Spaniard's mann-erisms. Putting the gamesmanship to one side, Rafa held his serve and then broke the Swede for 2-0. Then, typically, the rain came down again, ending Monday's play. It came at the worst time for Nadal, who was starting to pull away in the final set.

As the players returned on the Tuesday afternoon, desperate to get the match finished, Rafa seemed the favourite. He had had time to put his disappointment behind him and, crucially, he held the 2-0 lead. But Soderling had other ideas and, resuming at 30-30 on Nadal's serve, he broke back and then made it 2-2. With the match locked at 4-4, more rain left Rafa raging at the constant disruption, even though he understood it was unavoidable.

Back on court on Wednesday, the fifth set progressed to 5-5 as both players held their serve. It would probably come down to one break now and Nadal was desperate to grab it. He just clung on to his serve with a solid forehand to move 6-5 up. As Soderling served to stay in the match, Rafa was ready to pounce. He hammered some brutal shots to set up two match points but wasted them, hitting into the net and then wide. The Swede saved a third match point with a stunning cross-court winner but his luck ran out when he struck the ball wide and then long. Nadal had won an epic contest – but knew it should never have gone this far.

The Spaniard dropped to his knees in celebration. He had needed every bit of his incredible stamina to hold off Soderling. Incredibly, he had only just finished his third round match and was worryingly behind schedule now. It looked as though he would be playing round the clock in order to squeeze in all his matches. Speaking after the match, he revealed his unhappiness at some of Soderling's antics and admitted that he was stunned by the decision not to play on Sunday, despite the congested schedule.

'I don't understand why we don't play on Sunday when the weather was OK,' Rafa explained. 'They don't think very much about the players here, maybe.' He added with a smile: 'We have to play a lot of days in a row, although on the other side of the draw Roger [Federer] was having a holiday for the last week!' But Nadal had to forget all the resentment and frustration in order to concentrate on the fourth round, where he would meet Youzhny.

He found himself back on the court 24 hours after completing his marathon match with Soderling. Little did he know, he was about to enter another colossal bout. Youzhny was unsurprisingly fresher but the first set was extremely tight as both players served well and backed it up with powerful winners.

It was the Russian, against whom Nadal had struggled in the past, who had the edge. He served well to go 5-4 up and then broke Rafa's serve to win the set. Nadal looked weary and Youzhny capitalised, racing into a 3-0 lead at the start of the second set and displaying his brilliant backhand to devastating effect. Rafa chased and stretched but the Russian was always in the right place to deliver the finishing blow. He could not break back and Youzhny clinched the second set 6-3 as the Spaniard fired wide.

If Rafa was going to keep his title bid alive, he would have to go to five sets again. Having been two sets up against Soderling, he was now on the receiving end but managed to fire himself up to hit his way back into the match. He refused to give up on his Wimbledon dream and started playing with the freedom of knowing he had to go for his shots.

Nadal instantly looked fresher as he broke Youzhny in the

second and sixth games as his forehand began to leave the Russian panting. The fast-paced rallies started to stretch Youzhny and he could not match Rafa's power. The Spaniard served out the set to win it emphatically 6-1. Suddenly, it was all Nadal. Youzhny, who had been suffering with a back injury, simply wilted under the pressure. He had looked imperious in the first two sets but was already on the ropes as the fourth set started. Perhaps he had known that a fast start was necessary because of his back problems. Rafa broke his serve in the third game and quickly established a 3-1 lead. The Russian held firm for his next service game but in game seven he netted a forehand to give Nadal the double break. The Spaniard needed no second invitation to serve out the set – 2-2. 'Vamos!' was the cry from Rafa.

The crowd were on their feet as Nadal showed yet again that he had the stomach for a real scrap. He broke Youzhny in the third game of the deciding set after a delightful drop shot and moved 4-1 up with a break in the fifth game. By now, the outcome was no longer in doubt. The Russian tried to stay in the rallies but every baseline duel favoured Nadal, who was moving with the kind of agility that defied belief after so much tennis of late. The Spaniard missed out at match point in the seventh game but recovered to hold his serve in the eighth for a 4-6, 3-6, 6-1, 6-2, 6-2 victory.

He was into the quarter-finals but many wondered whether there was any energy left in the tank. Yes, he had utterly demolished Youzhny once he upped the tempo at the start of the third set. But he was living on the edge and faced a race against time to get his aching body ready for the next round. Nadal told the press: 'I thought I might be going home today.

Youzhny was playing very good. For me it was an important victory. The last three sets I never played like this on grass.' With Rafa due to play his quarter-final the next day, Youzhny believed that the Spaniard would be able to handle the non-stop action: 'Three hours is nothing for Nadal. He'll be ready for tomorrow for sure.' Rafa's hopes now rested in the hands of Titin, his XXXX, and his doctors

Czech Tomas Berdych would be Nadal's opponent in the quarter-final as the Spaniard tried to avoid another five-set marathon. Rafa got an early break in the first set but a fine Berdych forehand allowed the Czech to break back. The set stayed with serve and headed into a tie-breaker, which Nadal played to absolute perfection. He went 5-0 up with a couple of sizzling aces and Berdych contributed to his own downfall with some weak errors. Rafa won the tie-break 7-1 to clinch the first set. And he never looked back. He handled a troublesome wind and, after breaking in the first game of the second set, held the advantage. Berdych attempted to find the break but was unable to withstand Nadal's hitting, losing the second set 6-4. Rafa's serve was holding up well, answering some of his critics who still saw it as a weak point.

Just as Youzhny had appeared almost resigned to defeat at the start of the fifth set in the previous round, Berdych looked a beaten man here. Nadal broke the Czech's serve in the first game of the third set and then again to go 4-1 ahead. The crowd was thinning as a win for the Spaniard became inevitable. Berdych held his serve to reduce the deficit slightly to 5-2 but nothing could stop Rafa sealing the set and the match as the Czech made yet another unforced error to give Nadal a straight-sets 7-6, 6-4, 6-2 win.

After all the hours on court, Rafa could finally stop and reflect on what he had achieved. He was in the semi-finals again, despite a fatigue-inducing schedule, and was hitting top form at exactly the right time. The Spaniard spoke proudly after easing past Berdych: 'I played a very, very good match. I know I beat one of the best players in the world, especially on this surface.'

Djokovic beat Marcos Baghdatis in a dramatic five-hour, five-set marathon to set up a semi-final against Nadal. The Serbian had received treatment for a back injury during the victory and suddenly Rafa was going into a match as the fresher player, despite participating in two five-set contests of his own.

Rafa knew that Djokovic would be desperate to start strongly and avoid another lengthy match yet he was still unable to prevent the Serb from taking the first set in their semi-final. Djokovic broke Nadal in the second game and, although the Spaniard improved, the Serb hung on to take the set 6-3. Djokovic had always impressed against Rafa in previous matches but had not had the composure or experience to convert promising spells into dominant sets. Maybe this was about to change. But Rafa stepped up his game in the second set and gained momentum when he broke Djokovic in the second game, using Hawk-Eye to overturn a vital line call. Nadal broke again in the sixth game and served out to win the set 6-1. The Serb was clearly suffering with his back problems and could not keep up with the speed of Nadal and the ferocity of his hitting. The Spaniard was back on track and this meant big trouble for the Serb.

Djokovic called for the trainer, who attended to a foot

problem rather than his back injury, but even this pause could not throw Rafa off his game. He knew that he was in charge of the contest and that if he held his nerve, he would be in his second consecutive Wimbledon final.

Though Djokovic held his serve in the first game of the third set, it was only a matter of time before Nadal gained the ascendancy. He levelled at 1-1 and then won the next three games to take a commanding 4-1 lead. Again the trainer was called and on this occasion Djokovic decided he could not continue. He conceded the match, sending Rafa into the final. After the match, the Serb spoke to the press about the toe infection and blister he had picked up, as well as the back problems that had forced him to retire from the semi-final. Nadal then revealed his intention to win the final against Federer, who overcame Gasquet in the other semi-final. 'He is the favourite – there is no doubt about this. But I will try my best. I will try to go to the court believing in a victory.' And the Spaniard added his sympathy for Djokovic, saying: 'I'm sorry for him, he arrived in the semi-finals playing good tennis.' So, two weeks of toil would end with another Nadal-Federer showdown. Clearly, the Spaniard had made big improvements on grass since last year but had he done enough to match the champion? Federer was chasing a fifth straight Wimbledon triumph, which would equal Bjorn Borg's record, and had dropped just one set so far in the tournament.

Opinion was divided on who would come out on top. The majority favoured Federer, especially as he was the fresher of the two players and had the added motivation of matching Borg, but others felt Nadal was now ready to oust the Swiss.

A year ago, Federer had admitted his shock at seeing the Spaniard reach the final. This time, it surely came as no surprise. Rafa told the press: 'He [Federer] is the most complete player on the tour. But if I have the chances in the final, I will believe more than I did last year. If I win here, it will be the best moment of my career.' Borg offered the Spaniard a little advice, saying: 'Nadal needs to serve well, keep him at the back of the court and come in a little bit more.'

As the players walked out onto Centre Court, tennis fans everywhere were on the edge of their seats. It promised to be a special match.

Federer won the toss and elected to serve first. He took a 1-0 lead then broke Nadal in the Spaniard's first service game. Fans cast their minds back to 2006 when Rafa had been blown away in the opening set. Would it take him a set to get into his stride again? Surely, he could not afford for that to happen. But Nadal had learned valuable lessons that year and refused to be deflated by Federer's strong start. Going back to his chair 3-0 down was hardly the ideal start but he was only a break behind. There was plenty of time to draw level.

Rafa settled himself by getting on the scoreboard at 3-1, hammering a big ace to secure the game after using his forehand to manoeuvre Federer around the court. This was more like it. Nadal's calmness under intense pressure was then rewarded in the fifth game when he broke back. Despite being bamboozled by a Federer drop shot at the start of the game, Rafa conjured a couple of sublime passing shots to leave the Swiss flat-footed and then capped things off by smashing a backhand winner down the line to bag the break.

Rafa was into his stride now and was making Federer work

hard for every point. A solid service game levelled the set at 3-3 and suddenly it was Nadal who had won three straight games. The crowd waited with anticipation to see how the champion would respond. Federer, like Rafa, did not become flustered and, despite Nadal's efforts in chasing down seemingly impossible shots, the set went with serve. A brilliant forehand winner from Nadal levelled up the set at 5-5. It was gripping stuff on Centre Court and, after the terrible weather that had hit the tournament, everyone was thrilled that the rain was staying away.

Both remained rock solid on serve and Rafa wowed the crowd with a superb love service game, sending the opening set into a tie-break. Suddenly, the players looked edgy and the majority of the points came from unforced errors rather than glorious winners. Federer took control at 4-1 but Nadal refused to throw in the towel. Facing three set points, Rafa fought back to level it at 6-6 with the aid of Hawk-Eye and Federer looked furious with himself for wasting a handful of glorious openings. But the champion would not be denied, clinching the tie-break 9-7 with a backhand volley after Rafa had handed him the initiative with another unforced error. It was frustrating for Nadal to have played such a fine set yet finish with nothing.

However, he remained confident. Sitting down at the end of that first set, he refused to dwell on missed opportunities. He had begun brightly – a definite improvement on the 2006 final – and he carried plenty of positive energy into the second set. Rafa knew he had the character to bounce straight back – after all, he had triumphed in two five-set matches en route to the final and was fully prepared to go the distance again.

Federer's sheer presence, never mind his tennis genius, was enough to leave most men quaking when they stepped on a court with him. But it was different with Nadal and both players knew it. The Spaniard's superiority on clay meant he had experience of beating Federer and he was fast closing the gap on grass. Nadal had played well in the first set but he was even better in the second. He seemed to be hitting the ball harder than ever as he sought to gain a crucial break on Federer's serve. The Spaniard was troubling the champion with his lethal forehand and drawing errors but the set stayed with serve as Federer stayed firm to make it 2-2. Rafa had two break points in the sixth game after some dazzling rallies and more support from Hawk-Eye. He was beginning to take control of the lengthier rallies. But he could not convert these break points as Federer brilliantly conjured two stunning aces to keep the Spaniard at bay and was then relieved to see Nadal make unforced errors to help him get out of jail.

The Spaniard had a few jitters of his own at 4-4 as Federer earned a break point, but he held his nerve to force the champion to serve to stay in the set. Nadal had managed to pick up several points in Federer's service games but just could not get the break. He was running out of time to avoid another tie-break, which seemed to favour the champion's ruthless efficiency and big serve. Rafa's tireless running at the back of the court quickly had Federer in trouble in the tenth game. The Swiss was already angered by Hawk-Eye and Nadal's brilliance did little to help the champion's mood. The Spaniard delivered a winner while falling backwards and then slammed an unstoppable backhand past Federer to bring up two set points.

Nadal knew he had to take this opportunity – if he did, he would be level. This was a huge moment for the challenger. And he grabbed it. Rafa's backhand again proved decisive as he punched the ball stylishly past Federer to win the second set 6-4. Game on. There was no doubt that Federer had been thrown off his game a little by Nadal's refusal to be bullied in the rallies. He was hitting the ball harder than the champion and giving him by far his toughest test of the tournament. The Swiss had also uncharacteristically allowed the Hawk-Eye decisions to affect his game.

Nonetheless, Federer came out strongly in the third set. His serving was simply phenomenal as he gave Nadal few opportunities to break. Rafa had to save a break point in the first game and the Swiss always looked capable of picking up points on the Spaniard's serve. Meanwhile, the Swiss eased to 40-0 too often for Rafa's liking but there was little he could do as Federer unleashed ace after ace. Nadal was hanging on but his power helped him withstand Federer's onslaught. The Swiss levelled at 4-4 with a love service game, showing he too could hit ferociously as he sent Rafa scrambling all over the court. Fortunately for the Spaniard, his own serve was holding up well. It had certainly improved considerably since his final appearance at Wimbledon last year.

He created his best breaking opportunities towards the end of the set at 5-4 up and 6-5 up. But once again the Swiss stepped up a notch with a couple of classy touches. The third set headed into a tie-break. Nadal never found his rhythm in the tie-break as Federer took a 2-0 lead and used his powerful serve to devastating effect. Rafa answered with a stinging forehand and then an ace to cut the Swiss' lead to 3-2. However, Federer took control with an ace followed by two quick points after the changeover to gain an imperious 6-2 lead.

The Swiss was too good to waste so many set points, converting the second of them as Nadal overhit a backhand. Federer was back in the ascendancy but he had had to pull out all the stops. Once more, Rafa headed for his chair feeling aggrieved. He had produced another solid set but the tie-break had haunted him again as Federer pulled away. He reminded himself that he was playing very well and prepared to level things in the fourth set.

Federer returned from a bathroom break but must have wished he had stayed inside for longer as Nadal took the fourth set by the scruff of the neck. Rafa gained a break in the first game with a glorious forehand winner just as the Swiss seemed to be wrapping it up. It was the perfect start for the Spaniard. Nadal consolidated the break with more solid hitting. Federer had surged back to 40-30 but a well placed serve clinched the game for the Spaniard. He was on a roll now and he followed this with another break in the third game as Federer fumed over Hawk-Eye, telling the umpire: 'It's killing me.' Suddenly, Nadal was 4-0 up and within touching distance of his third five-set contest of the fortnight. The champion was threatening to self-destruct as the pressure mounted.

The Swiss held serve as he continued to seethe and a few words were exchanged between the pair as the tension went through the roof. Rafa needed the trainer to attend to a knee injury but it proved just to be a minor cut and, after receiving some spray and bandaging, he was back out on the court, ready for more. The crowd sighed in relief – this classic would continue. And Nadal was soon enjoying a 5-1 lead as Federer put a backhand wide after looking dangerous momentarily at 30-15 up. The Swiss stayed alive with some gutsy serving but the ball was very much in Rafa's court – he was serving for the set.

The Spaniard took his time, knowing the importance of the moment. However, the cushion of the double break eased the pressure somewhat. A lovely backhand put Nadal 30-0 up but Federer hit back with a whipped forehand winner. Rafa shrugged this off, though, and bagged the set as he outmuscled the champion from the baseline yet again. It was thrilling stuff and this epic was heading for a deciding set.

Crucially, there would be no tie-break in the fifth set and this was the only way that the Swiss had managed to shrug Rafa off thus far in the match. That had to count for something. The Spaniard knew his way around a final set and the experience he had gained against Soderling and Youzhny would be handy now. The momentum was with Nadal after his dominant fourth set but Federer had won the past four Wimbledon titles for a reason – he was the best grass court player in the world. It promised to be a classic final set. Notably, it was first time Federer had been taken to five sets at Wimbledon since his famous victory over Pete Sampras in 2001.

Both players scrapped for a glimpse of a break but the serving was perfect on the big points. Nadal whipped a delightful winner to earn two break points in the third game but Federer held firm, forcing the Spaniard into errors just as it looked like he would gain the initiative. Rafa had felt within touching distance of the title but the Swiss had come up trumps again.

Nadal put the disappointment behind him, holding his serve

for 2-2. He then tore into Federer's serve again with stunning power considering the energy-sapping nature of the contest. The Swiss was shell-shocked, first overhitting the ball and then putting a forehand wide. Nadal earned two more break points, giving himself another chance to power into the driving seat. He had never been in this position at Wimbledon. But Rafa just could not make them count. He made an unforced error on the first of them before Federer sent down a rapid ace at the perfect moment. The crowd were loving the drama but Rafa was furious with himself. More good opportunities had come and gone. He could not believe it and all these missed break points in the fifth set would haunt Nadal for months.

Relieved to still be level, Federer found top gear and pummelled Nadal's serve, earning three break points. It was a cruel twist and a crushing blow for the Spaniard, having seemed well-placed just minutes earlier. He bravely saved one as Federer's shot flew out but the champion cashed in at the second time of asking, producing a clever forehand winner to go 4-2 up. The Swiss celebrated – he knew it was the all-important breakthrough. It totally took the wind out of Nadal. He had failed to capitalise on numerous chances, then Federer had pounced instantly. He rattled through an easy service game, notching ace number 24 for a 5-2 lead. The end was nigh for Rafa but he still refused to believe he was beaten.

Federer began the eighth game strongly but the Spaniard fought back, taking it to deuce and giving himself hope. Nadal then stubbornly saved one Championship point as the Swiss fired long. The crowd cheered, hoping the entertainment would continue a little longer. But it did not. Federer created a second

Championship point and took it with an authoritative overhead smash. He fell to the ground and tears soon followed as he was overcome by equalling Borg's record. It was a truly fantastic achievement. Nadal was devastated but was dignified in defeat. He could have done little more that afternoon and could be thoroughly proud of his performance, though this did little to ease the pain. Rafa knew that on another day he would have been the man celebrating. It was simply that close.

He had finished second to Federer again at Wimbledon but not by much this time, and he could take comfort in knowing that he had pushed the Swiss harder than Federer had ever pushed him at the French Open. Nadal was getting closer to the title. But this loss remains one of the lowest lows of Rafa's career to date. The agony of being within touching distance of the trophy, only to falter in the crucial moments and see it snatched away, left him distraught. He blamed his own nerves and uncertainty for betraying him in the big moments on Centre Court. Federer, ever the gentleman, had nothing but praise for Rafa as he collected his fifth successive title: 'Each one is special but to play a champion like Rafa, it means a lot and equalling Borg's record as well.

'He's [Nadal] a fantastic player and he's going to be around so much longer so I'm happy with every one I get before he takes them all! It was such a close match. I told him at the net that he deserved it as well. I'm the lucky one today.'

Nadal had praise of his own for the champion: 'If he wins 14, 15 or 13 Grand Slam titles, his level is the best in history. Today was tough for me but at the same time it's good to play a final like this against the best in the world and to be playing at a similar level.'

After Venus Williams had made short work of Marion Bartoli in the women's final, everyone was delighted that the men's final had been such a classic. Many ranked it among the best ever finals at SW19. In fact, in a poll conducted by the BBC Sport website, the 2007 final earned 34% of the votes for being the best in Wimbledon history. Only the Borg–McEnroe final of 1980 collected more votes. With Nadal just 21 and Federer still 25, the future of their rivalry looked extremely bright.

As always, though, there was little time to reflect on positives and negatives – and this suited Nadal. One of Rafa's great mental strengths is his ability to shrug off defeats and focus on the challenges ahead without dwelling on past disappointments. He told *TIME* magazine: 'I give 100% on the court, so I do get upset when I lose. But it doesn't take me much time to recover. The first hours after the match are tough. After a while I forget, and I look forward to the next days back home in Mallorca. I love fishing and golfing there, for example – just being with my old friends. I'm a good loser.'

Nadal now had to recharge his batteries and prepare for the US Open. In order to do so, he headed to Stuttgart, where he beat Stanislas Wawrinka in the final to claim his 23rd career title.

Rafa followed this by performing well at the Rogers Cup in Montreal. He cruised into the quarter-finals where he met Canadian Frank Dancevic. Dancevic was willed on by the home crowd and produced some remarkable tennis, despite being ranked just inside the top 100. He took the first set 6-4, breaking Nadal in the final game to move ahead. But Rafa rallied, levelling the match with a 6-2 second set scoreline and then overcoming the vocal support for Dancevic to take the deciding set 6-3. Nadal advanced to the semi-finals but fell to eventual winner Djokovic in straight sets, losing 7-5, 6-3. It was disappointing for him, but at least he gained a few extra days of rest prior to the US Open while Djokovic went on to beat Federer in the Rogers Cup final.

Rafa arrived at the US Open hoping to avenge his Wimbledon defeat to Federer but his bid got off to a shaky start – it was an ominous sign. Facing the number 123 seed, wildcard Australian Alun Jones, Nadal struggled to find his usual tempo and was plagued by knee problems. As tendinitis flared up, he had to fight through the pain to stay in the hunt for another Grand Slam title.

The Spaniard took the opening set 7-5, despite trailing 4-1 after an early wobble, but allowed Jones back into the match in the second set. The Australian won it 6-3, again taking a 4-1 lead but this time holding his nerve to draw level. Rafa was looking totally out of sorts. Nadal then found himself 4-3 down in the third set after putting a backhand wide to give Jones the break. However, it was as if this disappointment sparked the Spaniard into life. He broke back immediately then won the next two games to take the third set 6-4.

The fourth set proved to be a formality as Nadal finally steadied himself and he won the first five games to leave Jones with no hope of an upset. Despite the pain, Rafa came through to win 7-5, 3-6, 6-4, 6-1. It had not been the convincing display that most had expected but the Spaniard had done enough to set up a second round match with

Serbian Janko Tipsarevic. Nadal was far from pain-free as he stepped out to face Tipsarevic but he produced far better tennis than in the opening round. Rafa raced into a two-set lead, capturing the first 6-2 and the second 6-3. His opponent had a muscle in his right side taped up early in the third set and, trailing 3-2, he decided he was unable to continue and retired. Nadal's displays had not been spot on so far but he had done enough. Rafa told the press that his knee had been troubling him at times but that it was improving and would be ready for the next match against Frenchman Jo-Wilfried Tsonga. Nadal told the press: 'I hope I continue to improve for the next match against Tsonga. I played better, too. I feel more comfortable with the forehand and with the backhand, too.'

The relentless ATP schedule was doing Nadal few favours and he was paying the price for his successful runs in Paris and London. It would take a superhuman effort for him to reach a third final at Flushing Meadows. Still, he would give it his best shot. Tsonga was an intriguing opponent. He had stunned Tim Henman in the previous round and was playing with great confidence and little pressure – a dangerous combination for Nadal to deal with.

The first set was incredibly tight and went to a tie-break, which Rafa won 7-3. Tsonga was deflated and the Spaniard wasted no time in ending the contest. The pair had appeared well-matched in the opening exchanges but Nadal ran riot in the second set, using powerful baseline hitting to secure a 6-2 scoreline.

Tsonga wilted further in the third set and Rafa wrapped up a 7-6, 6-2, 6-1 victory with the minimum of fuss. He was pleased to progress but also to keep the match to just three sets, ensuring his knee was not overworked. He wore strapping on both knees but needed no courtside treatment and was feeling better each day. Nadal's win set up an all-Spanish fourth round clash with Ferrer, who had survived a match point against Argentina's David Nalbandian.

Rafa's fitness seemed to be returning to optimum levels in time for the match and he appeared confident of reaching the quarter-finals. He began well but Ferrer matched him stroke for stroke and forced a tie-break. Nadal has struggled at times in tie-break situations, especially against big-serving opponents, but here he was brilliant, dominating the points and clinching the first set with a 7-3 scoreline. However, a gruelling first set was not good news for Rafa. The energy used up in the first set took its toll on his aching body and his knee problems resurfaced. To make matters worse, he also needed medical attention for a finger injury. Ferrer was in no mood for sympathy and produced some superb tennis to win the second set 6-4. Nadal fought hard in the third set but Ferrer was the fresher player and the number 15 seed moved 2-1 ahead, winning the tie-break 7-4.

Rafa was running on empty by this stage and his knees had deserted him. However, that should take nothing away from Ferrer's performance. One of the few players who can match Nadal's baseline speed, he repeatedly found the strokes to clinch vital points. He overwhelmed his compatriot in the fourth set and completed a 6-7, 6-4, 7-6, 6-2 victory to send Rafa limping out of the tournament.

As Nadal hobbled from the court, he knew the fitness gamble had not paid off. He told the media: 'I was having a very good season. I'm disappointed, I couldn't play at 100% in the tournament because of the knees, and maybe that affected a little bit my physical performance.' He refused to use injury as an excuse, though, and added his praise for Ferrer: 'He's a very good player, he's having an unbelievable season.' Ferrer told the media: 'Now I am very tired. To beat Rafa, I have to run a lot. I'm sorry for that, for my friend, for my partner, Rafa.'

Although his body was in great pain after the US Open, Nadal's season was not over as he steeled himself for a few more events. The long hours of practice and travel continued as he sought more silverware and prize money but he would be heading into tournaments at a clear disadvantage thanks to all the tennis he had already played during the season.

He competed in the Madrid Masters, reaching the quarter-finals before losing to eventual winner Nalbandian. He reached the final at the Paris Masters but Nalbandian again proved too good, winning comfortably 6-4, 6-0. All that remained for Nadal in 2007 was the Tennis Masters Cup – then he could put his feet up. In the round robin stage, Rafa earned victories over Gasquet and Djokovic but lost again to speedy compatriot Ferrer. Nonetheless, he progressed to a semi-final with Federer. Unfortunately for the Spaniard, it was just one match too many at the end of a long, gruelling year and the world number one picked him off with ease on the way to a 6-4, 6-1 victory.

As he looked back over the season, Nadal saw plenty of reasons to be pleased with his performances. Just like in

2006, he had been utterly dominant on clay yet again and there was still no sign of anyone being able to match him on that surface. People were already putting him among the clay court greats. He had also impressed everyone at Wimbledon. Admittedly, the trophy eluded him but his performance in the final was greatly improved. Nonetheless, his competitive nature meant that only the main prize could be considered a real success. There were a few low points, including his failures at the Australian Open and US Open again. He was determined to reach the final at these events next year and Toni believed his nephew was more than capable of producing such runs. But he would need to begin the year in brighter form and then hope that he was in good enough shape towards the end of the season to win in New York.

Undoubtedly, 2007 had been an excellent year for Nadal. He was developing and strengthening his game all the time. The warning signs were there for Federer – and everyone else on the tour – to see.

CHAPTER 4

CHASING GLORY DOWN UNDER AND DEFENDING HIS PATCH IN PARIS

Rafa entered the New Year on a mission. He had always stressed that he was content to be the world number two – and he was – but that did not stop him from targeting top spot and a cabinet full of titles along the way. He had picked out the areas of his game he wanted to improve and he hoped that 2008 would be the season when he won one of the other Grand Slams to go with more success on the clay of Paris. He did not want to keep hearing commentators calling him a clay court specialist.

Like the previous year, Nadal chose to prepare for the Australian Open by participating in the Chennai Open. After a disappointing end to the 2007 season, he was eager to begin well on the way to improving on last year's quarter-final exit in Melbourne. He had enjoyed a decent rest, allowing him to recharge his batteries. Strong displays in Chennai would boost his confidence before the Grand Slam and he trained hard to be in peak condition. He entered the Chennai Open as the top seed and marched into the semi-finals with the type of the ruthless, hard-hitting performances that he was now famous for.

He faced his friend Moya in an enthralling semi-final which lasted almost four hours. Nadal prevailed but Moya put up a tremendous fight. All three sets went to tie-breaks, with Moya grabbing the first 7-3. Rafa hit back, though, and grabbed a nail-biting second set tie-break 8-6 before taking the decider 7-1. This epic scrap equalled the record for the longest three-set ATP tour match. In the final, though, a weary Nadal was easily defeated by Youzhny 6-0, 6-1. The tiring effort against Moya had left Rafa below par and the Russian took full advantage with a flawless display. However, the Spaniard had gained what he wanted from the tournament – a good workout. His body felt ready for a Grand Slam.

The Australian Open began on January 14 and promised to be an exciting event as the competition hotted up at the top of the men's rankings. Federer remained the world number one but both Nadal and Djokovic appeared capable of knocking the Swiss player off the top spot. The pair had youth on their side and appeared unfazed by any challenge. There were other young players, too, such as Britain's Murray, who were threatening to join the party.

Rafa faced Serbian qualifier Viktor Troicki in the first round. Troicki was a player Nadal knew little about and initially the Serb was able to use this to his advantage. The first eight games went with serve as neither player showed the composure to break, and Troicki looked dangerous with a rapid first serve. Nadal finally edged in front with a break in the ninth game.

Troicki's fitness levels were severely tested as Rafa upped the power in the rallies and earned the advantage. To his credit, Troicki was unfazed and broke back immediately as Nadal's backhand faltered on a string of points.

Suddenly, Rafa was feeling the heat as Troicki held serve for a 6-5 lead and crafted a set point on Nadal's serve. Rafa escaped as the Serb tried an ill-advised drop shot and the set headed for a tie-break. And his experience told in the tie-break as Troicki's shot selection exposed him to his opponent's ruthless hitting. The Serb saved one set point with a brilliant volley but Rafa would not be denied and clinched the tie-break 7-3. Troicki headed for his chair knowing he had matched the world number two for the majority of the first set while Rafa worried about why he was having so much trouble again such a lowly-ranked opponent. The Spaniard did not appear to have found an answer as the Serb began the second set with more desire and Nadal was forced to scrap for every point. Such a dogfight was certainly not in the script.

The Serb grabbed a break in the third game and then moved 3-1 ahead. Rafa was having lots of problems on his backhand while Troicki, by contrast, was belting backhand winners. Unsurprisingly, the home crowd were cheering for the underdog and cranking up the pressure on Nadal. But Rafa had learnt to fight through tricky periods without losing his grip on a match. His experiences already in his short career to date told him to take things a point at a time and stay confident. He held his serve and got to 40-30 up on Troicki's serve before the Serb moved 4-2 ahead.

There was still no panic in Nadal's play and two games later he had levelled at 4-4. He moved swiftly through the gears in the eighth game, chasing and punishing loose balls from Troicki. The Serb saved two break points but Rafa conjured a beautiful lob on his third opportunity, erasing Troicki's advantage.

Undoubtedly, Nadal had the momentum now but Troicki's serve saved him on several occasions. The Spaniard guaranteed himself at least a tie-break as he moved 6-5 ahead with a solid service game. Faced with a relentless Nadal, Troicki could not hold his nerve or his serve. Previously, he had troubled Rafa with aces but serving to stay in the set, the Serb stuttered. Nadal wasted no time in pouncing on the opening, moving 40-0 up for three set points. Troicki saved one but then pulled a forehand wide to allow the Spaniard to double his advantage. A set that had begun in worrying fashion had had a happy ending for Nadal and, for all Troicki's efforts, he would soon be packing his bags.

The belief was visibly draining from the Serb as he returned to his chair. Rafa smelled blood and the third set was incredibly easy considering the tight nature of the first two. Troicki held his serve for 1-1 but Nadal moved up a gear and began to unleash the big guns, including a magnificent cross-court flick. He won the next five games to seal a 7-6, 7-5, 6-1 victory. The third set was one that Troicki would surely prefer to forget but he had shown prior to that that he had real quality. Aged 21, like Nadal, he appeared to have a bright future in the sport. Meanwhile, Rafa was left to reflect on a mixed performance. He had been good enough to get past Troicki but would need to play better if he wanted to reach the latter stages in Melbourne. Against Federer or Djokovic, Nadal would not have sneaked through the first two sets. 'I had to work hard and he played aggressive,' the Spaniard told the press. 'I was a little bit nervous at the beginning because it was my first big match of the season. But I played better on the important points and I changed my playing rhythm and serve in the third set.'

After the difficulties that he faced against the Serb, Rafa was eager to be more dominant in the next round. He took on Frenchman Florent Serra in the second round and produced a far more convincing display, dispatching his opponent in three effortless sets. This showing was much more like the Nadal who had thrilled crowds during the past few seasons.

Serra was overwhelmed by Rafa, who was clearly out to make a point after some of the struggles in his opening match. Serra was unable to hold his serve against Nadal's fearsome hitting and quickly became dispirited as Rafa started strongly on the way to hitting 39 winners. He won the first eight games as he took the first set 6-0 and the second 6-2. He moved Serra around the court with ease and seemed to have found a much better rhythm than against Troicki. Nadal wrapped up the contest in style, completing a 6-0, 6-2, 6-2 win in just 94 minutes.

The quick, emphatic victory allowed him to save energy as he awaited his third round opponent. The Spaniard was hitting the ball well on both sides and seemed ready to go beyond the quarter-finals of the Australian Open for the first time. The post-match feeling was very different to the previous round as Rafa beamed his way through interviews.

Nadal faced another Frenchman in the third round – Gilles Simon. He was another player that Rafa was far from familiar with. Simon, who would make rapid strides over the course of the year, started brilliantly and managed to knock his opponent off his game plan – something that so rarely happens to Nadal. The opening set was a brutal war of baseline hitting but the Frenchman was equal to everything Rafa sent at him. Simon's fine play was rewarded as he earned a string of set points – six in all. Unfortunately for the Frenchman, his inexperience proved costly. Nadal produced some excellent passing shots to fight his way out of danger and once Simon had missed his chances, Rafa took control.

The Spaniard was always ready to seize the moment and he moved around the court with an extra bounce in his step. Simon's disappointment at failing to take his chances was carried into the next few games, allowing Nadal to sneak the first set 7-5. The Spaniard knew he had dodged a bullet in snatching the advantage and upped his game accordingly. Slow starts were seriously threatening Rafa's Grand Slam bid. The second and third sets were far less of a contest as the crowd, who had believed an upset was on the cards during Simon's fine start, began to see the inevitable unfolding before their eyes. Nadal hit harder, finding the lines more consistently than before and forcing errors from his opponent, who was at full stretch just hanging in the rallies. Most importantly, Simon's serve became less of a threat as Rafa felt he could break at any moment. He did so impressively in the second set, racing to a 6-2 scoreline. There was no coming back from this for the Frenchman and, though Simon refused to throw in the towel, Nadal powered towards victory.

With Rafa in this type of form, it seemed as if no shot would be a winner against his tireless defence. Nadal clinched a place in the fourth round, winning 7-5, 6-2, 6-3. After a wobbly start, he had bounced back well and his resilience in the opening set showed his desire to succeed on hard court. Rafa was determined to win one of the other Grand Slams as soon as possible and believed this could be the moment. With Federer and Djokovic on the other side of the draw, things were looking up. Nadal admitted after the match that his initial tactics had been wide of the mark and that a change of plan was required to outfox Simon. The ability to think on his feet and use a plan B or C made the Spaniard an extremely dangerous opponent. He could easily have stuck stubbornly to the original tactics but had instead thought his way out of trouble. Again, the origins of this strength could be traced back to Toni's coaching.

His trend of facing Frenchmen continued in the fourth round as he squared off against number 23 seed Paul-Henri Mathieu. Mathieu had survived a five-set clash with Austrian Stefan Koubek, winning the final set 8-6. The match had taken its toll on the Frenchman and Nadal was ready to cash in. He knew from experience that, despite the adrenalin rush of winning a marathon contest, it was hard to bounce back from the wear and tear of a five-set match. His clashes at Wimbledon in 2007 against Soderling and Youzhny had been exhausting five-setters and these draining matches had played a part in his below-par end to the season.

The world number two wasted no time in attacking Mathieu's serve, catching his opponent off guard. He reached deuce in the first game and then broke to love in the third game. The Frenchman regained some composure to cut the lead to 3-2 but then immediately called his trainer for treatment on his shin. Nadal had worked Mathieu hard already and it looked highly unlikely that the Frenchman could last the pace against Rafa's powerful hitting. The Spaniard was in his element, lurking just behind the baseline and thundering shots into both corners of the court. Nadal continued to win his service games at will and force Mathieu to fight desperately on his own serve. The Frenchman held for 5-4, making Rafa serve for the set, and briefly threatened in the tenth game as he moved to 30-30. But Nadal was too strong, finding a timely ace and clinching the set 6-4. Mathieu had received more treatment after the seventh game. It did not appear to be a serious injury – simply aching muscles from the previous round. Nadal, by contrast, looked like a man in a hurry as he sensed the Frenchman's belief disappearing fast. Rafa broke in the opening game of the second set as his strokes down the line hurt his opponent.

The match was no longer a contest. He held serve to love then battered Mathieu's serve once more, outhitting the Frenchman to move 3-0 ahead. Mathieu threw his racquet to the floor as he was broken for the second time in the set and promptly retired, handing Rafa the victory. Clearly, his efforts against Koubek had come at a price.

With no sign of a serious injury, some questioned the decision, particularly at such a prestigious tournament. BBC Sport analyst John Lloyd said: 'It's strange, it doesn't look like he's limping. It's not the way to retire. You at least have to look as though you are in some kind of discomfort before you retire from a Grand Slam. I'm still in shock. It just looks like he was getting beaten and had enough.'

Nadal was pleased to be through but admitted the circumstances were not ideal. 'I was enjoying the match,' he told the press. 'I was playing my best tennis since arriving in

Australia. I'm happy to be in the quarter-final, but not like this way. I feel very good and I will have extra practice tomorrow to make up for my lost match time.'

The victory over Mathieu set up a quarter-final showdown with Finn Jarkko Nieminen, the 24th seed. As always against Nadal, the first set would be crucial. If Nieminen could grab a lead, his task would at least become a little easier. But letting Rafa get a flying start rarely gave an opponent hope of a comeback. Nieminen, to his credit, threw everything at Nadal in the opening set. The Finn would say post-match: 'I felt I was controlling the game in the first set.' Indeed he was. His shot selection was well thought out and he made the most of the opportunities that came his way. Leading 5-4, he crafted two set points as Rafa faltered.

As is so often the case with the world's best players, Nadal found the big shots to skip away from danger. He delivered two thumping serves and held on to level it at 5-5. Moments later, the Spaniard was celebrating breaking Nieminen's serve and then holding serve to win the opener 7-5. Title runs regularly succeeded or failed on these fine margins and Nadal was now an expert at grinding out the all-important points. The momentum had shifted massively in a matter of minutes and there was no coming back for the Finn. As Rafa got better and better, Nieminen faded. Nadal broke the Finn's serve at will and his crunching groundstrokes consistently found the lines. Just like against Simon, the Spaniard had weathered the early storm and now he was pulling away. He won the second set 6-3 and took a very one-sided third set 6-1. Though some critics focused on the faults in Rafa's early performances at the Australian Open, the Spaniard had yet to drop a set in the tournament and his defence was as dogged as ever. When opponents did not cash in early-on, Nadal rarely offered second chances.

He was delighted to have reached the Australian Open semi-finals for the first time and looked ahead to his match with unseeded Frenchman Tsonga, who was the talk of the tournament. Tsonga had blazed his way into the last four, eliminating seeds Murray, Gasquet and Youzhny. Rafa had defeated the Frenchman the previous year and knew that he would be seriously tested if Tsonga's recent form continued. Speaking after his win over Nieminen, the Spaniard said: 'I am very happy to be in the semi-final. It's a very important tournament for me to start the season well. I will be trying my best to continue on in the tournament and I'm playing very well here.'

Tsonga was well aware of the size of his task against Rafa. After his quarter-final success against Youzhny, he told the media: 'It's going to be difficult. I'm going to have to run again and again, so I will do my best and I hope to play like this.' Nadal was the overwhelming favourite as he stepped onto the court against Tsonga but his opponent had nothing to lose and everything to gain. The Frenchman made a terrific start and never looked back, racing into a 3-0 lead with two excellent service games and a fine break. Rafa tried desperately to gain a footing in the set but Tsonga continued to control the rallies. The Spaniard steadied his serve but the Frenchman's forehand caused huge problems, giving Nadal a taste of his own medicine as he scrambled around the court. At 4-2, Rafa reached 30-30 on Tsonga's serve but his opponent stayed calm and, trailing 5-2, Nadal had to serve to stay in the opening set. It ended as it had begun. Tsonga took control, moved to 40-0 up and grabbed the first set.

It was an incredible, frenetic start and the crowd were loving the Frenchman's stunning assault. Finally, someone had taken advantage of Nadal's early vulnerability – it had been coming after sluggish openings against Troicki and Simon. Rafa just could not handle Tsonga's serve and, with his opponent's fine forehand, he was forever chasing in vain along the baseline. He needed to change his tactics and find a way to gain the upper hand in the rallies. The first game of the second set was ominous, though, as Tsonga held to love. An opponent on top form and a noisy crowd left Nadal in real trouble. He showed his fighting qualities to level at 1-1 and then came close to breaking in the third game. Tsonga, however, showed maturity beyond his years to win the pressure points and hold his serve.

Nadal was clearly improving and he dug in to level again at 3-3. But Tsonga sensed that this was his day and he refused to give an inch to the Spaniard. He held his serve then bullied his way to a break point as Rafa was swept away in brutal rallies. Tsonga pounced on his opportunity and moved 5-3 ahead as the Australian fans roared him on.

Nothing seemed to be working for Nadal. His opponent was smashing unstoppable winners from all angles and his own game plan was being torn to shreds. Tsonga held serve to love and soaked up the applause as he secured a two-set lead. The louder the fans cheered, the more ruthless the youngster became. Rafa had rarely been thrown off his game so spectacularly and Tsonga again ruffled Nadal's feathers in the third game of the third set, producing yet another break as he continued to hit winners cross-court and down the line.

The writing was on the wall and everyone in the stadium knew it. It was just a staggeringly unexpected display from the Frenchman. Tsonga capitalised on more loose balls to hammer his way to a second break of the set and suddenly he was serving for the match. Typically, Rafa made the Frenchman work for every point as he tried to close out the contest. But Tsonga had come too far to falter now and Nadal had left it too late to show resistance. The Frenchman fought his way to 40-15 and then belted down a massive ace to complete the upset and move into the Australian Open final. Nadal had been brutally dissected and, despite all his improvements on the hard court, he would be missing out on the title again.

The media rejoiced in Tsonga's brilliance – and rightly so. After all, Rafa had not dropped a set in the tournament going into the semi-final yet the Frenchman had bagged an emphatic 6-2, 6-3, 6-2 victory. 'It is just amazing, unbelievable, nothing could stop me today,' Tsonga told the press.

Nadal was quick to highlight the quality of the Frenchman's 'unbelievable' performance, telling the press: 'I tried to play a little bit slower. I tried to play a little bit faster. I tried to play more inside the court, behind the court. No chance. Not today.' It was refreshing to hear such an honest assessment. There were never any excuses with Nadal. If he lost, it was because his opponent had played the better tennis.

A tournament that had begun so promisingly had ended with bitter disappointment. Federer lost out to Djokovic in the other semi-final and tennis fans were left to contemplate a

Grand Slam final featuring neither Federer nor Nadal. Such had been their domination of the sport that the final inevitably could not generate as much excitement without them in it. It was Djokovic who lifted the trophy as Tsonga fell short of the level he had produced against Nadal.

For Rafa, it was simply a case of learning his lessons and moving on. 2008 would offer him plenty more chances for glory and he needed to be ready to grasp them with both hands. He had to look at the positives – he had gone further in Melbourne than ever before, maybe 2009 would be his year there. Plus, he had the clay court season to think about – his favourite time of year. Toni, of course, was on hand to make sure that his nephew did not dwell on the failure against Tsonga.

Nadal threw all his energies into preparing for upcoming tournaments as his thirst for titles showed no signs of diminishing. And of course he was a massive fan favourite now wherever he went, delighting the supporters with his patient autograph-signing. He had always made every effort to be accessible to both the media and the fans. He stayed sharp ahead of the clay court season by appearing in a number of tournaments that saw him jetting all over the world. But he came up short on each occasion. While gaining match practice was important at such events, there was nothing like a winning run to build confidence and boost performance levels. Thus far, Nadal was still searching for his first title of 2008. He fell to eventual winners on several occasions. First, he was beaten by Roddick at the Dubai Tennis Championships and then by Djokovic at Indian Wells. The Serb bagged a convincing 6-3, 6-2 victory that had some suggesting that he might challenge Rafa for the number two spot. This brought additional pressure for the Spaniard. Nadal went a step closer in Miami where he put together some fine displays to reach the final. But Davydenko was too strong, winning the title 6-4, 6-2. Having started out with a bye, Rafa had claimed several decent scalps, including Paul-Henri Mathieu and the dangerous James Blake. He was getting closer.

Rafa was busy off the court in the early part of the year too. In Miami, he began blogging on his website, www.rafaelnadal.com, and this proved such a big hit that he has continued to keep his fans updated through this medium. In the first blog – on March 27 – he wrote with great honesty: 'Let me say that I want to thank you for this opportunity and that obviously, someone is helping me with it, with my English, with what I write, since as you all know my English is not that good. So this is not fake, simply I get some help so that you can understand it.'

So began Nadal's foray into documenting his experiences on the tour. On a similar theme, he is well aware of how fortunate he is to be playing the sport that he loves for a living and takes every chance to give something back – not just with entertaining performances on the court but also with charity work off it. This is a fine reflection of the way that his parents brought him up. He launched the Rafa Nadal Foundation in Manacor in February 2008 to tackle social work and development aid. His mother, Ana Maria, took on the position of chair with father Sebastian as vice-chairman as Rafa looked to keep the foundation in the family. He told the media: 'This can be the beginning of my future, when I retire and have more time. I am doing very well and I owe society.' Manacor

Mayor Toni Pastor expressed his delight at Nadal's plans for the foundation, telling Deutsche Presse-Agentur: 'Rafa was already great but he has grown even greater today.'

This was not the first charity project that Nadal had been involved with. He and Real Madrid goalkeeper Iker Casillas were among those who organised a football match to raise money for the fight against malaria. Rafa was always looking to make a difference, whenever and wherever he could.

The dawn of the clay court season cheered the Spaniard and sparked him into life. Now he was entering his most profitable part of the year and, sure enough, the titles started rolling in as he showed yet again that he was a cut above the rest. He had total confidence in his ability on clay and knew that if he was on song, he would crush everyone in sight.

Rafa bagged his first title of the year in Monte Carlo as he found the type of form that made him untouchable on clay. The tournament began on April 20 and it was his fourth straight title in Monaco. He beat Federer 7-5, 7-5 in the final after disposing of the likes of Davydenko, Ferrer and Ferrero. This was no mean feat and a victory over Federer was always welcome.

Nadal was not content with simply winning the singles title. The Spaniard also scooped the doubles title alongside compatriot Tommy Robredo. The duo overcame Mahesh Bhupathi and Mark Knowles in an epic final that kept supporters on the edge of their seats throughout. The Spaniards surrendered the first set 7-5 but levelled matters by claiming the second set 6-3. They then grabbed the decider 10-3. It was a fine week for Rafa and boosted his confidence before the tests that lay ahead.

He was thrilling fans with his tennis but one of his habits left some frustrated, much to Nadal's dismay. His constant fiddling with his shorts – pulling at the front and rearranging at the back – amused some but infuriated others. Rafa admits it is an issue he is trying to address. He told *TIME* magazine: 'It's not the fault of the clothes. It's a habit that I picked up when I was competing when I was young. I am trying to break the habit, but it's not easy.'

And this is just the beginning of his list of superstitions and habits. Like so many other sports stars, the Spaniard has a catalogue of things that have to be in place before he settles in for each point or game. These include taking one sip from each of his bottles of water and then placing them on the ground with the sponsor logo facing forward as well as pre-game rituals such as a cold shower and the careful positioning of his bandanna. He also likes to locate his family and team members in the crowd before play begins. It is all about going through certain processes – however bizarre they may seem to neutrals – which then help focus his mind on the tasks ahead.

Later that month, Nadal enjoyed more success – this time back in his homeland. The Spaniard travelled to Barcelona and made it three out of three on clay for 2008. He suffered a blip in Rome, losing early on to compatriot Ferrero, but he was happy with the way he was hitting the ball and the ease with which he was moving around the court.

In Hamburg, Rafa continued his fine form. The signs were ominous for his rivals with the French Open just around the corner – Nadal seemed to be at the peak of his powers. He was looking more likely than ever to capture another title at Roland Garros. Facing Federer in the Hamburg final, Nadal once again outlasted the world number one, winning a tight battle 7-5, 6-7, 6-3.

Rafa arrived in Paris with bags of confidence. His clay court form had been spectacular thus far and recent victories over Federer gave him valuable psychological points. But there was plenty of work ahead and Nadal knew he had a target on his back – everyone would be out to shoot down the three-time champion. The Spaniard had a flawless record at the French Open – would anyone be able to hand him a first ever defeat at Roland Garros? He might not have been the world number one but there was no player as feared on the clay as Nadal and the unlucky man to face him in the opening round was Brazilian qualifier Thomaz Bellucci. No one expected it to be a long match.

Rafa was determined to begin the tournament well. He had made stuttering starts at several Grand Slams and knew that it left him with an uphill battle. Against Bellucci, Nadal wasted no time in showing his clinical side. The match was interrupted a couple of times by rain, forcing the players off with the score at 1-1 in the first set. When they returned – two days after they were supposed to finish – Rafa lost his serve immediately, then battled back to 2-2. Bellucci, who had a string of clay court titles under his belt on the lower Challenger tour, was clearly up for the fight and impressed with his hard-hitting style. Seemingly endless backcourt rallies ensued and Nadal was stretched at times to live with the Brazilian's meaty forehand.

The Spaniard edged in front with a break of serve in the eighth game but Bellucci refused to throw in the towel. He held serve then stunned the world number two by levelling at 5-5. The Brazilian showed off a feathery touch to land a perfectly-played drop shot and put the pressure back on Nadal. If anything, though, losing his lead appeared to fire up the Spaniard. He produced a composed love service game and, dishing out a few shouts of 'Vamos', managed to up the tempo. Bellucci had hung around with great resilience but now faced the big test. Could he hold serve and force a tie-break with Rafa on the prowl?

The answer was no. The Brazilian moved to 40-15 up but Nadal pegged him back as a double fault pulled it level at deuce. Rafa crafted one set point, only to play a poor backhand. Bellucci saved a second with a vital forehand but, facing a third, succumbed to another double fault. It was a sad way for the Brazilian to surrender a set in which he had exceeded all expectations. Nadal bagged the set 7-5 and then romped home from there as he left Bellucci flailing desperately. A relatively nervy hour was shrugged off by the Spaniard as he roared into ruthless form. At 3-3 in the second set, Bellucci seemed to be doing a good job of frustrating the French Open champion, but Rafa cranked up his hitting and, in a matter of minutes, it was 6-3. The Brazilian had fought hard but was falling away now.

Rafa was clearly in a hurry to return to the locker room. He blitzed Bellucci early in the third set, breaking twice in the first three games. Before long, he was 4-0 up and cruising into the second round. The Brazilian looked exhausted and Nadal found yet another break to clinch a 7-5, 6-3, 6-1 victory. Considering the influence of the weather in Paris, Rafa was pleased to progress without any major scares. He told the press: 'The conditions were very bad and the wind was terrible. I had to wait two days because of the rain and could only practice for 20 minutes so it's difficult to come onto the court and find a good rhythm.'

The key was getting through this opening test and Nadal could now look ahead to a second round clash with French wildcard Nicolas Devilder. It promised to be another very one-sided contest if Rafa continued to strike the ball as cleanly as he did towards the end of the match with Bellucci. But the Spaniard was now slightly disadvantaged as the rain delays meant he was playing catch-up, which appeared to favour his rivals. In addition, the weather had also denied him valuable practice time. After bagging the first set 6-4, Nadal polished off the Frenchman with the minimum of fuss. Devilder showed some promising moments early on but he just did not have the weapons to hurt the Spaniard. Big serving and unstoppable winners saw Rafa take charge and, when his opponent netted a forehand, he completed an easy 6-4, 6-0, 6-1 victory, bagging 13 of the last 14 games.

This was not what the rest of the pack wanted to see. Nadal was already looking invincible and he had barely moved out of first gear. With the demolition of Devilder, Rafa stretched his winning streak at Roland Garros to 23. In the third round, number 26 seed Nieminen would be the next man to try to end the run. He and Nadal had done battle plenty of times and so the Spaniard knew what to expect from the Finn.

More rain swept into Paris, though, and gave Rafa an even trickier match pile-up. The delays in his match with Bellucci meant he was already disadvantaged in comparison to many of the other big guns in the draw and now showers were once again putting his bid for a fourth straight title in jeopardy. When he got on the court, Nadal was in splendid form. It was no exaggeration to say that he was pacing the locker room as he waited for the weather to clear up and he was into his stride immediately. The Spaniard left Nieminen in his wake as he raced into the lead. Rafa broke serve with ease, returning brilliantly and toying with the Finn as he clinched the opening set 6-1. He never looked back.

Nadal broke early in the second but Nieminen rallied to pull level at 3-3 before Rafa romped clear. He won the next three games for a two-set lead, crushing the Finn's hopes of a steely comeback. The end was clearly nigh. Rafa did not hesitate in going for the kill as Nieminen floundered against the sheer power of his hitting. Despite needing medical attention for blisters on his right foot, Nadal motored on to break serve in the fourth game for a 3-1 lead. He then bagged the next three games, clinching a place in the last 16 on his third match point. The 6-1, 6-3, 6-1 win had come in just less than two hours. Rafa's superior stamina was already looking like being a decisive factor. He was able to maintain his top level of performance throughout matches while his opponents, particularly those in the early rounds, visibly faded in the second or third sets. At such moments, the Spaniard pounced to seize control.

Due to the fixture mayhem, Nadal might not be getting any rest in the coming days but at least he had settled matters in three sets in each round so far. He was keeping himself fresh and was well aware that far tougher challenges lay ahead on the road to yet another French Open final.

An all-Spanish affair awaited the King of Clay in the fourth round as he squared off with Fernando Verdasco. Nadal had faced his compatriot five times and had never lost – not a good sign for Verdasco who would need to conjure up the performance of his life if he wanted to progress. Rafa, who is not always the best starter, began on the attack and never allowed his opponent to settle. Verdasco's big weapon – a stinging forehand – was kept at bay as Nadal eased into the lead. His compatriot's struggles with a thigh injury just made matters worse. A lack of mobility against Rafa of all people was a recipe for disaster and meant the odds were stacked against an upset.

The world number two wrapped up the first set in no time, using a string of winners to seal it 6-1. It got no better for Verdasco in the second set as Rafa continued his relentless form. His unwavering returns earned him three breaks as he doubled his advantage with a 6-0 scoreline. Moving the ball into the corners and finishing rallies with a flourish, the champion exploited his opponent's injury problem in typical fashion. There was no way back for Verdasco as he found Nadal in an uncharitable mood. Rafa was merciless against his opponent's serve and pounced on every loose ball. He moved into the quarter-finals in one hour and 54 minutes with a breath-taking 6-1, 6-0, 6-2 triumph. Had he even broken sweat? 'I wish all my matches were like this one,' Nadal told the press post-match. 'Here we don't want to have mercy for anybody.' It had been a gentle stroll in the park for the Spaniard and he was thankful to be conserving energy at a time when the tests were supposed to be getting tougher.

Looking ahead to the next round, where he would mark his birthday against another Spaniard in Nicolas Almagro, he said:

'He is a very good player. He has a beautiful serve, a very powerful serve. So I'll have to try and impose my rhythm, not let him take the initiative and make him run. It is probably going to be my toughest match this week.'

However, it proved to be a lot easier than Rafa himself could have believed. Even in his wildest dreams, he could not have foreseen a match as simple as his quarter-final with Almagro. His birthday wish had come true. The windy conditions did not help but Nadal seemed to handle the conditions far better than his opponent. Almagro's powerful serve helped him win his opening service game but this was a momentary peak in an otherwise humbling first set. Rafa secured breaks in the third, fifth and seventh games as he completed a totally untroubled set, winning it 6-1. Just like against Verdasco, Nadal went from strength to strength after taking the lead. He was bringing out all the shots as he followed a magnificent whipped forehand with a bullet ace. Almagro had no answer. Rafa broke for a 2-0 lead and, though his opponent finally held again for 3-1, he was undeterred. More emphatic shot-making brought two holds and a break, wrapping up the second set 6-1.

It had turned into such a walkover that the crowd were restless. It was a foregone conclusion but Nadal still refused to take his foot off the pedal. Almagro won the opening game of the third set which prompted a typical response from Rafa – he won the next six games. As Almagro shouted at himself for a string of errors, Nadal calmly tightened his stranglehold on the match as he fired forehands and backhands onto the line. In the blink of an eye, a 2-1 lead had become 6-1 and Rafa was acknowledging the applauding supporters. The final point summed up the match – Nadal refusing to deem any ball unreturnable and Almagro then netting an overhead lob.

It had not been close to a contest and the reigning champion was looking as good as ever. Djokovic would provide the next test before a potential final with Federer. But neither player seemed capable of toppling the Spaniard on current form.

After what some described as the most one-sided quarter-final in French Open history, Nadal refused to be complacent about his recent form. He told reporters: 'There is no such thing as a pre-written script before the tournament starts and anything can happen before any match. You never know if you'll make it to the semi-final, final, and win. This is something that we all have in mind. We all know that.'

Clearly, he would be taking nothing for granted against the number three seed Djokovic who had produced some fine tennis of his own during the tournament. The Serb would need to do all that and more if he hoped to end Rafa's 26-match winning streak at Roland Garros. Nadal had enjoyed his 22nd birthday celebrations but now it was time for business and the partying could wait. He was within sight of another final but Djokovic would be a tricky opponent with his speed and range of shots. With Federer expected to outmuscle Frenchman Gael Monfils later in the other semi-final, most of the attention was focused on Rafa's match. For the Serb, there was the added incentive of knowing that a victory would push him above Nadal in the rankings.

Rafa defended the number two seeding with a brilliant performance. What had been billed as a tight showdown turned out to be anything but for the Spaniard as he took charge of most of the rallies and left Djokovic exhausted.

Nadal took his opportunities on the Serb's serve, breaking in the third game with a brilliant backhand winner. This proved to be the decisive moment in the opening set and, though Rafa always looked capable of troubling his opponent's serve, the match went with serve for the rest of the set.

The Spaniard clinched it 6-4 with a solid service game that included code violations for both players – Rafa's for a time-wasting and Djokovic's for hitting a ball into the crowd. Nadal had not been troubled by the Serb thus far and was denying his opponent any scraps to feed on. Things got worse for the number three seed as Rafa made a rampant start to the second half. He broke Djokovic in the first game with some ferocious hitting and then held to love. The Spaniard seemed to have saved his best for this semi-final and was loving every minute of it. He was totally in his element and was playing some of the best tennis that Roland Garros had ever seen.

Djokovic earned a break point at 2-1 but Nadal, as usual, found something extra at the crucial moment as he unleashed a kick serve. Moments later, the Spaniard had held serve and was breaking the Serb for a 4-1 lead. Djokovic had failed to take his opportunity, Rafa had been ruthless. That is what champions do.

The point that sealed Nadal's double-break lead was a further example of why he was so tough to beat. The Serb had been in charge of the rally and, having fired a deep approach shot, he raced to the net. Rafa was being stretched to the limit but managed to dig out a brilliant forehand to leave Djokovic helpless. His ability to spring from defence to attack made him so dangerous. Nadal extended his lead to 5-1 before Djokovic held his serve and made the Spaniard serve for the second set.

Rafa duly obliged and, with six-time French Open champion Borg watching at Roland Garros on his 52nd birthday, he whipped a stunning forehand onto the line to take the set 6-2. He was really putting on a show for Borg and the rest of the captivated supporters.

It was hard to believe that this was a match between the second and third best players in the world. By rights, it should have been extremely close but instead it was one-way traffic and Djokovic was in danger of being blown away. Nadal had not dropped a set so far in the tournament so the Serb's chances of winning three in a row were bordering on non-existent. In the third set, Nadal picked up where he left off, pummelling Djokovic from the back of the court. Huge forehand winners helped Rafa break in the first and third games for a 3-0 lead as the Spaniard continued to cruise towards the final. But the Serb then enjoyed a brief purple patch, breaking Nadal and holding to cut the Spaniard's advantage to 3-2. With defeat looking more than likely, Djokovic seemed to finally loosen up and he produced the kind of tennis that had secured him a spot in the last four. Rafa faltered and suddenly it was 5-5 as Djokovic landed a perfect drop shot to set up a break point before drawing an error from the Spaniard. Two holds followed and the third set headed into a tie-break with the Serb carrying the greater momentum.

Yet again, though, Nadal showed his maturity and his ability to come up trumps under pressure. He seized the initiative by grabbing a 3-0 lead and upped the pace of the rallies. Djokovic began to make mistakes again as his display slumped. Rafa built a 6-0 lead and, though the Serb won the next three points, he clinched a 6-4, 6-2, 7-6 victory with a fine smash. Nadal celebrated jubilantly. He was heading into another French final Open and his record at Roland Garros stood at 27-0. It had been a sumptuous display against Djokovic and he was a deserving winner. He had managed to ignore the size of the occasion while the Serb seemingly got caught up in the moment and had failed to play with his usual freedom. But he was definitely not the first player to fall below their best when faced with the daunting prospect of taking on the world number two on clay. Speaking to Tennis X after the win, Nadal was thrilled with his performance. He said: 'The level of the two first sets was very good today. Almost perfect. Best match at Roland Garros so far, no?'

Watching Nadal play offers that rare treat of seeing genius at work. When people talk of it being worth the entrance money just to see it, this is what they mean. Performances at this lofty level are unique in their ability to reel in just about anybody. Naturally, tennis fans will be gripped by most of Rafa's matches but so too will sceptics or those who say they do not really follow sport.

Of course, similar cases of world class performance can be found across other sports as well. For instance, in the NBA – the US basketball league – LeBron James of the Miami Heat is in that bracket of elite players. There is something enchanting about the way James moves on the court: the power, the speed and the showmanship. It is all made to look so effortless, as if it is solely entertainment laid on for others. It is a show and stars like James never want to be anywhere but centre stage. Madison Square Garden was often LeBron's stage, Roland Garros was Nadal's. So Rafa had booked his place in the final and was just awaiting news on his opponent.

It would be Federer, who faced some testing moments before overcoming Monfils. The final that most neutrals had been hoping for was now in place and tennis fans worldwide would be able to watch the sport's top two players do battle again. Debate raged over the expected outcome of the final but most, while predicting a real battle, gave Nadal the edge. His track record at Roland Garros was, of course, flawless yet some experts suggested this might be his toughest test ever on clay.

Rafa tried to put thoughts of his flawless record and a possible fourth straight title out of his head. He just needed to focus on the match itself – all the accolades would come later. He had regularly outgunned Federer on clay so he had good experiences to draw upon and a solid game plan to stick to. Pat Cash, speaking on Radio 5 Live, said: 'Federer needs to go for the winners and absolutely drill them. Once we start getting into rallies, Rafa is going to nail him.'

Nadal made a dream start as he attacked Federer's serve. He missed out on his first break point but the Swiss handed him another and surrendered the opening game with a wild forehand. Rafa had to fight off a break point to consolidate the break for a 2-0 lead before Federer got back on track with a more assured service game. But the Spaniard was in relent-less form and made the world number one work for every point. A brilliant service game saw Nadal hold to love and he kept up the scorching intensity by breaking Federer to love in the next game. The first set was a formality from this point onwards as Rafa consolidated the double-break, held serve and clinched a simply stunning set with a third break.

Everything was working for the champion. He was pulling

off lobs, aces and mind-blowing passing shots on both sides. Federer had been below his best so far but only because Nadal had been out of this world. If Rafa maintained this level of play, it might be a very short final. Federer needed to start finding winners as the Spaniard looked imperious as soon as a point developed into a lengthy rally. It was easier said than done, though, as the Swiss was struggling to win points on his own serve, never mind find breaks of his own. With Wimbledon ahead, Federer did not want to surrender the psychological edge but he was helpless against Rafa's barrage.

There was no doubt that Nadal was totally in the zone. He opened the second set with another dominant service game and was making it all look easy. He was playing the world number one but one would never have thought it from the way Rafa steamrollered Federer. Soon after, it was 2-0 as the Swiss reached 15 unforced errors for the match. His belief was visibly seeping away as he struggled to make any inroads. Federer then momentarily steadied himself as he found two solid games to level at 2-2, leaving Nadal flat-footed with his best moments of the final. However, everything was a struggle for the out-of-sorts top seed.

The crowd were largely siding with the Swiss, especially as he was receiving a pummelling. Rafa ignored the applause that greeted every Federer point and focused on putting him to the sword. The Spaniard moved 3-2 ahead with ease, then Federer levelled with a solid service game. It appeared that a real contest was developing as the Swiss finally settled into the contest. He was holding his serve and beginning to unleash his stunning array of passing shots. But Nadal responded to Federer's improvements by finding a higher gear of his own and accelerating away. He had to fight hard to move 4-3 ahead and then he put a big dent in the Swiss' comeback hopes by steering a backhand down the line to seal his fifth break of the match.

Tennis fans everywhere were watching the final in disbelief. A tense scrap was turning into a gentle stroll for Rafa. He showed no sign of nerves as he moved Federer around the court before delivering the knockout blows. Having bagged the first set 6-1, Nadal doubled his advantage by sealing the second 6-3. Was there any way back for Federer?

Nadal answered the question emphatically. Most had already given up hope of a comeback from the Swiss but Rafa made sure that nobody was left in any doubt. He could see that Federer was on the ropes and he showed no mercy, breaking in the opening game of the third set after yet more errors from the number one. It had turned into a humbling day for the Swiss as he ran into Nadal in top form. But it would get worse. Rafa powered on, holding serve with a bullet into the corner and then terrorizing Federer's serve again. In the blink of an eye, it was 3-0 and the Spaniard was giving the top seed perhaps the most humiliating afternoon of his career.

A stunning backhand lob summed up how well Nadal was playing – everything was working perfectly. The atmosphere of the French Open final did not intimidate the Spaniard, instead it brought out the very best in him. Federer, who had performed with a classy swagger throughout the tournament, was staring defeat in the face with just four games to his name. The third break of the set left Federer on the brink and his body language suggested that he was in absolute shock over the way that the final had panned out. More phenomenal hitting from Nadal put him on the cusp of a fourth straight French Open title.

Nobody had a won a set 6-0 against Federer on any surface since 1999 but Rafa was just minutes away from doing just that. The Swiss thumped a forehand into the net but fought back to 30-30. However, it was too little, too late and yet another Federer error settled matters. Nadal had produced one of the greatest clay court displays of all time, completing a 6-1, 6-3, 6-0 victory and giving Federer the most torrid afternoon in memory. It was a fantastic moment for Nadal and the win ranked among his all-time best performances. He was ecstatic and, most worryingly, he was still just 22 years old. His domination at Roland Garros looked set to continue for many years to come.

Federer looked crushed. He had come into the final in good nick and felt he had a decent chance of coming away with the trophy. But Nadal had dismissed him with such disdain that the world number one, brilliant though he was, must have suffered a dip in confidence. He had not simply lost, he had been hammered.

Unsurprisingly, the media swarmed around Rafa after his Roland Garros domination. Everyone was desperate for a few words from the four-time French Open champion and the Spaniard was his usual patient self when answering their questions. After all, this was arguably the finest moment of his career to date and he wanted to savour it. He told the press: 'I did not expect a match like this. I think I played an almost perfect match. Roger played more mistakes than usual and I played more inside the court. I improved a little bit since last year. I have more control of the points, I am more aggressive than usual.'

Despite the quality of his display, Nadal refused to admit he was ready to take Federer's place at the top of the tennis tree. He explained: 'I feel like the number two because I am the number two and I am closer to the number three than the number one.' He also acknowledged that his relentless training regime had paid dividends in terms of the improvements in his game. He pointed to better execution of the slice, a greater ability to change direction in rallies more often and flatter shots, particularly on the backhand.

It had been an amazing fortnight for Nadal and Roland Garros had become even more like his own backyard. Anyone he faced in Paris was stepping onto his territory and he defended it with everything he had.

Emulating Borg's success at the French Open was particularly special. The aura of Borg is still a big influence on Nadal. He had grown up fully aware of the Swede's talent and achievements and was overwhelmingly proud to now be mentioned in the same breath as one of his heroes. Borg's ability to win on all surfaces put him among the greatest players to ever play the sport. And Nadal hoped to take a leaf out of his book. The Spaniard admitted if he could play a match against anyone in the history of tennis, he would pick the Swede. In *TIME* magazine, Nadal revealed: 'I'd choose Borg. He had such an incredible mental approach to the game. He had ice in his veins, and I'd love to see what I could do against him. If I had to say, I suppose he'd win.'

The nature of the tennis schedule meant Nadal had little time to savour the success in Paris. The ecstasy of that victory would stay with him but mentally he had to start thinking about the grass court season as he boarded a plane to England. It had been a big couple of weeks and he was on a roll. Could anyone stop the Spaniard? And what did his demolition of Federer at Roland Garros mean in terms of his chances at Wimbledon?

CHAPTER 5

A GOLDEN SUMMER

Returning to SW19, after going so close the previous year, Nadal had the perfect motivation. He had played brilliantly in the 2007 final, only to see the trophy slip through his fingers. That night, he had cried like an animal, in the words of his uncle. Now he was ready to make amends and end Federer's phenomenal run of victories.

Rafa's rivalry with Federer had the tennis world on the edge of their seats, anticipating a repeat of the thrills of the previous year. It had been a great spectacle but it was still a painful memory for Rafa – and one that he hoped to put to bed once and for all this time. Nadal had scored some psychological points with his demolition of the world number one at the French Open but Federer had brushed this defeat aside, claiming that playing on grass would be a different matter. However, it was clear to most tennis fans and pundits alike that Rafa was closing in on the

Swiss player on the surface that Federer had dominated for so long.

Nadal's transition from clay to grass impressed everyone. He arrived for the Queen's tournament eager to gain the necessary preparation for Wimbledon and delivered a fine showing. The fatigue that many had predicted after Roland Garros rarely slowed him down as he raced through the early rounds. He started with a bye and then eased through against Jonas Bjorkman of Sweden. He was not at his very best but every minute on the grass was aiding his chances of glory at Wimbledon. Rafa stepped up his game in the following rounds, sweeping aside his opponents to reach the final, where he met Djokovic.

The Serbian quickly established a 3-0 lead in the first set but gradually Nadal worked his way back into the contest, forcing a tie-break. Djokovic looked perplexed as Rafa clinched the opening set despite the stuttering start. With such an advantage, the world number three knew he should have closed out the first set. A tight second set proved again that the two were well-matched. But Nadal came up trumps when it mattered most and grabbed the all-important break to close out the match 7-6, 7-5. He had won a tournament on grass and he knew it was a very good sign ahead of Wimbledon. Provided that Rafa stayed injury-free, he looked set for a long run in the competition and he appeared to be better prepared than ever to go all the way. He had reached two finals, coming up short on both occasions. Now, he was focused on making it third time lucky.

After all the debate, Wimbledon 2008 finally began. Could Federer clinch his sixth straight title? Could Nadal dethrone the king of men's tennis? Could home favourite Murray achieve his dream of British supremacy at Wimbledon? In two weeks' time, tennis fans would have all the answers.

The draw for the tournament was favourable to Rafa. He found himself on the opposite side to both Federer and Djokovic, improving his chances of cruising through to the final. However, there was no hint of complacency in his play. He began against Andreas Beck, winning comfortably without ever being forced to find top gear. The third set tiebreak went in Nadal's favour as he completed a 6-4, 6-4, 7-6 victory, which gave him longer to rest ahead of his next clash. In truth, Beck just could not handle the ferocity of Rafa's play and it turned out to be the ideal warm-up for the Spaniard. The second round was a tougher proposition as Nadal faced Ernests Gulbis. He made a nervy start and dropped the first set 7-5. The crowd sensed a possible upset but Rafa had other ideas. He stormed back to level the match at one set all, then won a third set tiebreak to move into the ascendancy. It had been a rollercoaster afternoon but he did not look back after bagging the third set as he wrapped up a 5-7, 6-2, 7-6, 6-3 win.

This was the type of steely determination and self-belief that he would need if he hoped to overthrow Federer, who had made an emphatic start to yet another title defence. Nadal had looked jittery as the first set slipped away but he proved he could handle the high expectations with the manner in which he responded.

Routes to the final were rarely perfectly smooth and Rafa hoped that his play would continue to light up the tournament.

He was desperate to win Wimbledon, knowing that it would be a fantastic moment for himself and for his country. A Spaniard had not triumphed in the men's singles at Wimbledon since Manuel Santana in 1966 – a statistic he was eager to change. In the third round, Nadal took on Nicolas Kiefer of Germany. The opening set went with serve throughout as Rafa struggled to make inroads into the Kiefer serve. He had to hold his nerve to see off a surge from the German in the sixth game but in general his serve looked up to the challenge. Kiefer, the world number 27 seed, made a bold start to the tie-break yet Nadal kept coming back with more and more quality. A brutal groundstroke brought the Spaniard a 4-2 lead at the changeover and this soon became 6-2 as Rafa won a point at the net then forced a mistake from the German. Kiefer clawed one back with a well-placed serve but a relentless Nadal won the breaker 7-3 to draw first blood.

This seemed to simply be the Spaniard's warm-up because he came out with more intensity in the second set and pummelled the German into submission. Rafa grabbed the first break of the match in the second game of the set, then held for a 3-0 lead. Kiefer was hanging on by his fingernails and, while he recomposed himself on serve, he could not cause problems in the Spaniard's service games. As a result Nadal cruised on to 5-2 then clinched the set by breaking to love. Everything was firing by this stage – backhand, forehand, drop shot and volley. Whatever the French Open champion tried seemed to be coming off. It certainly left Kiefer bewildered because the veteran German just crumbled under the pressure. In the blink of an eye, the Spaniard was 4-0 up in the third set and seemed keen to finish the match in a hurry as night was drawing in. It was around 9pm by now and Nadal did not want to have to finish the contest the next day.

Kiefer finally sorted his serve out to get on the scoreboard at 5-1 down but surely this was only delaying the inevitable. Yet people began to wonder what lay ahead when the German broke Nadal to claim another game back, then held serve again. Why had Rafa suddenly gone off the boil? The Spaniard quickly refocused and crushed Kiefer's hopes of a comeback by wrapping up the match for a 7-6, 6-2, 6-3 victory. Nadal told the press: 'Kiefer is a difficult opponent on every surface but especially here on a faster surface. He's an aggressive player with a good serve, good volleys, but I played a very good tie-break and then played well after that.'

Rafa's style of play may have been founded on clay but he now looked every inch a grass court player. His speed and hard hitting were the key elements, making tennis look easy as he forced his opponent from one side of the court to the other.

Nadal's popularity with the English media and tennis fans ensured that he was always busy between matches, fulfilling all his duties. The longer he kept winning, the more interviews he would be involved in. Every player has their own routine for preparing for matches and dealing with rain delays. Some are always totally focused, not wanting to chat or relax. They stay in their match zone throughout. Others, like Rafa, manage to put tennis to one side when they are not on the court. Nadal enjoys playing computer games and unwinding during breaks in play, but he snaps back into match mode when he steps back onto the court.

As the second week of Wimbledon dawned, Nadal's desire was as strong as ever. He felt comfortable in the house he had rented for the tournament, (where, as he explains in his autobiography, he is "able to recreate the calmest sense of home") was delighted to see Spain win Euro 2008 and was even planning a possible sightseeing trip up the River Thames, as he explained on his website blog.

His fourth round opponent was familiar foe Youzhny and, with Djokovic crashing out against Marat Safin, every match pushed Rafa closer to a rematch with Federer in the final. It was the showpiece event that so many people were desperate to see. Nadal never looked too far ahead, though, despite the constant discussion. He has been fortunate to have such a supportive coaching set-up, keeping him on the right path, and they provide a stable environment for Rafa. The fact that his uncle is so heavily involved makes victories all the sweeter when it comes to the celebrations. They are very tight knit group and it helps Nadal's parents to know that Rafa is facing each battle with his uncle in his corner.

On paper, this looked a tough contest for the Spaniard but he made it look remarkably simple. His performance owed much to a strong start which left the Russian stunned and he never fully recovered from Nadal's early onslaught. The Spaniard actually slipped and tweaked his knee in the second game but such was his dominance that he rarely looked too troubled by the injury. Rafa broke in the fourth and sixth games to open up a comfortable lead, motoring on to take the first set 6-3. And things got no better for the Russian as Nadal hammered more winners in the second set. Youzhny continued to fire off target and the Spaniard broke in the opening game. The Russian scrapped his way back into the set but he did not possess the weapons to break back. Nadal played efficient tennis to keep his nose in front before finishing things off by breaking again to take the second set 6-3. It had been a woeful afternoon so far for Youzhny and he appeared to have little fight or confidence left.

The third set was the easiest of the lot for Rafa. Without playing anywhere near his best, he exploited the Russian's serve in a very one-sided spell, breaking twice and bagging a 5-0 lead. Youzhny was just going through the motions by this stage and, though he pulled one game back, defeat was clearly just around the corner. Rafa was pinging winners all over the court and seemed to be thoroughly enjoying such a routine contest. Youzhny was put out of his misery as Nadal cashed in on a second match point to secure a 6-3, 6-3, 6-1 victory. He was into the last eight and, but for dropping the first set to Gulbis, he was yet to blot his copybook.

Speaking about the first set slip and the comprehensive win, Rafa told the press: 'It's nothing very important that's for sure. I felt a little bit of pain and was a little bit scared because I felt something crack, but it's fine now. It was a very good result for me. I played a very good match and I am happy with the way I am playing and that I am in the quarter-finals.'

Having swept through to set up a quarter-final showdown with Murray, Nadal now had to prepare to become public enemy number one. Murray had produced a stunning comeback to dump Frenchman Gasquet out of the competition, despite trailing by two sets to love. The Scot would have raucous support as he and Rafa stepped onto the court for a contest that had the potential to be a classic. But Nadal was irresistible on the day as Murray looked a little jaded after his heroic display against Gasquet. The home support was noisy initially yet the sheer brilliance of Rafa's tennis soon left them gasping in disbelief.

Murray had been billed as a contender for the Wimbledon title – an outside bet perhaps – but this contest showed just how much improvement was needed before the Scot could compete with someone of Nadal's calibre. Rafa, Federer and Djokovic were still out in front and the rest of the pack had plenty to do if they wanted to overtake that trio.

Nadal began the quarter-final well, serving efficiently and taking his opportunities on Murray's serve. The Spaniard had a flawless record against Murray – 3-0 – but this was their first meeting on grass and the home favourite was on the rise. But Nadal was one of the most imposing athletes in the world of sport. Murray had flexed his muscles after beating Gasquet in the previous round but they still paled in comparison to Rafa's and every rally seemed to hammer home this point. Still, the Scot held his nerve to level at 1-1 despite suffering some nervy moments. And he did likewise for 2-2 with some solid serving. But the crowd were on edge. The match was just four games old but the menace of Nadal was already evident.

Rafa was serving expertly and conserving energy with which to attack his opponent. But Murray stuck to his guns, firing down the line and then finding a thumping ace to save two break points and level at 3-3. However, it seemed only a matter of time before Nadal cashed in on his superiority. He was in his comfort zone. Nothing Murray threw at him was having any effect. Another simple service game put the pressure back on the Scot as Rafa cruised into a 40-0 lead before clinching the 4-3 lead. Now he needed the break.

Murray's ill-advised drop shot gave Nadal a 30-15 lead in

the eighth game and moments later the Spaniard had two break points. The crowd groaned as the set continued to drift towards the world number two but they were on their feet as the Scot saved the first with a cross-court backhand. But he could not escape this time and Nadal broke for a 5-3 lead as Murray sent an overhead long. British fans at Wimbledon and in homes and pubs up and down the country let out a collective groan. It had been coming. Rafa had been the better player thus far and it was a deserved lead. His presence on court seemed to be stifling Murray's game and the Scot was now on the ropes. In truth, Nadal was not in top gear but he was still good enough to overwhelm his opponent. Yet another smooth service game gave the Spaniard the first set. There were few signs of encouragement for Murray.

After all the hype, the opening set had been massively one-sided and Murray needed to re-think his game plan. Rafa was happy to dictate from the back of court and cream winners with his opponent scampering around in desperation. Could the Scot come to the net more to put pressure on the French Open champion?

The second set began with Nadal looking even more secure on serve. At this stage, he was winning 94% of points on his first serve and 82% on his second serve. Murray was having to fight hard just to hold onto his service games. Rafa wasted no time in stamping his authority on proceedings again. He broke in the third game as the Scot contributed to his own downfall. He was feeling the strain and, in trying to gain the upper hand in rallies, made several key errors that he simply could not afford against someone of Nadal's quality. More hammering blows from the Spaniard's racquet consolidated the break as

Centre Court spectators sat in near silence, struggling to believe the demolition that they were witnessing.

Murray clung on to reduce Rafa's lead to 3-2 but he could not find even a glimmer of a chance to break on Nadal's serve. The four-time French Open champion was delivering a masterclass. At 4-2 up, he ripped into the Scot's serve again. He moved 40-0 up with unerring accuracy on scorching groundstrokes and his power was crushing Murray who just could not live with the onslaught. A split second later, Nadal had the double break sewn up with a stunning backhand. It was hard to know where Murray could go from here. The Scot's effort levels could not be faulted but he was simply not making any impression on the contest and this was more a result of Nadal's genius than Murray's mistakes. Another sizzling service game clinched the set 6-2 and a place in the semi-finals seemed all but in the bag for the Spaniard.

The home crowd were begging for a comeback but it never looked like happening. Murray loosened up a bit with the writing on the wall and produced some of his best moments in the match, matching Nadal with some resilient baseline striking. But he could not put these points together, making it impossible to earn a break. Meanwhile, Rafa was just lying in wait, ready to pounce on any opportunity. The chance arrived in the seventh game as the Spaniard gave his opponent the runaround once more. Murray looked exhausted and frustrated – and it began to show in his shot selection. Nadal forced more errors from the Scot's racquet and breezed into a 4-3 lead with his first break of the third set.

On this evidence, a Federer–Nadal was a near certainty and Rafa was in a hurry to clinch his semi-final spot. And the

Above Left: Rafa at his first Wimbledon Championships in 2003.

Above Right: Rafa kisses the French Open Trophy after his first win at Roland Garros in 2005.

Below: Spain's victorious Davis Cup team of 2004. From left: Juan-Carlos Ferrero, Tommy Robredo, coach Jordi Arrese, Rafael Nadal and Carlos Moya.

Above: Rafa collapses in joy after defeating Roger Federer in the 2006 French Open final. It was the start of an ongoing rivalry with the great player.

Below: Rafa's trademark – biting the French Open trophy.

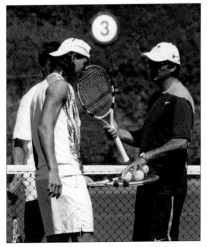

Above: As one of the biggest names in world tennis, Rafa often has media obligations to fulfil. Here, he is pictured in an underwater photo shoot ahead of the 2007 Monte Carlo Masters.

Below Left: Federer consoles Rafa after the 2007 Wimbledon final. Although the pair have a fierce rivalry on the court, off the court they are friends with great mutual respect for one another.

Below Right: One of the keys to Rafa's success is his close relationship with his coach Toni. Toni is always on hand to offer advice, as in this training session in 2008.

Rafa has always relished playing for Spain in the Davis Cup. In 2008, they won the trophy again in front of a home crowd in Madrid's Las Ventas bullring. Sadly, Rafa missed the final because of a knee injury, but his performances against Sam Querrey and Andy Roddick (*Above*) were instrumental in Spain's triumph.

Above: In action, and in control, against Federer in the final at Wimbledon in 2008.

Below: Nadal delighted the crowd by climbing up to the Royal Box after securing his win.

Rafa receives his
Olympic gold medal,
having just beaten
Fernando González.

Above: After reaching the peak of World No.1 in 2008, Nadal takes a well-deserved break on the golf course during the Castello-Masters Pro-Am in Spain.

Below Left: Rafa consoles a tearful Roger Federer after the Australian Open final in 2009.

Below Right: Rafa celebrates his 2010 US Open final victory, which made him only the seventh man in history to have completed a Career Grand Slam.

Above Left: One of Hollywood's greats, Will Smith, presents Rafa with the trophy after he defeated Novak Djokovic in an exhibition match.

Above Right: In November 2013, at the 75th Marca Awards, Rafa was honoured with the Legend Award, given to the greatest Spanish athlete of all time.

Below: After winning the 2013 French Open, his eighth victory, Nadal became the only male player to have ever won the same Grand Slam tournament eight times in his career.   All pictures © *Getty Images*

Swiss would need to bring his A game. More brutal hitting edged Nadal ever closer, extending the lead to 5-3. Murray kept the Spaniard waiting by holding serve but it simply prolonged the inevitable and Rafa put the home favourite out of his misery in the next game. He secured a 6-3, 6-2, 6-4 victory as Murray fired long. The weary Scot had gone out with a whimper. Rafa was delighted, telling the media: 'I played my best match here for sure. I tried to play aggressively all the time, and tried to attack his second serve, but a win like this is always surprising.' He added some consolation for his opponent: 'Probably he felt tired. It's always tough in Grand Slams, so that's normal. I feel sorry for him, but he's going to be in the top five very soon if he keeps playing like this and he has a good chance of winning Wimbledon.'

For his part, Murray was gracious in defeat, telling the press: 'He played so much better than me. I don't feel I played my best but regardless he was playing too well for me. His forehand was ridiculous. He was hitting the ball so close to the line and I felt rushed on every point. I had no chances at all on his serve and he deserved it.' The Scot added: 'If he plays like that and returns like that, he's very close to being the favourite for the title. He was close last year and he's playing better than that now.'

The match had been billed as 'The Battle of the Biceps' but Nadal hoped his brutal display had not alienated the British public. In his *TimesOnline* blog, he wrote: 'I hope that those of you fans of Andy are not too upset. I think I played my absolute best tennis on half of the first set and the whole second set. I felt really good today.

'But I wanted to mention specially the crowd. They were

just fantastic. I have said in the press conference that they were extremely fair but I would add now that they were simply the best crowd.'

Yes, the fans had been generous in their appreciation of Nadal's efforts but the Spaniard had a knack of making even die-hard supporters of his opponent offer their applause. When he was in that kind of mesmerising form, there were few more gripping sights in the world of sport. And it was not just the British fans who were impressed by Rafa's impact on the sport. Richard Bloomfield, the Brit who was at one time in the world top 300, reflected positively on the way Nadal goes about his business on and off the court. He said: 'I think he's brought more aggression and intensity to the game. Federer certainly raised the level but with Nadal it is a case of every point really mattering. He seems to get on with everyone in the locker room and naturally spends a lot of time with the other Spanish guys.'

Bloomfield admitted it was no surprise to see the Spaniard challenge Federer considering he is younger and fresher and suggested that British hopefuls could learn a lot from Nadal's approach. He added: 'I think the attitude Rafa shows in everything he does is undoubtedly good for any kids to learn from.'

Nadal had little time to celebrate his stunning performance because he had a semi-final to prepare for. His opponent would be Rainer Schuettler of Germany. The unseeded Schuettler had been the surprise package of the tournament but now he was facing a very different proposition. Though he was taking nothing for granted, Nadal must have seen the match-up as very winnable, considering some of the big names who might have reached the last four.

Rafa made a bright start, capitalising on the German's nerves. He captured the first set 6-1 in just 24 minutes, leaving many fans expecting an embarrassingly short contest. Nadal broke in the opening game and then the third game for a 3-0 lead as he unleashed some devastating winners. The Spaniard consolidated the double break before Schuettler finally got on the scoreboard at 4-1 with a fine forehand then a powerful ace. Nadal hit back with a love service game, followed by a third break. It was stunning stuff from Rafa, who was moving into top form at the best possible time.

Nadal's forehand was grabbing plenty of attention – understandably given the sheer ferocity of the stroke – but his serve was also proving a huge weapon. Murray had failed to make any inroads and Schuettler was looking equally at sea. Then, out of the blue, the German found some answers and bagged a break for a 2-1 lead. It took everyone inside Centre Court by surprise to see the underdog unloading some brutal backhands – Nadal included. Solid serving helped Schuettler maintain his advantage and, though Rafa scrapped hard for chances to break, the German held firm and, at 5-4 up, had the opportunity to serve for the set and level the match. But he wasted the opening. It is probably unfair to place the blame squarely on Schuettler's shoulders because Nadal peppered him with heavy baseline bombs and eventually the underdog succumbed, firing a string of errors as he was rushed by the velocity of the Spaniard's returns. It could have been the turning point for the German but Rafa was level at 5-5 and had regained the momentum.

To Schuettler's credit, he kept his head and took the set into a tie-break. It was do or die really, though, for the

German. If he lost the second set, there was surely no way back considering the form that Nadal had shown in the last few rounds. And the pressure again threw Schuettler off his game. Nadal played the tie-break expertly, delivering the big serves on cue and forcing forehand errors from his opponent. The German crumbled and a 7-3 scoreline gave Rafa a seemingly decisive two-set advantage. Nadal had one foot in the final, where Federer was waiting for him after a very professional victory over Safin in his semi-final. Schuettler's successes against Rafa in the second set would have given the Swiss encouragement as he sought to extend his brilliant Wimbledon record.

Rafa failed to sweep the German away in the third set but he was also leaving a lot in the tank. Schuettler began well, holding to love, but Nadal's ability to hit brilliant passing shots on the run earned him a break in the third game. And this was decisive. The set continued with serve as the German worked stubbornly to make Rafa toil for the victory. At 5-4 up, the Spaniard served for the match and a place in the final for the third year on the trot. Nadal did not falter as Schuettler had when serving for the second set. Instead, he dished out a ferocious forehand down the line and booked a re-match with Federer with another bullet ace.

The 6-1, 7-6, 6-4 victory had been stylish at times but, most importantly, Rafa had kept himself fresh for the final. It promised to be another thriller if last year's epic was any indication and the debate was once again raging as to who would have the edge. BBC commentator Tim Henman said: 'The final will boil down to who can win the key points. With the way Rafael Nadal has been playing recently, he's going to fancy his chances against Roger Federer even more than last year.'

All eyes would be on Centre Court on the Sunday as the two finest tennis players on the planet squared off in their third successive Wimbledon final. Most pundits had predicted it would end up this way but they could not decide on the winner. As it happened, five excruciating sets of tennis, disrupted by several rain delays, would be required to determine the champion.

The day before the final, Nadal did his best to stay calm. He explained in his blog that he practised for a couple of hours in the morning until he was happy with the way he was hitting the ball and then faced the media. The evening was spent with friends and family at dinner and playing darts - with no discussion of the match ahead.

The players received an overwhelming ovation as they walked onto Centre Court - all the waiting was over and it promised to be a sensational scrap. Federer won the toss and elected to serve first, which suited Rafa just fine. Both competitors made positive starts on serve but it was clear that the longer the points went on, the better chance Nadal had. Just like on clay, his game was suited to long rallies. He would hit returns all day if necessary. There was little evidence to suggest that the humbling defeat at Roland Garros was affecting Federer in the first couple of games but then Rafa landed the first blow of the match by breaking in the third game. His returns were finding the mark and Federer was broken for only the third time in the tournament.

Nadal consolidated the break with a gutsy hold. From 40-0 up he slumped back to deuce and then had to save a break point but his resilience got him into a 3-1 lead. Federer held to love, putting his previous service game behind him, but Rafa's aggression was keeping his nose in front. The Swiss was looking dominant on serve again but Nadal held the advantage and unless Federer found a break, the set would go to the Spaniard. The world number one delivered another love service game to cut the deficit to 5-4 but Rafa would serve for the opening set.

Federer made Nadal toil, earning break points but wasting them. He was making more errors than usual as he seemingly overcompensated for the Spaniard's power. Two backhand mistakes handed Rafa the set 6-4. Henman, in the BBC commentary box, had seen enough to nail his colours to the mast. He said: 'I think I would favour Nadal. He has looked so comfortable from the start.' Rafa knew he had a long way to go still but for the first time in his three Wimbledon finals he had captured the opening set.

Federer came out fighting in the second set, winning the first game to love. Apart from the third game of the first set, the Swiss had been very confident on serve but he had failed to capitalise on the break points that he had earned on Nadal's serve. He put this right in the next game, playing with more freedom and punishing the Spaniard with some exquisite forehands. A fine cross court winner sealed his first break. The on-song world number one quickly consolidated the break, moving into a solid 3-0 lead.

The momentum had certainly shifted but Rafa refused to panic. There were bound to be patches in which Federer dominated. He just had to ride them out and stay in touch. Some well-constructed points saw the Spaniard get on the scoreboard before the Wimbledon champion produced another flawless service game for a 4-1 lead. He kept telling himself that he was only a break down. Nadal was not making an impact on Federer's serve in the second set and knew he had to up the tempo or kiss his advantage good-bye. He stepped up a gear and made the Swiss toil on serve for the first time in the set, cranking up the power of his groundstrokes and drawing mistakes from the world number one. With a few gritty points, Rafa engineered a break point and grabbed it with both hands as Federer fired long. For all the Swiss' second set dominance, Nadal was right back in the mix.

Rafa held for 4-4 despite giving up a break point. Federer's frustration became evident as he snapped at a spectator who called 'out' during a rally but this outburst was triggered by the way that Nadal had muscled his way back into the set. And the challenger was suddenly rampant again, cashing in on the champion's loss of concentration. Federer's disappointment at missing out on a break in the previous game carried over into his next service game and Rafa pounced on the opening. Taking the lead in rallies again, Nadal forced break points. The Swiss saved one but a brutal forehand earned Rafa a second straight break and Federer would have to break back to stay in the set.

It had been an amazing turnaround. Federer had led 4-1 just minutes earlier but Nadal had bagged four games in a row and stood on the brink of a two-set lead. It would be a long way back for Federer if Rafa held his nerve. A cross-court backhand passing shot brought up a set point but Federer saved it. The champion stubbornly hit back and an inexplicable drop shot from Nadal gave the Swiss a chance to level at 5-5. But Rafa came up trumps again, battering his opponent and surviving the scare. Moments later, Federer netted a backhand, handing Nadal a two-set advantage. It was a huge moment in the contest.

The equation was simple now for Rafa: he had to win one out of three sets to become Wimbledon champion. But Federer, of course, would not surrender his title without an almighty fight. He was a five-time champion for a reason and he began the third set well with a love service game. He then got to 40-30 up on Nadal's serve but a wayward forehand allowed the Spaniard to draw level.

There was a brief scare in the third game as Rafa fell as he charged along the baseline, injuring his knee. He picked himself up and opted against taking the medical time-out. Federer had upped his game now and the crowd were firmly behind the world number one. They wanted to see this spectacle go on for a few more sets, just as the supporters had cheered the Swiss in Paris as he limped to defeat in the French Open final. Nadal showed his steel by fighting off a couple of break points in the fourth game, frustrating Federer by winning a call challenge by the finest of margins. But the Spaniard was having to work overtime to hold his serve at the moment with the champion on the charge. Meanwhile, Federer was motoring through his own service games. The difference so far had come partly in the form of unforced errors: Federer had 20, Nadal just 11.

Rafa faced four more break points in the sixth game but remarkably escaped again. These were the passages of play that determined champions from the rest of the pack and

Nadal was coming through when the stakes were highest. Federer looked dismayed as he headed for his chair having taken just one of 12 break points thus far. The Spaniard almost cashed in on a rattled Federer, racing to a 40-0 lead on the Swiss' serve but missing out as the champion bagged five straight points. The weather was taking a turn for the worse and suddenly a delay looked inevitable. Nadal stayed focused, though, and enjoyed his easiest service game of the set as he held to 15.

With dark clouds set to put a dampener on proceedings, Federer stuttered to 30-30 and the crowd knew a few bad points would hand Nadal the title. But the champion found some big serves and moved into a 5-4 lead. Then came the rain.

As Rafa left the court, he could reflect on a brilliant display so far. But against someone like Federer, the job was never truly done until the very last point. He recalled the final against the Swiss early in his career when he had been beaten despite taking a two-set lead.

The delay allowed pundits to properly digest the Nadal masterclass that they had witnessed in the past few hours. Boris Becker, speaking on BBC1, said: 'This is a big surprise for a lot of people out there. Federer gets to break point and then seems to get nervous. He seemed confused in the first set, looked like he was going to win the second and then Nadal rattled off five straight games.'

Coming back after a break of more than an hour was never going to be easy for either player but it was especially tough on Rafa, who would immediately have to serve to stay in the third set. However, such was his current confidence that he shrugged off the tricky situation and breezed into a 40-0 lead with some breathtaking serving. Anyone who had questioned the Spaniard's serve in the past must surely have changed their opinion after his efforts in recent months. Federer refused to crack nevertheless and, with the aid of a successful challenge, he heaped the pressure back on Nadal. The Spaniard, though, was up to the test. His experiences in the Wimbledon final in 2006 and 2007 were standing him in good stead as he held to love with an ace – tie-break time.

It was no secret that Federer had an excellent record in tie-breaks and he looked to make his mark early with a booming ace. Nadal hit back to lead 2-1 but the Swiss was fighting for his life and at last found some openings. Two fearsome forehands moved the champion into a 5-2 lead and, despite Rafa's tireless chasing, Federer was within touching distance of the set at 6-3. Nothing in this final was easy for either player and Nadal dished out a fine volley and a heavy serve to save two set points. Could he escape yet again? The answer came emphatically in the next point as Federer delivered a powerful ace out wide and clinched the tie-break. Game on.

The comeback was on now for the Swiss but Nadal tried to stay calm, reminding himself of how far he had come in this match already. The crowd were enthralled as Federer suddenly seemed to have come out of his shell. Henman was certainly impressed, saying: 'Unbelievable response from Federer – there were the big forehands and the second serve returns and the big inside-out forehand winner and a big ace to finish it off. He certainly hasn't given up this match.'

But Nadal was thinking inwardly, he did not let it show. He remained unflappable and made a bold start to the fourth set, holding to 15. He would need to be rock solid to hold off the Federer fightback. With the Swiss' forehand finally finding its mark, the champion was a far bigger threat and he levelled things with ease.

The quality of play was absolutely dazzling and spectators were enjoying a rare treat. Two true greats were going toe-to-toe and, just when viewers thought they had seen it all, they would produce another rally of stunning brilliance. Despite a few wobbly moments, the set stayed with serve. Federer had stepped up his play but Nadal was matching him stride for stride, shot for shot. If there had been a more captivating final than this, few pundits could think of it. It was even better than the epic that they had provided last year. Rafa moved 4-3 up with a love service game, Federer levelled with a well-placed forehand.

The Spaniard created his best chance of the set at 5-4 and 30-0 up on Federer's serve but, like a true champion, the Swiss played the big points brilliantly, leaning on his serve and hammering forehand winners. Nadal had been just two points away. There was simply nothing to choose between the pair in the fourth set and it moved inevitably into another tie-break.

The tension was rising to a whole new level now and the drama did not disappoint. Nadal bounced back from losing the first point to go 2-1 up as he pounced on Federer's serve. Seconds later, it was 4-1 as Rafa delivered two vital serves at the perfect moment. The Swiss cut the lead with his 62nd winner of the match – an incredible statistic which showed how hard he had had to work to win points. And he was still trailing! The drama was only just beginning. Rafa edged into a 5-2 lead and, with two serves to come, he could sniff the prize. But he seemed to falter facing the magnitude of the moment and he squandered the chances with a double fault and a backhand into the net. The momentum shifted and, with a stunning forehand, Federer drew level at 5-5. With Rafa still shell-shocked, the Swiss' powerful serve earned him a set point. From 4-1 down, Federer had turned the tables on the Spaniard. But he too wasted the opportunity, firing an inviting forehand wide – 6-6.

It was so delicately poised now. It was almost sudden death. Federer sent a forehand long but saved a match point with a big ace. Then came perhaps the most incredible rally of the entire match, maybe even the history of the tournament. With the champion in charge of the point, Nadal was charging from side to side to keep the rally alive. Federer seemed to have won it until Rafa sprinted along the baseline and, at full stretch, whipped a seemingly impossible passing shot down the line. Amazing.

Presented with a second match point – this time on his own serve – the Spaniard was undone by a backhand from Federer that was only marginally less staggering than Rafa's previous winner – 8-8. The atmosphere inside Centre Court was absolutely electric as the Swiss, encouraged by his heroics in saving two match points, hammered yet another massive forehand winner to bring up set point. Nadal then netted a backhand and, after four pulsating sets in which Rafa had been the better player overall, it was suddenly all square at two sets all.

The crowd were on their feet, delighted that this epic contest would now go the distance. Rafa still did not look dispirited, despite missing out on two Championship points.

His short career to date, especially last year's final, had taught him that success depended in part on handling the ups and downs of a match. He was still playing brilliantly and could easily have won the fourth set tie-break on another day. Federer, for all his talent, had needed tie-breaks to clinch four of the five sets he had won against Rafa across the past two finals. The media had devoted countless inches of column space to discussions of how mentally scarred Federer might be after the French Open final massacre. But here he was, refusing to surrender his crown. Could Nadal lift himself for one more push?

With both players surely on their last legs, one break would possibly be decisive at this stage. Rafa had a slight chance to break in the first game of the final set but Federer shut the door. With rain in the air once again, the Spaniard had an equally tricky time on serve but he too prevailed.

There was no such thing as an easy service game by now. Nadal got to deuce in the third game but again Federer got out of jail, keeping the crowd on the edge of their seats. The Spaniard responded in style, though, to make it 2-2.

Henman watched in awe as the spectacle unfolded. He said: 'It is just an unbelievable effort from Federer to keep himself in this match. I can only imagine it must be so difficult for Nadal not to think about those opportunities that he had – 5-2 with two serves to come and then two match points but not be able to cross the line.'

To the dismay of viewers everywhere, the rain interrupted the contest again. At two sets all and 2-2, it could not have come at a tenser time. It was almost 8pm and the chances of finishing the marathon match were decreasing by the second.

However, the shower passed and the delay proved to be just half an hour. Play resumed with Federer in the midst of a nervy service game – but the champion powered through to go 3-2 up. Who would handle the break better?

Nadal answered with a very composed service game, cruising to 40-0 and then finishing the job. Federer found a love service game to keep the drama going. Rafa endured the first worrying moment since the rain delay as the Swiss ploughed into his serve and crafted a break point. The Spaniard stepped up with a breathtaking forehand and held his nerve to level at 4-4. With no tie-break in the final set, there was a feeling that this set might just go on and on. Henman pointed out in his commentary that there had now been 346 points played in this epic match with Federer narrowly ahead 174-172. The Swiss was now playing the type of tennis that had made him untouchable on grass for the past five years. The question was: where had this Federer been during the first two sets? He cranked up the power on his serve and eased into a 5-4 lead – just a game away from title number six. Nadal needed to come up with an answer.

Rafa had come too far to wilt now and, though he was pegged back at 30-30, he showed the character to keep his title dreams alive. Toni and the rest of the Nadal camp urged him to push on and make inroads into Federer's serve. He did just that, bringing up two break points with a curling forehand, but the Swiss replied with some devastating serving and an emphatic forehand. Every point seemed to be raising the bar, providing the best possible advertisement for tennis. It was the kind of match that in years to come fans would be discussing and explaining where they were when it took place.

Nadal was once again serving to survive but remained cool as ever, levelling at 6-6 and somehow managing to look relatively fresh at the same time. All those hours of fitness training were paying off now. As predicted, this set was going beyond 12 games.

One slip up could now be decisive. Federer seemed to be in trouble at 30-0 down but, as he had done numerous times in the match, the world number one dug deep and, with the aid of his 24th ace, held off Nadal. The Spaniard then rallied, dishing out a forehand to make it 7-7 to the delight of his camp. Something had to give eventually and Rafa decided to make sure it went in his favour. He attacked Federer's serve with more gusto than ever, conjuring up a superb cross court backhand and bagging two break points. The Swiss saved both with an ace and a crunching forehand; but Nadal would not be discouraged and he would not relent. This was his moment. This was his day. He earned and missed out on a third break point but brought up a fourth when Federer wavered on his forehand. And this time the Spaniard seized his chance, tempting the Swiss into another off target forehand and grabbing the break. He would serve for the title.

The crowd were exhausted. It was one of those matches where even watching on television was an emotional, nerve-shredding rollercoaster. Rafa was one game away from the most spectacular achievement of his career, one game away from adding his name to the greats who had triumphed at Wimbledon. Could he handle the pressure?

He made the worst possible start with a wild, nervy forehand and Federer began to hope again – maybe the Spaniard would blow it. Rafa tucked away an important volley for 15-15 then another for 30-15. The champion refused to roll over, though, and drew an error to pull level at 30-30. It was on a knife-edge. Toni watched on nervously as his nephew prepared for the biggest points of his career. But Federer eased the tension slightly by firing a backhand wide. Nadal had another Championship point. Surely this was the end. After all the blood, sweat and tears, Rafa was almost there. But the world number one again slammed the door in the Spaniard's face with a bullet return.

Nadal regrouped and earned another chance with a thumping ace. He took a deep breath, grabbed his towel, adjusted his shorts and tried again to clinch the title. After the exertions of the day and the nerves of the moment, it was a wonder that Rafa managed to get his serve in play at all - but he did, even with the memories of last year's tears. Federer had dodged the bullet several times already in the contest but he had run out of lives. He netted a forehand and Nadal had done it - he was the Wimbledon champion.

The Spaniard fell to the turf in a mixture of joy and exhaustion. After a warm embrace with Federer at the net, the celebrations began. Pundits agreed that this was the greatest final in Wimbledon history, if not the greatest tennis match ever played. It was that good.

Rafa amazingly still had the energy to climb into the Royal Box to collect a Spanish flag and take the plaudits from his fans. Nadal's family, friends and coaches joined in the party as Federer came to terms with the end of his fantastic Wimbledon run. There would be no sixth successive title.

Then came the ceremony. Federer collected the runners up

plate before standing aside to allow Rafa to walk forward and lift the main prize. Emotions were running high all round. Nadal raised the trophy, becoming the first man since Borg in 1980 to win the French Open and Wimbledon back-to-back.

Federer was dignified as ever as he addressed the media. The pain of the defeat was written all over his face but he still found the words to praise his opponent's achievement. He said: 'I tried everything. Look, Rafa's a deserving champion. It's been a joy to play here. It's shame I couldn't win it but I'll be back next year.'

Nadal was equally respectful: 'It's impossible to explain how I feel. It's a dream. I never imagined I would win this tournament. It's very tough to play Roger – especially here – he is excellent when he wins and when he loses. He's still the number one and he's still the best. He's won five and I've only won one.'

Witnessing a match of such quality was truly a once in a lifetime experience. And Nadal had come out on top. He had conquered the grass and toppled the seemingly invincible Federer. It was among the proudest days of his life and he would never forget it. It was the trophy he prized most. The well-deserved celebrations went on well into the night as he soaked up the atmosphere at the Wimbledon Champions' Ball, along with fellow winners including Venus Williams and 14-year-old Brit Laura Robson, who had triumphed in the girls' singles. It was the perfect end to a perfect fortnight.

It had been a stunning few months for Rafa but, with the Olympics in Beijing just around the corner, there was limited time for rest. Nadal pulled out of a tournament in Stuttgart in order to rest his right knee and recharge his batteries back in

Mallorca, where he predictably received a hero's welcome. He was able to relax, go fishing, see family and let all his recent success sink in. It was exactly what he needed.

Next up was a trip to Toronto for the Rogers Cup. Having mastered the adjustment from clay to grass, it was now a case of switching back to the hard court again. The Olympics and then the US Open would be played on hard surface and, despite his aches and pains, Nadal wanted to get as much match practice under his belt as possible.

The Spaniard headed to Canada on the crest of a wave. He felt invincible and wanted to continue his faultless run of results. Nadal was already being asked plenty of questions about the Olympics and what it would all mean to him. Federer had outlined his desire to win a gold in China and Rafa admitted that he too was focused on topping the podium.

Nadal enjoyed the luxury of a bye in the first round of the Rogers Cup, allowing him more time to get over the strain of the past few months. He was soon into his stride though and a solid, if unspectacular, second round showing against American Jesse Levine set up a third round clash with Igor Andreev. The Russian had troubled Rafa at times but the Spaniard now seemed to have all the answers against any opponent. And it would be a nice change to go back to playing best-of-three-sets tennis.

After a blistering start, Nadal wrapped up the first set 6-2 and exuded total confidence in his ability to break Andreev's serve. But he was not at his clinical best, converting just two of his nine break points. The second set was a tighter contest yet Rafa came up trumps when the key points were on the line. It went to a tie-break and Nadal overwhelmed his opponent, taking the breaker 7-1 and booking his place in the Rogers Cup quarter-finals. He was pleased with the improvements from his previous display and was eager to press on towards yet more silverware. He told the press: 'It was much better for me than yesterday. I'm happy to get to the quarter-finals for the first time in Toronto. I played well today but I'll have to work on my break points.'

Ever the perfectionist, Nadal knew he could always improve aspects of his game and was training as hard as ever. In the quarter-finals, he surrendered a marathon first set tie-break to Frenchman Gasquet but then bounced back to dispatch him with stunning hitting in the final two sets. Gasquet brought his A game in the first set, forcing a tie-break and holding off Nadal before claiming the breaker 14-12. Against most players, the Frenchman would have been able to use that momentum to power on to victory. Instead, Rafa proved that nothing could knock him off his game. He levelled the match with a breathtaking second set, taking it 6-2.

Then there was only going to be one winner. Nadal did not waste any time either, swatting Gasquet aside 6-1 in the deciding set and marching on. He had now won an incredible 27 straight matches. Murray awaited the King of Clay in the semi-final, German Nicolas Kiefer and Frenchman Gilles Simon would contest the other.

Murray presented Rafa's toughest test of the tournament so far and the Scot was a genuine threat on the hard court surface. But, despite Murray's obvious talent, he was unable to cope with Nadal. The Spaniard had to rely on his tireless scrapping more than usual, though, and the victory owed a lot to his mental toughness. The transition from grass to hard courts was looking as smooth as his switch from clay to grass. He had to work hard to defend his serve in the first set as Murray blazed away from the back of the court, matching Rafa in some hard-hitting rallies. The pair headed into a tie-break but Nadal showed his class by stepping up a gear in the breaker, winning it 7-2.

Murray did not crumble but Rafa was half a step sharper in the second set and when the Scot gave Nadal a glimmer of a chance, the Spaniard seized it. After a tight start, the set was locked at 3-3 but in the blink of an eye it was all over as Rafa gave yet another lesson in dominant tennis. It had been a test but it would take more than this to put an end to his run. Only Kiefer stood between the Spaniard and another trophy.

Kiefer might have been a surprise finalist but Nadal was leaving nothing to chance. He got into the zone and prepared to give the Canadian fans another glimpse of his genius. After a cagey start, Nadal took charge of the opening set. He broke in the fifth game as Kiefer netted a drop shot and then clinched the set 6-3 with another break in the ninth game. It was hard to see how the German could hurt Rafa as everything he threw at the Spaniard was coming back with interest.

Against players like Nadal, it is imperative to snatch every half-chance on offer. Kiefer created a great opportunity to get back into the match when he earned a break point in the fifth game of the second set. The game included six deuces as the German finally made inroads into Rafa's serve. But, when the dust settled, Nadal was still in charge as he held off the German's attempts to break. Having missed out on this golden opportunity, Kiefer fell apart. The disappointment left the German distraught and, as he dwelt on the blow, Nadal reasserted himself. Counting himself fortunate to be 3-2 up, Rafa upped the aggression and Kiefer contributed to his own downfall as two double faults gave the Spaniard a 4-2 lead. Just moments later, Rafa was celebrating another title. He served well in the seventh game then broke again in the eighth for a 6-3, 6-2 victory. It seemed like just another day at the office for the French Open and Wimbledon champion. Could anyone knock him off his perch?

Nadal was in buoyant mood after all the recent success. He told the press: 'I win on every surface, no? I win on grass, on hard, on indoor and on clay too. So if I am playing my best I can win on every surface, no?'

He was a big favourite with the fans in Toronto and, while some of the other big guns had made early exits, Rafa was there until the last to thrill the fans. Bagging his second Rogers Cup was a special moment and he knew that five straight tournament wins was close to perfection.

Rafa then headed back to the US for the Cincinnati Masters. He had gained a lot of ground on Federer in the hunt for the number one spot and it seemed just a matter of time before Nadal overtook the Swiss genius. Depending on results, the Spaniard's rise to pole position could be confirmed in Cincinnati. While he told the media yet again that he was not thinking about the rankings, it was inevitable that Rafa was aware of the possibilities. He knew that a good run in this tournament could see him sitting at the top of the tennis tree. A first round bye gave Nadal more time to rest and, after a slow start, he cashed in against Frenchman Serra. Serra upset the formbook initially as he took the first set 6-4, bewildering Rafa, who looked well below par.

Nadal fought back, though, surviving a few nervy moments to win the second set tie-break 8-6 and stay alive in the contest. Serra stuck at it but just could not pull off the upset as the Spaniard sneaked it 4-6, 7-6, 6-4. It was rather unconvincing stuff from Rafa but then he could not be expected to hit top form every time he went out onto the court. The victory was all that mattered at the end of the day.

He faced Tommy Haas in the third round. The German had progressed in his previous match after Gael Monfils retired late in the first set. But he had beaten 14th seed Youzhny in the first round so could not be underestimated. Nadal did no such thing. He put together an improved performance to wrap up the match in straight sets. Haas had a few openings but just could not grasp them. Rafa played the important points well to grab the first set 6-4 and then produced a flawless tie-break, winning it to love.

And, in a way, it was a double celebration, too, as news reached Nadal that Federer had lost his third round clash against Ivo Karlovic. The Croat's 7-6, 4-6, 7-6 victory opened the door for Rafa to claim the number one ranking. Could he take the opportunity? He would need to reach the semi-finals to make sure of top spot.

In the quarter-finals, he took on Nicolas Lapentti of Ecuador. It promised to be a test of Nadal's aching body as he took the final step towards taking Federer's place as the world's number one player and capping a sensational few months. The first set was a gripping battle as Lapentti showed no fear and seemed to relish the prospect of being the party-pooper. But Rafa showed his class in the tie-break, winning it 7-3. Lapentti offered little resistance in the second set as Nadal took total control, dominating the Ecuadorean's serve and finding a string of perfect passing shots. He wrapped up the match 7-6, 6-1 and with it ensured that he would move into the number one spot by August 18 at the latest.

It called for big celebrations. Nadal told the press: 'I am happy because I have been fighting a lot these last three years, although I was happy as number two as I won a lot of tournaments. But for sure, number one is a goal and I am very happy.'

Djokovic awaited in the semi-finals as Rafa attempted to win yet another tournament. The Serb had enjoyed a consistent year and was a serious contender for the Olympics too. Perhaps the jubilation over gaining top spot distracted Nadal. Perhaps Djokovic was just on top of his game. But either way the Serb made short work of the Spaniard and moved into the final. Rafa just could not cope with Djokovic in the first set as the Serb climbed into his serve and seemed capable of breaking with ease. He bagged it 6-1 and, with it, moved into the driving seat. Nadal eventually settled into the match but by then it was too late. He scrapped in typical fashion but Djokovic had all the answers, clinching a 6-1, 7-5 victory and ending the Spaniard's streak of tournament successes.

It was an impressive performance from the Serb and it came as a surprise when he was outgunned in straight sets – both tie-breaks – by Murray in the final. Rafa was disappointed with the loss against Djokovic but it was just a blip in a stunning few months and he felt that he was playing as well as ever at the moment. It meant he was travelling to the Olympics in Beijing with unbelievable momentum. It was no secret that Nadal was extremely excited about competing at the Olympics. He told reporters: 'It is a special tournament and certainly provides a special motivation as it only happens once in four years.'

Having watched the Olympics as a boy, Rafa knew all about the interest that the Games generated across the globe and he could not wait to play a part in the action. He always loved representing his country and wanted to make all his family and friends proud back home. As he made the trip to China, though, there were some experts predicting it would be one event too far for the Spaniard. They questioned whether he had the energy to pull off yet another triumph. But Rafa ignored their doubts. He could not wait to sample the Olympic atmosphere and mix with the other competitors, including US stars Kobe Bryant and Michael Phelps.

Viewing figures for the Games reached the staggering heights of 4.7 billion but Nadal was driven on by all the attention rather than overawed. He opened his bid for gold against Italian Potito Starace and, though the Spaniard was the overwhelming favourite, he still expected to graft for every point. And as it happened, the Italian put in a very creditable display. Nadal never found top gear but did enough to reach the second round. A routine first set saw Rafa break Starace at will for a 6-2 scoreline and the smart money said the contest would be over in two sets.

However, Nadal faltered in the second set and Starace pounced on the opportunity. Sloppy forehands contributed to the Spaniard's downfall and his opponent showed no nerves as he wrapped up the set 6-3. Suddenly, everyone was paying attention. Surely Rafa would not suffer a shock first-round exit?

He did not. Nadal upped his game in the deciding set and shut the door on Starace's dreams of an upset. Hitting with increased power, Rafa battered the Italian into submission and claimed a 6-2, 3-6, 6-2 victory. Having played only doubles in Athens in 2004, this was Nadal's Olympic singles debut and he was delighted to progress. Life in the Olympic village was proving a wonderful experience for the Spaniard and he was desperate to stick around. He told the press: 'I am very happy to be here. Just trying to enjoy 100 per cent the experience, and later try my best on court.'

Nadal was also a winner in his first round doubles match. He and compatriot Tommy Robredo overcame Swedish duo Bjorkman and Soderling 6-3, 6-3. Playing twice in a day was gruelling but Rafa had his eyes on two gold medals. The action came thick and fast. Nadal took on Australian Hewitt in the second round and brushed aside the former world number one. Hewitt made his name as a scrapper who could chase down seemingly impossible shots. But this was Rafa's speciality now and he made the Australian toil on the way to a 6-1, 6-2 victory.

Hewitt, exhausted after a lengthy doubles match, could not handle the pace and Nadal was in relentless form. Speaking to the media after the match, he said: 'I played very well. It was one of the best matches I have played.'

In the next round of the doubles, Hewitt gained revenge by eliminating Nadal and Robredo. He and Chris Guccione collected a 6-2, 7-6 victory. While it lightened Rafa's workload and surely improved his chances of singles glory, the Spaniard was disappointed to see one of his gold medal opportunities pass him by. Focused on just one event now, Rafa steeled himself to give everything to achieve his goal. In the third round, he clashed with Andreev, who was emerging as a very talented player. But he was no match for Nadal.

Rafa bagged the first set 6-4 and went from strength to strength as he secured a place in the next round by winning the second set 6-2. It was an extremely impressive performance and would have been painful viewing for his fellow medal hopefuls. Could anyone live with Nadal in this type of form? There would be nobody queuing up to face him. But the unlucky man to take on the Spaniard was Austrian Jurgen Melzer. Melzer had shown flashes of brilliance in the earlier rounds, disposing of ninth seed Stanislas Wawrinka, yet few believed he represented a genuine obstacle on Nadal's path to gold.

Unfortunately for Melzer, Rafa seemed determined to prove the pundits right. He started like a house on fire, dominating the Austrian's serve and outhitting his opponent in almost every rally. The match had been delayed by rain in Beijing and Nadal was keen to finish the contest as quickly as possible.

In less than 30 minutes, he had bagged the first set 6-0. It was a humbling experience for Melzer, who just could not live with the quality of tennis that Rafa was producing. The second set was more even but the Spaniard clearly had numerous gears to move into if necessary. Eventually, he managed to grind Melzer down and grab the decisive break, earning a 6-0, 6-4 victory. It was a very easy night's work.

He would take over the world number one slot after the Olympics and he was certainly playing tennis befitting of that ranking. As Federer crashed out against Blake, it seemed more likely than ever that Nadal would be the man topping the podium. Blake and Chilean Fernando Gonzalez would contest the first semi-final before Nadal squared off against Djokovic, the number three seed. With Federer out, the Serb seemed the best bet to outgun Rafa.

Many speculated that the winner of Nadal–Djokovic would be the eventual gold medal winner, so the pressure was on. Rafa made the brighter start, just as most pundits had predicted. The heat of Beijing seemed to make little difference to Rafa as he pummelled Djokovic from the back of the court. He snatched his opportunity to break to win the first set 6-4. But the Serbian showed his character by bouncing straight back in the second set. He was made of much sterner stuff than some of the players that Nadal had eliminated en route to the semi-finals. Rafa began to struggle and lost his way on his serve, allowing Djokovic to gain the upper hand. The Serb took the set 6-1 and seemed to have the momentum heading into the deciding set.

The biggest disappointment was that neither player produced their best tennis on this lofty stage. Breaks of serve came via errors rather than staggering passing shots, which was a crying shame considering the immense talent on show. Nadal knew that he was still only an hour away from the gold medal match and the prospect of this huge prize seemed to will him into reasserting his authority.

The final set was incredibly tight and tense with both players crafting and then wasting opportunities to move ahead. But Rafa reacted quicker to the disappointments and finally edged in front. At 5-4 up, he found himself with match point. Yet the pressure of the moment allowed the Serb to escape. However, Djokovic could not repeat the trick. Nadal grabbed a second match point and clinched a 6-4, 1-6, 6-4 victory as his opponent sent an overhead smash just out. The Spaniard threw himself to the floor – exhausted and delighted. It had not been a classic but his spirit had helped him prevail and his incredible journey continued.

His mission when he arrived in Beijing had been to win a gold medal – nothing less. There had been no talk of Rafa just aiming to get on the podium. There was only one medal that interested him and it had been a great incentive all week. Now only Gonzalez, the victor in a heated semi-final with Blake, stood in Nadal's way. The Chilean had stunned Rafa in the past, could he do it again with such a big prize at stake? The Spaniard remembered his defeat to Gonzalez in the Australian Open quarter-final in 2007 and sought to gain revenge in Beijing. The final would be a five-set contest, unlike all the previous rounds. If anything, this played into Nadal's hands. He fancied his chances of outlasting Gonzalez. The Chilean would now need three sets rather than two for victory and, on current form, the Spaniard looked unlikely to be charitable. Cheered on by hordes of travelling Spanish fans, Rafa made an excellent start. The nerves of the occasion certainly seemed to hinder Gonzalez as Nadal got his nose in front and motored towards a 6-3 first set scoreline.

The section of the crowd adorned with red and yellow rose

jubilantly as Rafa clinched the opening set. He was looking a cut above his Chilean opponent and was rising to the occasion once again. It was so long since Nadal had lost in a major tournament that his confidence was sky high. Winning so many matches in the past few months gave him great belief and plenty of good memories to draw upon.

The second set was tighter as Gonzalez began to let loose. He made Nadal sweat as he scampered along the baseline. Rafa had to fight off two break points with some brave tennis and in the end he settled for a tie-break as his opponent stretched him to the limit. The Chilean had arguably missed his best chance of a fightback and he found Nadal too hot to handle in the breaker. Rafa was everywhere, chasing down likely winners and producing remarkable returns. His all-round tennis was just on a higher level than Gonzalez – and every other player on the circuit at present. The Spaniard saw the finishing line in sight and bagged the tie-break 7-2. He was one set away from claiming the gold that he coveted.

It was amazing to see Nadal on the brink of making a brilliant year even better. Had any other player produced such a stunning set of results in a calendar year? He just did not miss when he got into a rally – every return landed perfectly and rushed his opponent into rash shots. Gonzalez was fast losing patience and the more he sought out winners, the more errors he seemed to make. Rafa picked his opponent apart again early on in the third set as he dominated the Chilean's serve and motored on towards the top of the podium.

Despite a few nervous moments as he tried to close out the

final, Nadal got there eventually. He cashed in on his fourth match point as Gonzalez fired into the net, clinching a 6-3, 7-6, 6-3 win. Now the party could really start – Rafa was the Olympic champion. He had tasted his fair share of success in 2008 but this was still a massive moment for the Spaniard. His heartbreak at missing out four years ago had made Beijing an even more significant occasion and he had put together a week of sublime tennis, fit to grace the Olympic Games. He was a worthy winner.

The statistics spoke for themselves. Nadal had won 38 of his past 39 matches and was heading for the world number one spot. Rafa was undoubtedly enjoying the form of his life yet he kept his feet on the ground, despite the attentions of the media circus. He told the press: 'I just want to enjoy this moment because I'm having an unbelievable year. It's more than my best dreams so I want to enjoy the moment. I know how difficult it is to win these things. Winning here for me is unbelievable.'

Hot on the heels of his gold medal success, Nadal was able to savour the moment that he officially overtook Federer in the rankings. While it had been confirmed during the Cincinnati Masters, the handover officially took place on August 18. The Swiss, who had been utterly invincible at times during the past four or five years, had held the number one ranking for a record 237 weeks but it was now time for a changing of the guard. Rafa had enjoyed a stunning year and that was always going to be what it would require to dislodge Federer at the top. Nadal told the media: 'I'm very happy but the feeling doesn't change much because the last years I did well too. For sure there's satisfaction but at the same time I don't have time to celebrate. I play New York [US Open] in one week.'

It was a glorious moment for the Spaniard. He had held the number two slot since July 2005 but, with Federer installed as top seed from February 2004 onwards, there had been little chance of Nadal overtaking the Swiss. Now, though, Rafa was reaping the rewards for a simply phenomenal season.

Rafa could easily have taken his foot off the gas following his French Open and Wimbledon triumphs. But he had not. Federer's form had dipped since losing at SW19 but Nadal had motored on.

How would this change things for the Spaniard? As top dog, there would inevitably be greater pressure for every tournament and opponents would be even keener to beat him. But, in truth, he was already regularly in the public eye and, more often than not, was expected to win his matches. Perhaps there would be higher expectations but there was also the joy of officially being the world's top tennis player.

Federer, for his part, took the loss of the top spot in his stride. His rivalry with Nadal had always been founded on mutual respect rather than animosity and the Swiss was quick to praise Rafa's fine season so far.

He told reporters: 'That's what I expected and hoped for many years ago when I got to number one, that if ever somebody were to take it away from me, he would have to play an incredible tennis schedule, win the biggest tournaments, dominate the game basically, and then like this he can take number one.

'I didn't want it to happen that I would play completely bad and somebody would pick up number one in the world. So I think Rafa totally deserves it.'

By his own impeccable standards, the Swiss had had a troubled year. Having lost out to Djokovic in the Australian Open semi-final, he managed to reach the finals in Paris and Wimbledon but was foiled by Nadal on both occasions. With the US Open as the last remaining Grand Slam, there was a genuine possibility that Federer could end the year without scooping one of the big prizes. It was amazing to consider how things had changed. No one would have believed this possible 12 months ago. Many still wondered how much psychological damage Nadal had inflicted with his 6-1, 6-3, 6-0 demolition of Federer at the French Open. The Swiss had not been the same untouchable star since that afternoon in Paris. Could the Spaniard now embark on a run at the top to rival Federer's stunning stint as world number one?

As he left Beijing, Nadal could reflect on not only a great triumph but a fantastic experience. He had met so many fine competitors across a range of sports and the spirit and atmosphere of the Olympics was something he would really miss. But for now, Rafa had to look ahead to the next challenge in his path – the US Open.

It had been an exhausting few months and this fact was well documented in the press. In his blog, Nadal mentioned that he had had no time to relax in Mallorca since the start of the Rogers Cup in Toronto. From there he had gone to Cincinnati then on to Beijing.

CHAPTER 6

PAYING THE PRICE FOR HIS SUCCESS

It remained to be seen how the rest of the year would pan out. So far in his career, the latter months of the season had not been fruitful for Nadal. He tended to peak during the clay court season and he had been successful at Wimbledon, but then results often went slightly downhill from there. However, this year had been like no other for Rafa so it was impossible to tell. Would all the drama finally take its toll on his body?

Nadal arrived at the US Open at the top of his game and with the prizes to prove it. But how much longer could he carry on shrugging off the incredible number of matches he had played? His body appeared immune to the taxing nature of life as one of the world's finest sportsmen yet it was hard to tell from the outside whether or not he was struggling.

In the first round, Nadal faced German qualifier Bjorn Phau. Rafa was determined not to become complacent but his body did not allow him to play his best tennis against Phau. In fact, it was a real grind for the world number one. He grabbed the first set tie-break 7-4 to earn a slender advantage. The Spaniard improved in the second set and it was one-way traffic as Rafa upped the tempo, taking more chances on Phau's serve. The German struggled and Nadal was able to break, bagging the set 6-3.

Most expected the qualifier to crumble as Rafa cruised towards the second round but Phau showed great resilience as he took the third set to a tie-break. Unfortunately for the German, his gutsy efforts went unrewarded again as Nadal exhibited his ruthless streak. The Spaniard rose to the challenge on the big points and clinched the victory, winning the tie-break 7-4. The media unsurprisingly focused on the hectic schedule that Rafa had faced since the start of the French Open and questioned how much he had left in the tank. Did he really have the energy to compete for the US Open crown? 'To win in three sets is always a good result,' he told the press. 'I had some difficult moments, so that's going to help me a little bit to be prepared for the pressure moments. I played well today when I had the pressure moments. I am a bit tired, yes, but it is the US Open so I have to try my best here.' He was making all the right noises in front of the microphones but speculation continued as to the state of his body. Nadal's opponents hoped that he was indeed beginning to feel the aches and pains of his victory spree.

Anyone who watched his clash with Phau would have admitted that Rafa was below-par. He was still easily good enough to progress but could he match up with Federer or

Djokovic after so many battles over the past six months? Nadal steeled himself for the next challenge – posed by American qualifier Ryler De Heart. De Heart, ranked number 251 in the world, had stunned Belgian Olivier Rochus in the opening round and could not be taken lightly. Rafa seemed desperate to make quick work of the American, making a bright start and dominating De Heart's serve at will. On this type of form, few players' serve could have held up against Nadal's onslaught. The Spaniard bagged the first set 6-1, leaving all those watching in no doubt as to his commitment to winning the tournament.

As Nadal dominated again in the second set, pundits began to mull over the possibility of Rafa picking up a third Grand Slam of the year. Would he become a contender for the greatest player of all time? On current form, nobody could live with the world number one and it did not seem to matter how many matches Nadal had played in recent months. He boomed down an exceptional 70% of first serves against the American.

De Heart was swept away as Rafa completed a straight-forward 6-1, 6-2, 6-4 victory and booked his place in the third round. Nadal's only difficulty came in the third set when his opponent managed to take his only break point of the contest. But any hopes that the American might have had of a comeback were smashed as Rafa won the next five games to seal the victory. He refused to get carried away with the performance, though, as he sought to make the most of a rest day. The Spaniard seemed content with his display when he addressed the media. 'The important thing was I had to come back in the third set and I'm happy with the victory,' he said.

'Now I'm in the third round, I'm happy. For me, it's an important tournament.'

His next test came in the form of Serbian Viktor Troicki, who had overpowered 25th seed Philipp Kohlschreiber in the previous round. Troicki was a familiar opponent for Nadal, having faced the Serb at the Australian Open in January. Anyone hoping to witness an upset was in for a disappointment as Rafa continued his improved form and cruised through. The opening set saw the Serb hold his own at times in punishing rallies but Nadal was more clinical on the vital points, taking the set 6-4.

Troicki made a storming start to the second set, imposing himself and earning a well-deserved break. Leading 3-1, he was certainly in the driving seat. Against most players, the Serb would have gone on to clinch the set but Rafa's power brought his opponent crashing back to earth. As if greatly aggrieved to have surrendered the break, Nadal cranked up the ferocity of his hitting and sent Troicki scurrying around the court. In no time, the Spaniard had turned a 3-1 deficit into a 6-3 scoreline, moving two sets ahead.

The third set was always going to be a formality. Troicki was still in shock after Nadal's five-game blitz and the Spaniard was capitalising on every short ball. Rafa broke serve with ease as he opened up a comfortable lead and then accelerated away, taking a hugely one-sided set 6-0. Another three-set victory kept him on track for a place in the final. There was still a long way to go, of course, but Nadal was pleased with the way he was hitting the ball and his movement across the court. Up next would be another home favourite, Sam Querrey.

He told the media: 'The truth is that I was practising much

better yesterday than the first few days. I think I am ready to play a good match in the fourth round. I know I have to play a good match if I want to win.' Nadal had played the American only once before, winning in three sets in Cincinnati in 2006, so there was plenty of preparation to take care of. He knew Querrey would have massive support and would be able to play with freedom. The American had nothing to lose – a dangerous scenario for Rafa.

Querrey certainly gave Nadal his biggest test thus far. The Spaniard came flying out of the blocks, tearing the American's big serve to pieces and punishing him with ferocious groundstrokes. It looked like being a short match as Rafa clinched the first set 6-2. He looked less imperious in the second set but still posed plenty of threat to Querrey's serve. The pair swapped breaks before Nadal struck again and moved 5-3 ahead. A two-set advantage seemed just moments away for the Spaniard. But then things changed in a hurry. Nadal lost concentration and Querrey pounced on the opportunity. The American broke back to level at 5-5, held for 6-5 and then cashed in on the momentum by breaking Rafa for the third time to sneak the set. The crowd were on their feet and Nadal was stunned. He had let the set slip through his fingers – now it was all square.

Rafa's serve was suddenly very shaky and every winner from Querrey's racquet was met with deafening cheers. The Spaniard's usual assurance was missing. He opened up a 4-2 lead in the third set but, uncharacteristically, let the American back in with loose forehands and a disastrously-timed double fault. The pair headed into a tie-break where Nadal at last returned to his best form. He built up a lead and never looked like relinquishing the advantage, strolling to a 7-2 scoreline and moving 2-1 ahead. Some felt Querrey would wilt in the fourth set but the American emerged with great credit as he fought hard for every point. Nadal got the vital break in the fifth game but had to call on all his resilience and know-how to stave off seven break points in his next service game. Querrey knew this would be his final opportunity, as his head understandably went down. Rafa, now far more assured on serve, held his nerve and booked his place in the quarter-finals with a 6-2, 5-7, 7-6, 6-3 victory. But he had certainly been made to sweat over it.

Nadal admitted the clash had been 'very tough' but preferred to reflect on reaching the quarter-finals at the US Open for the first time. He told the press: 'I'm very happy for the victory. Now I'm in my best round at the US Open and I hope to play better in the next round.' Querrey, whose performance was heavily praised by the media, admitted that Rafa just had too much quality on the day. He said post-match: 'I was just taking my forehand and trying to rip it as hard as I could. He's just too good.'

Nadal knew he would have to make adjustments if he wanted to reach the last four, though. He faced yet another American in the quarter-finals in big server Mardy Fish. It guaranteed yet another noisy night but the Spaniard thrived on the big match atmosphere and hoped he could silence the American fans with a dominant performance. Incredibly, Nadal and Fish did not start their quarter-final until 11.30pm on the Wednesday night. Murray and Del Potro then the Williams sisters played lengthy matches, forcing Rafa's contest to be pushed back.

The late start did not seem to bring out the best in Nadal as Fish overwhelmed him in the opening set. The effect on a player's body clock should not be underestimated in these circumstances and Rafa appeared to be paying the price. But, of course, it was the same scenario for both players and the American was simply handling it better. Fish came to the net with great success in the opening set and returned Nadal's serve with interest on numerous occasions. The American bagged a 3-0 lead and held on to take the first set 6-3. Would this wake Rafa from his slumber?

It certainly did. Nadal responded with a far better effort in the second set. He found a rhythm on his forehand and began to manoeuvre the American around the court with ease. He broke Fish's serve twice to level the match at one set all. Clearly, this battle was destined to go into the early hours of Thursday morning. Fish scrapped to stay in the third set but Nadal was everywhere now. The American's tactic of rushing in had been inspired in the first set but Rafa was ready for it now and unleashed a string of brilliant passing shots, leaving Fish helpless at the net.

Rafa clinched the third set 6-4 and moved to within a set of the semi-finals. But he never took his eye off the match in hand. After a cagey start to the fourth set, Rafa made more inroads into the Fish serve and, two breaks later, had earned a 5-2 lead. Nadal rarely choked badly under pressure and once again he refused to falter with a first-ever US Open semi-final up for grabs. He held his serve and sealed a 3-6, 6-1, 6-4, 6-2 victory. The match finished at 2.11am but New York was still buzzing after witnessing a gripping contest. Rafa, who was certainly buzzing himself, had eliminated another American but received a warm ovation from the home fans nonetheless. 'The night session here is always unbelievable,' he told the media – but he admitted he preferred finishing much earlier than 2am! He also praised his opponent's efforts, adding: 'Mardy played great in the first set. He was serving very well.'

In beating Fish, Rafa clinched a proud record of reaching the last four of every Grand Slam in 2008. He had won two of them and hoped to seal a third later in the week. But Murray, his semi-final opponent, would provide the toughest test so far. The Scot had put his disappointing showing at the Olympics – and the subsequent bad press back in Britain – behind him and his form in New York had been terrific. Murray's clash with Del Potro had shown his fighting spirit and ability to win the big points. Now he was determined to earn a first ever win over Nadal.

Rafa was boosted by the memory of annihilating Murray in straight sets at Wimbledon just months earlier but knew the Scot was currently full of confidence and certainly came into the contest fresher than Nadal. The British media were heaping praise on Murray and Sky's viewing figures rocketed up with every victory. But question marks remained over the Scot's ability to beat the very best players – could he prove that he belonged in the same league as Nadal, Federer and Djokovic?

Federer and Djokovic contested the first semi-final and, despite the Serb enjoying some promising moments, it would be the Swiss who booked his place in the US Open final with a four-set victory. With the Federer–Djokovic match still in progress, Nadal walked out for the second semi-final. He was the favourite and the world number one – it was hard not to feel pressure in such circumstances. Rafa was playing in the Louis Armstrong Stadium for the first time during the fortnight and would have to adjust instantly. He won his first service game, shrugging off pressure at 30-15 down, but things soon headed in Murray's favour. The Scot broke in the third game and consolidated it for a 3-1 lead with some brilliant serve-volleying. Rafa's forehand errors were costing him dearly and he had to battle to hold serve for 3-2. Murray sensed he had gained the initiative and he delivered some thumping aces to keep Nadal at bay. He was making life very uncomfortable for the Spaniard.

Murray earned a second break in the seventh game and held his serve to snare the set 6-2.

Nadal had plenty to think about as he returned to his chair. British fans were jubilant and Radio 5 Live Sports Extra's Jeff Tarango announced: 'Murray's like a cobra. He just sits there and then every time he sees that forehand down the line he takes it.'

It was far from over for Rafa but it was now apparent that he was in for a huge battle. He improved in the second set but remained tentative and below-par. Murray was regularly grabbing a couple of points on Nadal's serve, forcing the top seed to play under immense pressure. The Spaniard saved three break points in the third game while Murray held to love in the fourth. It told the story of the players' contrasting levels of confidence and fitness. But Nadal was doing enough to hang on in the contest and in the seventh game finally managed to hold serve with ease. At the same moment that Federer clinched victory over on the Arthur Ashe Stadium, Murray levelled for 5-5 with his 11th ace. Nadal cranked up the pressure on the Scot by moving 6-5 and 30-15 ahead but Murray forced a tie-break with more dominant serving. Rafa had played almost two sets now and still had not found his rhythm. Murray deserved great credit for throwing Nadal off his game. In the tie-break, the Scot moved to a 3-1 lead but the Spaniard hit back for 3-3 at the changeover. As the tension mounted, Nadal picked the right time to deliver some top class serves and moved 5-4 ahead. But Murray's head never dropped. He received some luck with a net cord which bounced on Rafa's side but there was nothing fortunate about his bullet serve that brought up set point. Nadal faltered again, sending a backhand wide and handing the second set to Murray. The crowd were largely behind the underdog and the stadium filled with cheers as the Scot returned to his chair with a two-set lead. Rafa was stunned but vowed to hit back.

The day's play came to an abrupt end soon after, denying the Spaniard the chance to make amends. The rain that had been forecast duly arrived, just as Nadal was beginning to gain the upper hand. He had secured a break in the third set to lead 3-2 but weather intervened, sending the players off to the locker room.

While Rafa was ahead in the third set, the rain delay at least allowed him to clear his head. Murray, on the other hand, was surely frustrated that his opponent had been granted a reprieve. The rain continued to fall and an official decision was later announced, explaining that the remainder of the semi-final would be played the following afternoon.

The task was clear for Nadal. He had to secure the third set and then throw everything into his bid to win the final two sets. But Murray was hitting the ball brilliantly and the Spaniard knew he faced an uphill battle. When the pair returned on the Sunday afternoon, the crowd continued to give Murray their support. The Scot had been open about his love for New York and the fans had taken the youngster to their hearts. But as Nadal moved 4-2 ahead, the supporters cheered him on – they understandably fancied the prospect of a five-set epic.

Murray held to love with an impressive service game but Rafa appeared content with his break, safe in the knowledge that holding his own serve would be enough to clinch the set. This strategy looked like costing the Spaniard as Murray battled back. Nadal squandered a set point and then had to save a break point. But the Scot was powerless to stop Rafa clinching the set as the world number one belted a forehand onto the line to cut the deficit to 2-1.

He was pumped up now and Toni was on his feet in the stands. Part one of the mission had been completed but could Nadal keep it going? Rafa certainly seemed in better form and was hitting the ball noticeably harder than the previous day. The results were speaking for themselves. Murray was showing no signs of nerves, though, and continued to viciously attack Nadal's serve. Leading 1-0 in the fourth set, the Scot earned seven break points in the second game but just could not make them count, allowing Rafa to escape with his serve intact. 5 Live's Jeff Tarango admitted: 'Nadal played great shots on all those break points.'

Nadal punished Murray's profligacy by breaking in the next game. He raced into a 40-0 lead and the Scot then sent a backhand wide. Moments later, despite going 30-0 down,

Nadal held serve to move into a 3-1 lead. It looked ominous for Murray. But Rafa could not keep the initiative. Murray, still the fresher of the two, showed that he had greater steel now than in previous meetings with the Spaniard. The Scot earned his 18th break point of the match in the sixth game and another Nadal forehand error pulled Murray level at 3-3.

Now the Scot was on top again and Rafa rued missing the chance to push on and seal the set. Murray moved 4-3 ahead with a freak shot that looped over Nadal and all the pressure was back on the Spaniard. He surrendered a 19th break point of the match but stepped up his game to hold serve as he brought an error from his opponent. The Scot rattled through his next service game with the type of confidence that suggested he was ready to earn a first ever Grand Slam final appearance. His serving had been a revelation and Nadal had been unable to handle the spate of aces. Murray had enjoyed success on Rafa's serve throughout the contest and the tenth game was no different. Nadal's weary body tried to put up one last fight but the Scot had come too far in the tournament to miss out now. Murray forced deuce then earned a match point with a neat volley at the net. Rafa knew the end was nigh. On the next point, he raced into the net but was passed by a clever Murray backhand and his US Open dream was over. The Scot would face Federer in the final.

Nadal could reflect on his US Open experience with few regrets. He had arrived on the back of a draining schedule yet had produced glimpses of brilliance on the way to the last four. He could not argue with his defeat to Murray – the relatively new kid on the block had deserved it. But it made Rafa even more desperate to win in New York in the near future. Nadal admitted: 'I'm disappointed but at the same time I'm happy. I did a good semi-final and when I arrived I had too many matches on my shoulders. I leave the US Open with positive memories.' He added: 'I go on court all day with calm, try to fight as much I can, going home knowing I tried everything. I had my chance in the fourth set. I just didn't come back.'

Murray, meanwhile, was jubilant. He said: 'It's awesome to beat him, a great feeling.' The Scot would go on to lose in straight sets to Federer in a rather one-sided final but he had proved he could mix it with the best in the world. Nadal's sadness at not reaching the US Open final lingered but he could look back happily at his achievements at the 2008 Grand Slam tournaments. He had outgunned or matched his previous efforts at each one. In Melbourne, he had reached the semi-finals for the first time, he had been invincible once again in Paris, he had finally toppled Federer at Wimbledon and last but not least he had reached a first US Open semi-final. It was a superb set of results, especially when you threw in a stunning gold medal at the Olympics. He was due a decent break from the game but that would have to wait. There was more tennis on the agenda.

The Davis Cup was just around the corner for Rafa and he was excited to be representing his country again. Spain faced the USA, Davis Cup winners in 2007, in Madrid and Nadal would have an immediate opportunity to put his US Open heartache behind him.

Unsurprisingly, Rafa was back with a bang as he sparked his compatriots in front of passionate home support. He drew first blood for Spain by edging out Querrey in the opening match.

The American outlasted Nadal in a first set tie-break but it proved a false dawn as Rafa roared back to complete a 6-7, 6-4, 6-3, 6-4 victory. Those who felt he had little left in the tank were forced to think again.

Drawing inspiration from Nadal's strong showing, Ferrer then clinched a huge win over Roddick in the second match of the day. Despite losing the second and third sets, the Spaniard stuck to his guns and won the final set 8-6. It was a tough day for the Americans – Nadal and Ferrer had crushed their hopes. Mike Bryan and Fish kept US hopes alive in another classic contest, winning in five sets against Spanish duo Feliciano Lopez and Fernando Verdasco. It meant that Nadal headed into his clash with Roddick knowing he could clinch victory for Spain. He loved that kind of pressure. The nation would be watching: and he did not disappoint the feverish crowd. After the start was delayed for almost two hours, Rafa edged the first set 6-4 but was troubled throughout by the American's big serving. Nadal then found the perfect rhythm in the second set and blew Roddick away, hitting some stunning winners along the way to a flawless 6-0 scoreline. It was easy to forget that the American was a top ten player as Nadal ran him into the ground. A place in the Davis Cup final was now in the Spaniard's sights and every point Rafa won was cheered enthusiastically by the crowd inside Madrid's Las Ventas bullfighting arena.

Nadal cruised to a 6-4, 6-0, 6-4 victory and the party began. He was hoisted high by his team-mates and the Spanish team could look ahead to the final later in the year. The champions were out and Ferrer's match with Querrey became a dead rubber. Rafa told the media: 'It was great to win at home. There is no atmosphere like this.' He admitted that his energy levels were lower than usual after the exertions of his incredible year but he was quick enough to punish any mistakes from Roddick. The American attempted to serve-and-volley his way to victory but Nadal was always there to pick off loose balls and drill immaculate passing shots. Roddick was dignified in defeat, adding: 'I don't think you can draw up a tougher scenario than playing Nadal on clay in front of a crowd like this. He's the best clay courter of all time, but I'm not that great a clay courter.'

It had been a massively intense few days for Rafa as he returned to winning ways and moved on from the US Open defeat. It was perfect timing really as the home fans had managed to lift his performances and give him some extra motivation. He was always so proud to represent his country and bringing success to the Spanish people was extremely satisfying. He got another chance to impress on Spanish soil at the Madrid Masters. Having thrilled spectators during the Davis Cup semi-final, Nadal was clearly in good form and, so long as his body did not betray him, seemed to have a strong chance of winning the tournament.

Playing in Madrid, in front of home supporters, was always special for Nadal. He was determined to end the year on a high – something that he knew he had not done the previous year. He tried to forget about all the triumphs of 2008 as he threw all his energies into chasing this latest trophy.

He began well, working his way through the tournament with his usual ruthless streak. Elsewhere, Federer and Murray were both impressing and Rafa knew he would need to find his best form if he wanted to add another trophy to a brilliant year. The Spaniard's form so far in his short career suggested that the exertions of the French Open and Wimbledon tended to leave him a little below par for the final months of the season but he tried to shrug this off. He was troubled by a shoulder injury throughout the event but nonetheless reached the semi-finals with a solid win over fellow Spaniard Feliciano Lopez. The semis paired Nadal with Gilles Simon and Federer with Murray. It seemed to be set up for another titanic clash between the world's top two players.

Rafa was confident of reaching the showpiece final but, despite an excellent start, his challenge wilted against the intense play of Simon – a player who was enhancing his reputation with every tournament. Nadal had been the clear favourite going into the match but he soon found out that he was in for a fight. Rafa bagged the first set 6-3, winning some punishing rallies; but his shoulder seemed to impede him at key moments and Simon levelled things, claiming the second set 7-5. The momentum was with the Frenchman and he capped a fine week of tennis by taking the decisive third set tie-break 8-6, sending Rafa out and denying him the chance to compete for the title.

Despite this defeat, Nadal would still end the year as the world's top seed after Federer lost out to an in-form Murray in the other semi-final. And the Spaniard remained positive about his tennis, praising his opponent's fine fightback: 'I didn't play well on the backhand and he was playing with unbelievable confidence. Simon was putting all the balls inside the lines. It was disappointing not to win, it's tough to lose a match like this after a big fight. I tried my best, I'm happy with myself for that. I was not under any big pressure, not after the season I've had.'

Nadal dragged his aching body to Paris next in the hope of producing the same form that had seen him extend his unbeaten streak at the French Open earlier in the year. The city held great memories and he was keen to add another title to his haul for the season. But this particular quest was destined for an unhappy ending.

He began well. After receiving a bye in the opening round, he made quick work of Frenchman Serra. Nadal was far too strong and wasted no time in picking apart his opponent's serve. The Spaniard had soon wrapped up a comfortable 6-2, 6-4 victory. The 16th seed Monfils awaited Rafa in the third round but proved no match for Nadal's hitting. The Spaniard was able to find the break points on Monfils' serve and cashed in to bag the first set 6-4. The second set also went with the formbook as Nadal burst into the next round without having to play his best tennis.

Winning matches with the minimum of fuss was very important, considering how exhausted Rafa was after his year's exploits. The more rest he could cram in, the better his chances of progressing to the latter stages of the tournament. In truth, though, he was on his last legs. The efforts earlier in 2008 had left him shattered. And in his quarter-final with Davydenko, Rafa's body finally refused to take the strain any longer. He had to withdraw from the match after just one set as he was unable to bend his right knee. The tendinitis problem had reared its ugly head again. Almost as distressing was the chorus of jeers from the supporters as the Spaniard limped away. He had thrilled them at the French Open and they repaid him like this! Rafa had lost the opening set 6-1 but would have given anything to stay out on the court to fight back.

While missing out on fighting for the BNP Paribas trophy – eventually won by Tsonga against Nalbandian in the final – there were bigger concerns for Nadal as his involvement in several other competitions was now in jeopardy. Much to his disgust, his body was in no condition to return to the court any time soon. After being checked over by his medical team, Rafa's worst fears were confirmed as the tendinitis injury was serious enough that he was forced to pull out of the Masters Cup in Shanghai. It was dubbed as the year-end tournament that pitted the top eight players in the world against each other – yet the world number one would not be there. It was a huge blow for both Rafa and the tournament organisers. To make matters worse, the media were quick to point out that this was the first time that a number one seed had not played in the Masters Cup. The Spaniard was devastated to be letting people down but there was nothing he could do about the injury. Due to his brilliant form, he had played a mammoth 93 singles matches so far in 2008 and the toil had finally caught up with him.

A gloomy Nadal told the media: 'This is one of the most difficult decisions in my career due to the importance of the event and, above all, my will to be with the fans in China and the tournament organisers who always treated me in such a special way.' He also sent a message out to his supporters, explaining the tricky time he was having. He said: 'I am deeply saddened and disappointed for my fans around the world that expected to see me fighting in every match.'

Without the Spaniard, the Masters Cup did not have the same glamorous appeal but the show did indeed go on. Federer lost his first match against Simon while Murray made a good start with victory over Roddick. In the end, though, the Swiss and the Scot both bowed out before the final, in which Djokovic outgunned Davydenko to scoop the trophy. While keeping an eye on events in China, Rafa was also nervously looking at the upcoming Davis Cup final. Would he recover in time? It was no exaggeration to say that the hopes of a nation were resting on his shoulders. If he failed in his race against time to be fit, the consequences could be dire. Inevitably, there was plenty of pressure on him to be ready to represent his country.

Argentina would be Spain's opponents in the final, boasting talented duo Nalbandian and Juan Martin Del Potro in their squad. Losing Nadal to injury would present the Spanish selectors with a major selection headache. How could they possibly find a suitable replacement for the world number one? Ferrer, Feliciano Lopez and Fernando Verdasco – the other key men for Spain – were all talented players but none of them had the wow factor or aura that Rafa brought onto the court. It promised to be a nervous wait for all Spanish tennis fans as the Mallorcan did his best to overcome the tendinitis problem.

Despite his best efforts to recover in time, Nadal had to throw in the towel as the injury refused to heal sufficiently. Ever since his earliest Davis Cup appearances, Rafa had been in love with the tournament and the atmosphere created by representing his country. It was clear that this injury was a major concern as the Spaniard would not have ruled himself out if there was even the slightest chance he could battle through a few sets. 'After a long and very positive season, it pains me to miss Shanghai and the Davis Cup final,' he told the media. 'It's a difficult time, I did everything to try and make this final.'

It was a tough patch for him as he tried to get used to a spell without tennis. It allowed him to relax more than he could usually but this was little consolation to him. On his website, Rafa added: 'I am used to playing with pain but this was a new and different pain I cannot control.' The tendinitis problem was clearly a short-term problem for the Spaniard but people soon began to wonder whether there were long-term implications too. Could this be a career threatening injury? The Spanish Davis Cup team doctor Angel Ruiz-Cotorro suggested that such concerns were unnecessary but that three to six weeks of rest were imperative.

Unfortunately, rest and Rafa rarely go hand in hand and it was a big ask for his coaching team to wrap him up in cotton wool for so long. The positive side to the injury was that it had come at the end of the season and would at least allow Nadal to begin 2009 in top condition. However, the worry was that his style of play was starting to deal out serious punishment to his body. He was still a young man yet the wear and tear of each year on the tour was overwhelming, especially 2008. Some pundits felt the Spaniard might need to rethink the intensity of his training and his all-action playing style: but such an idea was unlikely to appeal to Nadal.

It was disappointing for Rafa to see his performances tail off again in the latter part of the year but it had been a stunning season. He was world number one. He had always publicly played down his desire to move above Federer in the rankings but he was thrilled to have made the step up. Now, more than ever, he had a target on his back. In the past, he had simply been the man to beat on clay. But his success at Wimbledon and then the Olympics in Beijing meant he was the all-round top dog. And his fellow big guns would be eager to respond.

There were plenty of players to watch out for as Nadal began to think about the next season. Obviously, Federer would be back hungrier than ever and desperate to take back top spot. Djokovic had continued his improvement and always posed a threat. And Murray had thrown his name into the hat too with a brilliant final few months of the season. Then of course there were the likes of Simon and Tsonga who were eager to make a big impression and break into the elite group at the top of the game.

Nadal knew he would have to be at his best again if he wanted to hold onto his place at the top of the tree.

CHAPTER 7

THE WIZARD OF OZ
AND INJURY HELL

Without doubt, 2009 promised to be another landmark year for Nadal. Though bettering the previous season was bordering on impossible, the Spaniard had high expectations for the months ahead. As had been the case for the past few years, the Australian Open and the US Open were high on the hit list for Rafa as he was still to triumph there but all the Grand Slams obviously carried great significance.

The year did not begin as Nadal would have liked. The early season tournaments are momentum builders and he had benefited in the past from some solid runs at such events; but it was all about Murray as 2009 kicked off. The Scot was the form player and he proved it by claiming two early titles, piling the pressure on Rafa, Federer and the rest of the field. The ominous signs were there in early January when Murray beat Nadal in an exhibition event in Abu Dhabi. While the Scot saw the 6-4, 5-7, 6-3 victory as a clear indication that he could beat the Spaniard in a close match, Rafa was more concerned with gaining match practice following his knee injury. After the defeat, Nadal told the media: 'I made some mistakes today but I think that's to be expected after two months out. I think I'm playing well, I did a lot of running and I feel great. Today was a very good test for the knee. It was two hours 45 minutes of high quality [tennis] and I'm feeling very well.'

This was the key. He wanted to be ready for the Australian Open in order to give himself the best possible chance of reaching the final for the first time. Losing out to Tsonga in 2008 had been a big blow and he knew he was capable of bettering that effort. But Murray kept raising the bar. He claimed the first ATP tour event of 2009 in Doha at the ExxonMobil Open as he continued to stake his claim to be considered an elite player. Rafa had some bright moments early in the tournament but fell in straight sets to Monfils in the quarter-finals. He had to watch as the Scot continued to look the form man.

Nadal did not have to wait long to make amends, though, as he and Marc Lopez contested the doubles final the following day. They had entered as a wildcard pairing but they shrugged off the challenge of highly-rated duo Daniel Nestor and Nenad Zimonjic to clinch the title 4-6, 6-4, 10-8. After a slow start, Rafa had come through with some inspired winners and it was always enjoyable to take the chance to participate in the doubles. Both players received trophies and Lopez even joined Nadal in biting the prize to celebrate! Rafa told the press: 'It was disappointing to lose in the singles yesterday so I feel a bit better having won the doubles.'

There were few real concerns in the Nadal camp, despite

Murray looking in devastating form. The biggest stages tended to bring out the best in the Spaniard – this was the best way to look at the situation. The draw for the Australian Open meant that Rafa and Murray were again mentioned in the same breath. The world number one and the tour's in-form player were in the same half of the draw and were on a collision course for a semi-final showdown.

Nadal put all the hype to one side and concentrated on his own preparation. This tournament was sure to test the strength of his grip on the number one spot. Having become the first left-hander since John McEnroe to finish a year atop the rankings, the Spaniard was eager to keep his rivals at bay.

His first round opponent in Melbourne was Belgian Christophe Rochus and Nadal immediately took the chance to send out a message. Yes, he had been injured. Yes, Murray was in fine form. But Rafa was the number one and someone would have to play out of their skin to take that away from him. Nadal, wearing a new look kit with a short-sleeved top rather than a vest, despatched Rochus in three effortless sets of serene tennis. He had been reluctant to change to the new outfit during the latter part of 2008 and risk jinxing his strong run but it appeared to be bringing him good luck in 2009. He produced ten aces and 37 winners in a 77-minute cameo. He smashed the Belgian off the court in the first set, sealing it 6-0. His serving reached 198 kilometres an hour as he bagged the next two sets for a 6-0, 6-2, 6-2 victory.

It was a timely reminder of the Spaniard's brutal power. Nadal remained focused despite the dominant display, admitting that his concentration would need to stay at peak levels if he wanted to enjoy a long run in the tournament. But he was moving well on the hard court, which he admitted was similar to the surface in Beijing when he bagged the gold. Rafa then wasted little time in sweeping into the third round with a comprehensive win over unseeded Croatian Roko Karanusic. His tally of aces and winners were not as impressive as against Rochus but a 6-2, 6-3, 6-2 victory was a formality nonetheless. Nadal was looking closer to his formidable best. Meanwhile, Murray was matching him stroke for stroke with two easy wins of his own.

The Spaniard, blogging for *TimesOnline* during the tournament, wrote: 'Today I played my second round match and I am again having those good sensations I have been also having during practice. I feel I am playing well and with confidence so great.'

His blog for *The Times*, which he has produced at several Grand Slams, also offers fans to post their own messages for the Spaniard and send questions to the world number one. In fact, the sincerity of the blog has drawn praise from numerous quarters, emphasising how the public appreciate Nadal giving up the time to address his supporters. And this is something that he clearly takes very seriously. On his website www.rafaelnadal.com, he has a separate blog which he updates as he travels the world.

A third round clash with German Tommy Haas appeared to be a more challenging prospect but Nadal was an overwhelming favourite. Federer looked in serene form as he dumped Safin out with ease and the chasing pack were reminding Rafa that he could take nothing for granted. They were all after his number one ranking.

Nadal again delivered a performance worthy of a top seed.

Despite going 2-0 down in the first set – and losing his serve for the first time in the tournament in the process – the Spaniard regrouped and powered his way back into the contest. He won six of the next eight games, including four in a row, to snatch the first set. Haas' success had been short lived and there was little he could do to counter Nadal's 53 winners. Once the Spaniard had shaken off the slow start, his hitting was as accurate as ever on the way to registering just eight unforced errors. The 6-4, 6-2, 6-2 victory sent Rafa through to the last 16 in style and there he would face Chilean Gonzalez, who had ended Nadal's Australian Open hopes back in 2007.

And Gonzalez fell in similar fashion to Haas. Rafa, who received a boost prior to the match when Murray crashed out to Verdasco, was ruthless as he continued his exceptional form. Any question marks that may have existed regarding the Spaniard's fitness or form were quickly being blown away. He took the opening set 6-3 then ripped into Gonzalez's serve with great success to move two sets ahead. The Chilean was gutsier in the third set but nothing was going to stop Nadal on current form and he wrapped up a routine 6-3, 6-2, 6-4 win.

The Spaniard's rhythm was improving and there were some anxious faces amongst the rest of the locker room. Nadal just focused on preparing himself for Simon, his quarter-final opponent, admitting that he needed to crank up his serve for the latter stages of the tournament. Losing out to Simon in Madrid in October 2008 had hurt and Rafa vowed not to make the same mistakes again.

In fact, Nadal was a little off the pace against Simon. He

was desperate to step up his game but he appeared to be trying slightly too hard. Nonetheless, Rafa outmuscled the Frenchman in a solid first set, taking it 6-2. But he struggled thereafter and had to rely on his ever-dogged defence to withstand his opponent's fightback. The doubts over Nadal's title credentials resurfaced as he looked rusty in the second and third sets. But like a true champion, he soldiered on and hit his way through the difficult patch. His sheer grit and never-say-die attitude helped him bag the second set 7-5 and he repeated the trick in the third, clinching an off-colour 6-2, 7-5, 7-5 victory.

The key point was that Rafa was into the last four – however, he was alarmed by some of his shortcomings. 'I don't know how I won, really', he told the press. 'Today was tough because I couldn't play exactly my rhythm. Gilles is very good player, much improved in last few months, and it's a bit difficult to play in conditions like this – the ball is faster and it is very hot.'

It was reassuring for the Spaniard that he could still scrap his way through though when his shots were not hitting the mark. Compatriot Verdasco now stood between Nadal and a first ever Australian Open final. He had come into the year determined to make his mark in Melbourne and New York and he remained on course to do so. Verdasco, though, was in sublime form and had enjoyed a fine run so far in the tournament. What followed between the compatriots was an epic that would live long in the memory. Nadal, of course, had not dropped a set yet at the 2009 Australian Open but that record quickly changed as his opponent took the opener.

The match began in cagey fashion and, with both players

wasting chances to break, the first set stayed with serve and headed into a tie-break. Even the breaker was a tight affair but at 5-4 Verdasco received a fortunate net cord and capitalised on this to claim the first set. Nadal took a little time to recover from the setback but peppered his opponent's serve in game eight of the second set, only for Verdasco to play brilliantly on several massive points. Two games later, however, Rafa finally cashed in. Having already missed out on four break points in the set, Nadal unleashed a brilliant forehand to earn a fifth and then saw Verdasco fire long. The world number one was level.

Rafa had the momentum and Verdasco fans were fearing the worst when Nadal broke early in the third set with more ferocious forehands. But his opponent managed to hang on in the contest, breaking back immediately. The pair exchanged breaks again and, much to Rafa's disappointment after some bright moments, the set headed into another tie-break. This time, Nadal was not caught napping. It was Verdasco who stuttered, firing a string of unforced errors that pushed Rafa within sight of claiming the third set. The world number one dished out a stinging forehand and then clinched the breaker 7-2 with an ace. But Nadal was having to pull out all the stops. Federer had seen off Roddick in the other semi-final and fans were already discussing the prospect of another classic Federer–Nadal final.

Verdasco had other ideas. Despite needing treatment for a calf injury, he refused to let Rafa cruise into the semi-finals. The serving had been below-par in the previous set but the fourth set was a major improvement as neither player managed a break point. Nadal had promising moments but could not put a string of winners together. Rafa was outgunned 7-1 in the breaker as Verdasco stunned fans all over the world by ensuring this marathon match would go the distance. Time after time Nadal saw his compatriot smash winners past him. Now it was anyone's match. It was effectively a one-set shootout and Rafa upped his aggression as he chased an early break. Federer was gaining plenty of rest while his potential opponents sweated it out on court. Nadal just could not find a way to kill off Verdasco's charge and the longer the match went on, the more hope Verdasco clung onto.

Eventually, Nadal's class and unquenchable desire told. He moved 5-4 up with more thumping groundstrokes and Verdasco, who mustered an incredible 95 winners, faltered at the last. Rafa was on hand to profit as his opponent double-faulted to give the world number one three match points. Verdasco kept at it but another double-fault handed victory to Nadal, which as Rafa admitted in his autobiography, was just as well given that he was breaking down from the sheer emotional exhaustion of the moment. After a gruelling five hours and 14 minutes, Rafa could celebrate a 6-7, 6-4, 7-6, 6-7, 6-4 win. Nadal somehow found the energy to savour the moment but his mind was already racing ahead to the final – his first at the Australian Open. He told the media: 'It was very tough to play aggressive against a player like Fernando. He played unbelievable. Only when you're playing very well can you have these wins.

'Roger has a bit of an advantage over me. He's resting right now. But I want to try my best. It's very important for me to be in this final. Whatever happens on Sunday, I've started the season my best ever.'

Verdasco admitted that it would take time for the wounds of this defeat to heal. He explained to reporters: 'Both of us played unbelievable. I will have this match in my mind for the rest of my life. It is a pity for Rafa that he had to play such a long match ahead of the final when Roger only played three sets. I want him to be 100% to play in the final. I lost but he is a big friend and I hope he wins on Sunday. I wish him all the best.'

And so, Nadal rumbled on towards his date with destiny. He had steadily improved since his first appearance in Melbourne and had bettered last year's semi-final exit. But there was a problem. His body was a wreck and he feared even his team's healing hands might not be able to repair the damage in time. Fortunately, he was surrounded by knowledgeable, trusted experts, including good friend and physio Titin, physical trainer Joan Forcades and doctor Angel Ruiz Cotorro. Together, they had always come through for Rafa.

Ice treatment and massage slowly had an impact but Nadal admits in his autobiography that he went to sleep the night before the final unsure of how he could possibly compete in the final. He felt no better in his training session a few hours before the final. But, after some stirring words from Toni, coupled with all the work that his team had put in since the semi-final, he found a way to compete. Federer was gunning for a 14th Grand Slam title and the chance to equal Pete Sampras' haul but Rafa had a target of his own – winning his third different Slam. Everyone remembered the pair's stunning show at Wimbledon the previous year and so the expectations were high. However, both made nervy starts, dropping serve and making uncharacteristic errors. Federer recovered quickest to break Nadal in the sixth game of the first set and move 4-2 up. Would Rafa's marathon match against Verdasco be the decisive factor here? How much did he have left in the tank? Federer was hitting the ball nicely but Nadal bounced back instantly with a couple of unbelievable points that turned the set on its head. The Spaniard's speed allowed him to reach almost-certain winners from the Swiss and the world number two served up a double-fault as Rafa broke back, then levelled at 4-4.

The contest was not yet at the mesmeric standard of some of their previous clashes but the pair remained inseparable. Federer's first serve percentage was letting him down, though, and ultimately this would cost him in the opener. Nadal was able to dictate the rallies with more success and, after holding to 30 for 5-5, he profited from a string of Federer errors before bagging the break with a forehand pass. Despite his desperate state a day earlier, the Spaniard was not looking like a man struggling to shake off the effects of playing a five-set match two days previously. But Federer was certainly giving him a helping hand and this trend continued as Nadal served for the first set. The Swiss made three unforced errors and Rafa clinched it with another breathtaking shot from a seemingly impossible position. Yet again he was displaying his incredible knack of turning defence into attack in the blink of an eye. He would be at full stretch on the backhand before charging across and nailing a forehand winner. Federer had held a 4-2 lead but, in taking five of the next six games, Rafa was on top and Toni, to whom his nephew often glanced after big shots, appeared delighted.

Did Federer still have the belief that he could beat Nadal? After all, the Spaniard had snatched away his grass court superiority. The Swiss almost wobbled badly in the first game of the second set as Rafa continued to return every shot with interest. Nadal got his reward in game five as Federer found no answer to his breathtaking shot-making. Three glorious winners earned the world number one a break. As the pressure mounted, though, Federer pulled himself back into the match. Like the true champion that he is, the Swiss kept pressing and Nadal threw away his hard work in the previous game as Federer made it 3-3. And the Swiss was not finished. He held serve and broke Rafa again as his forehand began to show signs of hitting top form. Federer calmly held again and suddenly it was one set all. Nadal had lost four straight games and, with it, the momentum. He appeared tired and it was a worrying sign for his supporters that he had struggled towards the end of the set. He had simply been smothered by the efficiency of Federer's hitting. So, what next? The answer was more back and forth scrapping. The set stayed with serve but both players engineered glimmers of hope early on. Nadal then went close to a break in the fifth game but Federer managed to escape. And after, it was the Swiss' turn to make inroads, earning three break points but falling victim to Rafa's ferocious defence. After a gentle start, this set had turned into an epic with both players having to pull out all the stops to stay in it.

At 4-3 up, Nadal called for the trainer and the crowd collectively held its breath. He received a quick massage to address pain in his thigh but was not moving comfortably as he headed back onto the court. Federer instantly levelled at

4-4, heaping more pressure onto a weary Rafa. The desperation of the scrambling defence and the blistering speed of the attack showed that they had lost none of that Wimbledon magic. They just did not seem to have boring matches. But would the Spaniard's body hold up? Retiring was never going to be an option for Nadal, though, however bad the thigh became. He gritted his teeth and continued to do what he does best – play every point with incredible intensity, as if it is his last. He got to 5-4 up, received more treatment and prepared himself for more superhuman effort.

Federer was in a groove and his serve was beginning to hit the spot. It made life even tougher for Nadal. The Swiss levelled again and then played some brilliant points in Rafa's next service game. Federer earned three break points but the Spaniard would not quit; he would not throw in the towel. He defied his fatigue and, despite looking exhausted, found the strength to stave off Federer's charge. Nadal saved all three break points and clinched the game with an emphatic forehand. Federer responded by narrowly denying Rafa a stunning set-winning break and it moved into a tie-break. Breakers had hurt Nadal against the Swiss at Wimbledon and the decider definitely appeared to favour Federer's pinpoint serve. But this time Rafa refused to budge. At the changeover it was 3-3 but the Spaniard then took the tie-break by the scruff of the neck. He was everywhere and Federer was clearly under pressure to find the perfect shot to secure a winner. Nadal won three quick points, including a fine forehand and an exceptional backhand volley, before Federer surrendered the breaker with a double fault – almost unheard of from the Swiss. Nadal had looked down and out but his sheer determination had helped him overcome the thigh problem and fight back.

Everyone knew, though, that this was far from over and Federer began the fourth set on a mission. He held to love and followed that with a break set up by a flowing forehand down the line. The Swiss looked a relieved man, having already squandered 13 of his 18 break points. His joy did not last long, however. Nadal is never quiet for long and he was back to his relentless best as he took the next two games to level things up. Rafa then missed several great opportunities in game five as Federer became rattled. The Swiss was supposed to be the fresher man but he was finding it impossible to grind Nadal down. However, Federer's resilience got him out of jail as he survived five break points and seven deuces to move 3-2 up. It was as if a switch had been flicked, because the Swiss suddenly looked invincible again. He showed how much this final meant to him as he celebrated breaking Nadal in the next game with some monster forehands. Federer then held serve and, although Rafa pegged him back to 5-3, the former number one would serve for the set. Hawk-Eye gave the Swiss a 30-15 lead and he motored on to square things up again. These two would go to five sets again on the big stage.

Some pundits wondered whether Nadal's fatigue would haunt him in this deciding set but he appeared as fresh as ever, bouncing over to the back of the court ready for one last push. It was the first time the Australian Open final had gone to five sets in 21 years. Nadal made a bold start, holding serve and getting to 30 on Federer's serve before the Swiss held on. Rafa sensed he had the upper hand, with his opponent looking nervy, and a love service game showed that the Spaniard was on top. The belief was visibly seeping from Federer and his serve deserted him at the worst possible moment. He gave Nadal a glimmer of a chance and the Spaniard snatched it ruthlessly, forcing the Swiss to net a backhand on break point.

Rafa's serve, in contrast, was functioning brilliantly and he consolidated the break for a 4-1 lead. Federer looked a beaten man – was there any way back for the Swiss? Previously, Nadal had been the King of Clay and Federer was head and shoulders above the rest on every other surface. Now, Rafa had triumphed at Wimbledon and was on the brink of a hard court Slam. Fans began to sense that they were witnessing the start of the Spaniard's total domination.

Cheered on by supporters who did not want this classic to end, Federer held to love but breaking Nadal was beyond him as the Spaniard moved to within a game of the title with a love service game of his own. Rafa could have simply relied on his next service game to clinch the prize but he went after Federer's serve instead. At 40-15 up, he was within touching distance, only to blow it as the Swiss fought back to deuce. But a belting backhand winner gave Nadal another chance before Federer fired long to hand Rafa the title. The Spaniard fell to the floor in now familiar fashion. He had bagged three of the last four Slams and had added success at a hard court Slam to his career highlights. Nadal and Federer shook hands at the net, with the Swiss absolutely devastated. It had been another epic contest but, in four hours and 23 minutes, Rafa had come up trumps again.

And Nadal was his typical charming self when he collected the trophy, saying: 'Roger, I know exactly how you feel. Just remember you're a great champion and you're one of the best in history and for sure you're going to match Sampras. To receive this trophy from Rod Laver is a dream for me.' Before Rafa's speech, Federer had collected his runner-up silverware and had spoken tearfully of his disappointment. He said: 'I've felt better. Maybe I'll try later. God, it's killing me.' In yet another sign of the friendship and respect that exists between the pair, Nadal was there to comfort Federer with a hug. After all the blood, sweat and tears of this final, they were able to stand side by side and be friends. But where did the Swiss go from here? Nadal had looked a goner in the third set as he struggled with injury yet he had pegged Federer back. Psychologically, this defeat seemed as painful and significant as the loss at Wimbledon and it would take a long time for Federer, still regarded by many as the greatest player ever, to get over this huge setback.

For Nadal, it was the perfect way to kick off a year that he hoped would bring him plenty more thrilling moments. But the heroic victory in Australia proved to be a false dawn as the remainder of 2009 brought more frustration than glory. Injury problems were nothing new for Rafa by this stage and he was no stranger to the notion that his playing style ate away at his body. Nonetheless, even Nadal could not have envisioned the woes that lay ahead.

His knees just refused to continue enduring the frantic impact of high level tennis and, much as he attempted to fight his way through the pain, the ever-improving competition on the tour made it impossible to be 50% fit and grind out a victory. Federer, Djokovic and Murray presented obvious challenges but beyond them a chasing pack was emerging too, led by Argentine Del Potro and a revitalised Roddick. Put simply, it was not a time to be struggling for fitness.

Having blasted his way through opponents for the majority of the 2008 season, Nadal had rightly taken his place at the top of the tree. But a fall was always a possibility given the staggering number of hours on court the Spaniard had logged over the past 12 months.

Initially, the severity of the niggling knee problems was not entirely apparent. In Rotterdam in February, Nadal willed his way to the final – toppling the likes of Tsonga and Monfils en route – only to lose to Murray in the final. The Scot played well for his 6-3, 4-6, 6-0 win but Rafa was visibly hampered by pain in his knee. Shaking his head throughout and unable to serve at full power, only Nadal's relentless drive forced the contest into a third set but he had nothing left as Murray upped the ante. Despite the constant treatment – prior to the match and during it – the Spaniard's mobility was lacking. In truth, the discomfort reached a level where most players would have simply retired but, though he considered that option, Nadal refused to surrender the final under such circumstances.

And so it began. Losing to Murray was nothing to be ashamed of but his fitness was a big worry. Just weeks after arguably the most courageous victory of his career, Nadal was facing more time on the treatment table and, as Murray admitted, nobody wanted to see that. The Scot, who counts himself among Rafa's fans and has spoken about the enjoyment he gets from watching the Spaniard, told the media: 'I don't want to see him get hurt and make his knee worse. I was thinking to myself, "He should stop the match, it's better for him and his knee."'

Though Nadal has rarely admitted as much, his reluctance to admit defeat when carrying injuries has exacerbated his problems at times. Admittedly, he would reasonably argue that he would not have an Australian Open title in his trophy cabinet were it not for his never-say-die approach – but his successes have come at a heavy price. This final in Rotterdam was the latest example of the Spaniard's heart ruling his head.

As February dragged on, Nadal found himself on the mend and capable of taking his place at Indian Wells for the Masters event in mid March. In fact, despite his setbacks, Rafa was still many experts' pick to win the tournament – after all, Federer had not played an event since the Australian Open and Nadal could not face the Swiss or Murray until the final.

The Spaniard began with a bye and then headed onto what was deemed to be a tricky path. But after trouncing German Michael Berrer and ambling past Dmitry Tursunov, Nadal was into his stride. He might have been short of full fitness yet he never stopped fighting. Against Nalbandian, Rafa survived five match points to beat the Argentine for the first time. He then conquered Del Potro, crushing the youngster 6-2, 6-4 in a gentle reminder that the Argentine had work to do before he could be mentioned in the same breath as Nadal and Federer.

The victory over Del Potro booked Rafa's place in the semi-finals, where he took on home favourite Roddick. Buoyed by home support, the American gave Nadal one of his toughest outings thus far with his unstoppable serve and a shrewder range of groundstrokes. But the Spaniard remained rock solid, winning the first set 6-4 and moving ahead in the second before careless lapses helped Roddick recover and force a tie-break. Nadal would kick himself later for throwing away the ascendancy but he managed to control his emotions on the court and grab the tie-break 7-4.

Another final against Murray awaited Rafa, who was eager to put the disappointment in Rotterdam behind him. He was the number one seed and knew that he needed to do everything possible to keep that ranking. What followed was a brutal and mature performance that cut the Scot to shreds. It was no secret that Nadal was focusing a lot of his efforts on improving his hard court game – an approach that had been fruitful at the Australian Open – and, watching him demolish Murray, it was difficult to believe he was ever considered a one-trick pony. Clay still felt like home but his all-round game had come on leaps and bounds since lifting the trophy for the first time at Roland Garros in 2005.

The wind in California made life tough for both players yet only Nadal mastered the conditions, adapting to the elements and dictating the rallies. He had played in enough big games by now to know how to handle gusty winds and, most pleasingly, his knees did not appear to be hindering him. Murray, who had outlasted Federer in the semi-finals, had no answer. Rafa raced into a first set lead, building a platform for a 6-1, 6-2 victory and earning yet another trophy. He told reporters: 'Conditions today were really difficult but I have a good strategy and I played a really good match with those conditions.'

It was an important psychological victory too after Murray's wins at the US Open and in Rotterdam. Though none of the top seeds would admit it, it was always an advantage to have had the upper hand in the most recent contest and

Nadal had thumped the Scot here, capturing his 13th Masters Series title.

Rafa was less successful at the Miami Masters later in the month, though, as Del Potro dumped him out in the quarter-finals. He offered up no excuses in the post-match interviews but question marks remained over his fitness as the clay court season approached. With the energy-sapping nature of clay court tennis, this portion of the year would provide the most accurate indication of just how near to 100% Nadal was.

The results boded well as Rafa added gloss to his clay court record. In Monte Carlo, he waltzed his way through to the final without losing a set, making short work of some talented opponents. Ljubicic and Murray both suffered at the Spaniard's hands before Djokovic at least took a set from him before Nadal wrapped up a 6-3, 2-6, 6-1 victory.

It was a momentous fifth straight Monte Carlo title for Rafa, who became the first man to achieve this feat. The atmosphere and glamour of the city has made it Nadal's favourite Masters Series event and, as a result, he raises his game another notch when it rolls around on the schedule. It was the perfect way to kick-start the clay court season but, ever the perfectionist, he found areas to fine tune ahead of Roland Garros. Rafa told the media: 'In this tournament I didn't serve very well. Especially my second serve, sometimes it was 120 kph, so that's a disaster.' While this was true, it had hardly mattered.

The next week, he strolled to a fifth straight Barcelona Open triumph. It was almost taken for granted by now that Nadal would win these tournaments and it was important for him to stay focused despite the ease with which he was picking off the other contenders. His dominance since winning the French Open in 2005 demonstrated the consistency with which he was playing and he was hitting the ball as cleanly as ever. Rafa cruised past Davydenko and Ferrer to lift the trophy.

And it was the same story in Rome at the end of April. Nadal had lost the final to Djokovic the previous year but he made no mistake this time. It might have been a different year with new threats but Nadal just seemed to own this part of the season. After a little stutter against Seppi in the second round, the Spaniard knocked off Soderling, Verdasco and Gonzalez to reach the final, where he handled everything Djokovic could muster and won 7-6, 6-2. This result and Rafa's performances in Monte Carlo and Barcelona pointed emphatically towards a sixth French Open success at the end of May. Even a loss to Federer in the final in Madrid – Nadal's first loss to the Swiss since 2007 – felt like a blip at the time, even if he did not look his usual self for reasons that would later become apparent.

For years now, there had been no debate over who was the favourite for Roland Garros. Nadal had earned that lofty status with his flawless French Open record and an easy win over Marcos Daniel in the first round did little to change the general consensus. But what was unknown at this stage was the status of Rafa's knees. Coming into the Slam on the back of a string of tournaments had done wonders for his form – but what had they done for his health? Though he remained upbeat in front of the cameras, he was pushing his knees to the limit and needed extensive treatment just to make it onto the court.

With his knees still troubling him, it would be critical for

Nadal to keep each round to just three sets and he did just that in eliminating Teimuraz Gabashvili and Hewitt to reach the fourth round. Hewitt, in particular, took a pounding as he won a measly five games across the three sets and was powerless to stop the Spaniard picking up a 31st straight win at Roland Garros.

Speaking to the press, Hewitt admitted: 'You have to start well as he is such a great player when he's in front. He goes for his shots and dictates all the time so it gets harder and harder. He's hitting the ball extremely clean and he has that heavy spin. He makes you rush, he hits passing shots on the run and makes you try harder.'

Then the impossible happened. Nadal headed into his fourth round clash with Soderling in good form but never found the level of play that had left Hewitt helpless. Rafa had famously rowed with Soderling at Wimbledon in 2007 during a five-set marathon that the Spaniard edged. This time, the Swede was out for revenge.

The ominous signs were there from the start for Nadal. The Spaniard, sporting a pink top for the tournament, dropped the first set 6-2 as Soderling unveiled an aggressive, in-your-face approach that immediately bore fruit. He took chances with ambitious strokes and was rewarded with winners, he served solidly and he displayed few nerves considering this was his first appearance in the fourth round of any Grand Slam.

Nadal returned to his chair, pondered a disastrous opening set and plotted a comeback. But Soderling had clearly decided today was the day for an upset of epic proportions and there was no drop off in his attacking tactics. Rafa, though, improved, settling his serve and dictating a greater percentage of the points. The second set headed into a tie-break and the Spaniard kept his head to level the contest.

The expectation now was that Soderling would quietly fade over the next two sets – after all, he had taken a set off Nadal and could be pleased with that alone. It is quite possible that nobody outside the Swede and his coaching team believed that a shock was still on the cards as the players returned to the court for the third set and history suggested that Rafa would go on to clinch victory number 32.

As expected, the rest of the match was one-way traffic, only it was Soderling, not Nadal, in the driving seat. Sensing the Spaniard was having an off day, Soderling continued to attack and force errors. He got his nose in front, never stopped believing and took the third set 6-4. As tennis fans all over the world pinched themselves, the Swede was one set away from arguably the biggest shock in Grand Slam history.

Nadal had hammered Soderling 6-1, 6-0 in Rome just weeks earlier but was struggling to come close to that level of play and the errors crept in as he lost his composure. Soderling refused to back down and, having forced a fourth set tie break, he dominated it from start to finish, collapsing on the clay as he sealed a simply stunning victory. Rafa was disconsolate at surrendering the French Open title but he had been wildly out of sorts on the day and Soderling had cashed in.

While numerous questions focused on Nadal's fitness after the match, it would have been a discredit to Soderling had Rafa sought out excuses. Typically gracious, the Spaniard heaped praise on his opponent but his pained expressions throughout hinted that his mobility was restricted. Without a doubt, he had arrived in Paris in worse shape physically than in 2007 or 2008 and this time he had come up against a man who produced the best performance of his career.

Federer would go on to finally win the French Open, beating Soderling in the final, and Rafa could only watch it all unfold. With Wimbledon the next thing on everyone's minds, Nadal sought to shake off his disappointment and prepare for the grass court season. Instead, his knee problems came back to haunt him.

The Spaniard has been very open about his concerns over the number of tournaments crammed into the tennis calendar, even claiming that his injury problems could be attributed to the hectic schedule. And as the season entered June, Nadal's successes on clay seemed to have left him in serious pain. He pulled out of the AEGON Championships to rest the injury but travelled to England in a desperate bid to test his knees and make a final decision about his participation at Wimbledon.

Such was his determination to defend his title that he arranged exhibition games against Hewitt and Wawrinka to gauge his progress. Facing Hewitt at the Hurlingham Club, Nadal looked rusty. It was his first match since the French Open and it showed. The Australian prevailed 6-4, 6-3 and capitalised on the sluggish nature of Rafa's performance. Things were little better against Wawrinka, leaving the Spaniard with a tricky, emotional decision to make.

After updates and meetings with his coaching team and the doctors, and with the All England Club holding its breath, Nadal gave his verdict. He would not be part of Wimbledon 2009. For the first time since Goran Ivanisevic in 2001, the Wimbledon champion would not defend his title. And in making the decision public, Rafa came clean about the state of his knees and the on-going struggles he had bravely put to one side. He told the press: 'Not to play at Wimbledon is one of the toughest decisions in my career. No one is more disappointed than me and the Wimbledon crowd must understand I tried my best.

'I've played with some problems in my knees for a few months but I always felt I'd try and try. You don't know what your limit is, but I have now reached the limit. I'm going to try very hard to come back and when I come back I'm going to come back with 100% mentality because when I play now, I was thinking more about the knee.'

His comments shed a little more light on his struggles against Soderling at the French Open, but most of all, they sparked concerns over his future in tennis. While all reports suggested that it was not a chronic problem, it would require rest and careful treatment. He had little choice but to listen to his body and spend more time on the sidelines. Federer and a number of others revealed their disappointment that Nadal would not be among the contenders for Wimbledon, strengthening the sense that the Spaniard was a popular figure on the tour. The event had suddenly lost some of its appeal.

And things got no better for Nadal as news of his parents' separation hit the headlines. It was an off-court issue that had weighed on Rafa's mind during a number of tournaments and he had first heard the beginnings of the situation after the Australian Open. While he was programmed to continue fighting on the court, the joy just was not there. The Spaniard had always treasured family life and it was taking time to adjust to the news. It was as though Rafa was carrying a burden on his shoulders in each match and, as he himself admitted, he was not mentally prepared to beat the world's best. As Rafa explained in his autobiography, "My parents were the pillar of my life and that pillar had crumbled.

Speaking later in the year, when he had had more time to take in his parents' split, Nadal told the *Guardian*: 'I am OK now but you need time to accept. And it's more difficult to accept when you are outside home and don't know what's happening. At least the injury gave me time to be with my friends and family.'

But there were knock on effects as he tried to cope. In the same interview, he added: 'I played with less calm. One of the reasons was the pain in the knees. And I was down because of the divorce. I wasn't ready, mentally or physically, this year.' The whole experience left Rafa drained and emotional and, combined with the injury problems, it was the toughest patch of his career on the tour.

Meanwhile, in London, Federer went on to clinch his sixth title at SW19, beating Roddick in a gripping five-set final, breaking Borg's record of five Wimbledon triumphs and reclaiming the number one seeding from Rafa. Just 12 months ago, Nadal was lifting the trophy in the midst of his golden summer and there was understandable sadness for the Spaniard as he saw others profit in his absence. With his knees requiring a lengthy break from tennis, Nadal made the tough call to pull out of Davis Cup duty for Spain too.

It was now unclear as to when Rafa might return to action and whether he would ever return to the kind of form that saw him light up 2008. The trouble was that there was no easy solution. Nadal had honed his tactics and style of play over years of practice and was not about to make huge adjustments.

His speed, resilience and power were big strengths and he needed to be mobile around the back of the court. His serve, though solid, was not going to win him enough points on its own in the manner that Roddick or Ivo Karlovic often cruised through service games.

Having set the US Open as a target, Nadal first rested then worked round the clock to prepare for the Grand Slam. A triumph at Flushing Meadows had thus far eluded him and it was no secret that this provided major motivation. Despite some suggesting he forego tournaments until the US Open, Rafa returned to action at the Montreal Masters as the defending champion and number two seed, having been surpassed by Federer. A second-round victory over Ferrer proved to be the highlight before a 7-6, 6-1 loss to Del Potro.

Though he remained positive about the condition of his knees, Nadal was non-committal about whether he would be at full fitness for the US Open. Nonetheless, it felt good to be back on the court. He told reporters: 'After two months out of competition it's tough to play at that level – I needed to concentrate more than usual. I have to be happy with the tournament. Del Potro is playing very well and I was at the same level as him in the first set.' But the fact that the Spaniard was simply relieved to have matched a rival for one of the two sets was a telling sign as to his current expectations.

A quick turnaround did not prevent Nadal from playing in the Cincinnati Masters, where he improved on his efforts in Montreal. He reached the semi-finals but lost out to Djokovic. The writing was on the wall after the Spaniard dropped the first set 6-1 and he continued to look a step slow in the rallies.

The countdown to the US Open was almost over and his chances of making the final looked mighty slim.

Nadal entered the US Open in the unfamiliar position of third seed, meaning a tougher draw and the prospect of a quarter-final against Tsonga and a semi-final with Murray. He knew he was going to need to summon every ounce of fighting spirit to go deep into the tournament but gritty tennis helped the Spaniard conquer Gasquet, Kiefer and Almagro and set up a fourth round clash with Monfils.

Yet he never had the look of the 2008 Nadal. He was not brushing opponents aside and could not sustain his dominance for long stretches as he had before. The scurrying defence and mind-boggling winners were still features of his play but everything seemed to be coming at a price.

Against Monfils, Rafa had to dig deep once more. After dropping the first set tie-break, things could easily have slipped away from the Spaniard. Still regaining confidence in his body and seeking to rediscover a rhythm, Nadal found himself in a tough spot and, to make matters worse, he was also carrying an abdominal injury form the third round that was preventing him from being in peak condition. But he leaned on his steely resolve to escape. He was more aggressive on Monfils' serve and suddenly the breaks came in floods, pushing the Spaniard to an impressive 6-7, 6-3, 6-1, 6-3 victory.

But the action did not end there as a spectator broke past security and raced up to Nadal's chair to kiss him. All in all, it had been a strange day and, considering his questionable fitness, Rafa was just happy to get through it and set up a quarter-final against Gonzalez. Nadal told the media: 'I'm very happy now after the last two matches I played. I had a few problems in those but now I'm in the quarter-finals for the third time in my career here.'

And not even the court intruder could dampen the Spaniard's spirits after the win. 'For me it wasn't a problem. The guy was really nice, he was a great fan, he said I love you,' Nadal said.

Gonzalez posed a major threat for Rafa, who knew his body might not hold up in a five-set marathon. The key would be to limit the match to three sets – and he managed to do just that. The Chilean had toppled Tsonga in the fourth round but Nadal was a tougher nut to crack. With the rain pouring down in New York, the match began on Thursday but spilled over until the Saturday. The first two sets were tight and both headed for tie-breaks as neither player kept control for long enough to make their mark. And it was the Spaniard who held his nerve to take both breakers. Trailing by two sets to none, Gonzalez fell apart and Rafa completed a 7-6, 7-6, 6-0 victory.

Nadal was doing a good job of hiding his injuries but an in-form Del Potro was waiting in the last four. Rafa admitted that he had profited from the rain delay for once, taking the chance to rest his body and return fresher to finish off Gonzalez. The Spaniard told reporters: 'It was important to have one day off to get better for today. I played well, that's very important as well.'

In truth, it was a slight surprise for Nadal that he had made it to the last four of a Grand Slam, given his injury hell since winning in Australia in January. He vowed to fight on but there was little left in the tank. Del Potro, meanwhile, was a man on a mission, arriving in peak condition and brimming with confidence. He simply overpowered Rafa from the get go, crunching winners and appearing considerably fresher. Nadal's serve was shaky, largely owing to the strained abdominal muscle, and he made few inroads during the Argentine's service games.

There was no stopping Del Potro as he raced to an emphatic 6-2, 6-2, 6-2 victory. It was a humbling loss for Nadal but he accepted it graciously and acknowledged the fact that his weary knees and injured abdomen had made a victory almost impossible. As he willingly admitted himself, he was not mentally or physically ready to win a Grand Slam and, instead of displaying his usual calmness, he was edgy and agitated when the going got tough.

The Spaniard explained to the media: 'It was a little bit unlucky [this] year for me. I started the year playing really well but that's sport. I had a problem with the right abdominal and it was difficult for me to serve.' There were simply too many obstacles for him to overcome.

There were just a few commitments left for Nadal in 2009. In Beijing in early October, the Spaniard reached the last four once again but was outclassed by Croat Marin Cilic – and his misery was deepened by Madrid's failure to land the 2016 Olympics. On his website, Nadal wrote: 'Spain, keep your head up high, we were very close. We made it to the final round and now we have to stay close to each other and support the organizers of our campaign more than ever.

'We knew there could only be one winner at the end and unfortunately it wasn't us. Nevertheless, the key is to keep on fighting. I know next time we will win because we deserve it.

Madrid deserves it and as it has always been the case, I will be there to help as much as I possibly can for whatever you need.'

Then, back in China for the Shanghai Masters event a week later, Rafa lost to Davydenko in the final. And in November, Nadal lost to Djokovic in the Paris Masters semi-finals as the Serb continued to chase the Spaniard in the rankings. Titles were eluding Rafa and his frustration was mounting.

The season-ending World Tour Finals in London brought more heartache for Nadal. Drawn in what appeared the easier of the two groups, he lost all three games and headed home as Davydenko went on to lift the trophy. The Spaniard knew he was letting himself down with recent performances but he was still trying to adjust after his injury problems and understood that he would only feel fully comfortable again in the New Year.

Switching his attention to Davis Cup action was the perfect remedy and Nadal played his part as Spain beat the Czech Republic in the final, enjoying the chance to be part of a team after spending so much of the year fighting solo. It allowed Rafa to end a physically and emotionally challenging year on a positive note but, having not won an ATP title since May on the clay in Rome, he certainly had questions to answer.

However, he was determined to enjoy the moment with his team-mates. He told reporters: 'You have to be sure to enjoy these moments when they happen because you don't know when the next victory will come. To finish the second half of the season with this ending is very important and nice, especially after all of the problems I had over those two months.'

The beginning of the 2010 season provided plenty

of motivation for Nadal, with the likes of Djokovic, Murray and Del Potro closing in with every passing week. He put together a good run in Qatar to reach the final but, after winning the first set 6-0, he threw away the ascendancy and lost to Davydenko.

The Australian Open had been a happy hunting ground for Nadal in 2009 but, as he returned to defend that Slam, it was again apparent as to how things had changed in the past year. Rafa was still considered a contender but he was playing catch up to compete with the rest of the field after his injury problems. He now appeared to be close to full fitness but the Spaniard would have to pull out all the stops to outlast Federer, Murray and company.

The hard surface was bound to take its toll on Nadal's knees, if any lingering pain remained, but the defending champion made a bold start, securing straight-sets wins over home favourite Peter Luczak and Slovakian Lukas Lacko. With his surge gathering pace, Rafa accounted for Philipp Kohlschreiber in four sets and, though he dropped the third set 6-2, there were flashes of the 2008 genius, including one sumptuous whipped forehand winner from a seemingly impossible angle. It had been a scrap but the Spaniard had survived.

Now Karlovic stood between Nadal and a spot in the last eight. When Rafa and his team discussed the match, handling Karlovic's dangerous serve was the main talking point and the Spaniard had clearly found some answers because he weathered the Croat's serving barrage. Apart from some stutters in the second set, Nadal remained in control, picked up the breaks he needed and earned a 6-4, 4-6, 6-4, 6-4 victory. So far, so good on the injury front. Nadal gained a lot of confidence from progressing to the quarter-finals to face Murray – but he told reporters he would be on a plane home if he got his game plan wrong.

The showdown with Murray was a mouth-watering prospect and tennis fans worldwide crossed their fingers that it would be an epic contest. Unfortunately, they were to be disappointed. The pair had fought out some enthralling matches in the past and the Scot had certainly closed the gap on Nadal. Well beaten by the Spaniard at Wimbledon in 2008, Murray had developed his game impressively since then.

While Nadal had often said that Murray's future was bright, the Scot was yet to win a Grand Slam. This was bound to be playing on his mind and the Spaniard hoped to capitalise. But much had changed over the past 18 months and Murray was entering the match in good form and looking fresh, as he showed in the first set. Though Rafa defended with typical resilience, he was broken twice as the Scot took the first set 6-3.

The second set saw flashes of the Nadal of 2008. He took control of the rallies and left Murray flailing with a string of punishing forehands. Having secured the break for a 4-2 lead, the Spaniard seemed on course to level the match but then things took a turn for the worse. Murray broke back immediately to crush Rafa's revival and he then forced a tie-break, which he dominated and won comfortably. From a strong position, Nadal now found himself two sets down.

And, as the crowd were about to find out, he had bigger concerns than just losing the quarter-final. Competing with an on-song Murray was proving a tough task and, sadly, the Spaniard's knees could not take the strain. Early in the third set, trailing 1-0, Rafa called for the trainer as he winced in pain and, two games later, he made the sensible decision to retire. It was the first time he had ever retired from a Grand Slam match. He desperately wanted to make it into the last four but he was at last learning to listen to his body.

As Murray celebrated a 6-3, 7-6, 3-0 victory, yet more questions were heading Nadal's way regarding his knees. It had now reached the point where fingernails were bitten every time the former number one stretched for a ball or charged to the net. He told the press: 'It was a similar thing that I had last year. It was impossible to win the match.'

Murray took no pleasure in Rafa's downfall, telling reporters: 'I've known Rafa since I was 13 or 14 and he is someone I always looked up to when I came up through the juniors. I am a bit gutted for him.' The hope was that Nadal's decision was more precautionary than anything else.

And the medical assessments brought mixed news. Doctors believed that the injury was a tear to the back of his right knee but, on the positive side, it was not deemed to be related to Rafa's tendinitis woes. The outcome? More time on the treatment table – four weeks to be precise, made up of a fortnight of rest followed by two weeks of rehab work. Nadal downplayed the injury but the medical opinion suggested he would not be back on the tour until the Indian Wells Masters in the middle of March.

Losing out to Murray dealt further blows with regard to the world rankings as Djokovic moved into second place and the Scot climbed to third. From being the undisputed number one in late 2008, Nadal had slumped to fourth spot – his lowest seeding since May 2005. The Spaniard was visibly becoming more and more frustrated with his constant injury problems but, nonetheless, he told the press: 'It is not important for me the ranking issue and losing a few spots, that's normal when you are not able to compete.'

While his fall in the rankings was hardly a disaster, it illustrated the extent of the disappointments in 2009. And on top of that, he was back into the agonising routine of resting and staying off his feet as much as possible. This was not how it was supposed to be.

CHAPTER 8

COMPLETING THE CAREER GRAND SLAM

As concerns grew over Nadal's long-term future, the Spaniard simply blocked out the doubters. A full month without competition was a bitter pill to swallow, but he committed himself to following the rest-and-rehabilitation instructions.

Back in action at Indian Wells at the BNP Paribas Open, where he was the defending champion, Nadal progressed to the semi-finals as he felt his way back into rallies and tested out his knee. The disappointment of an eventual loss to Ivan Ljubicic was cancelled out by winning the doubles title with Marc Lopez. 'For me it's a pleasure to play with Marc,' Nadal explained. 'He's a very close friend of mine, and we do really well. After losing important singles, the victory in doubles makes me happy.'

Making his return during the clay court season – his favourite part of the year – was looking like a shrewd move.

He was a semi-finalist at the Sony Ericsson Open before beginning a fine winning streak that ensured he arrived at the 2010 French Open on top form. He saw off compatriot Verdasco in Monte Carlo, out-hit Ferrer in Rome and defeated Federer in Madrid. This meant he had grabbed all three Masters crowns on clay – the first time a player had achieved the feat – and it helped him climb back to No. 2 in the seedings.

'Winning here at home is a dream,' the Spaniard said after the win in Madrid (a record 18th Masters 1000 title for Nadal). 'Never in my wildest dreams did I imagine I would win all three of these big events.'

Returning to Roland Garros, Nadal was full of confidence, as you would expect from a four-time champion. Of course, all the warm-up victories would count for little if he blew the chance to recapture the French Open title – but he was arriving in the right frame of mind and in good health, unlike the previous year.

Nadal began in ruthless fashion, crushing teenage wildcard entrant Gianni Mina 6-2, 6-2, 6-2 in the opening round. Argentine Horacio Zeballos fared little better, being swept away 6-2, 6-2, 6-3 in round two. At this early stage, it seemed doubtful that Nadal would lose a set, never mind a match.

While Murray and Djokovic faced some early scares, Rafa booked his place in the fourth round by outlasting Hewitt 6-3, 6-4, 6-3. It was his biggest test thus far but the Spaniard just had too much power for the Australian, who had become a familiar foe at Roland Garros. Hewitt drew criticism and attention for swearing at various points in the match but never threatened to take Nadal the distance.

The French Open schedule was calling for night matches in challenging conditions, and Nadal admitted that he was rushing to complete his win over Hewitt to reach the more welcoming confines of the locker room. 'I saw the clouds gathering,' he said. 'I kept looking at the sky because I really wanted to wrap up the match. I did not want to continue playing this match [on Sunday].'

Thomaz Bellucci offered some resistance in the fourth round, but it was another three-set win for Nadal – 6-2, 7-5, 6-4. Rafa felt comfortable with his knee – or at least able to manage any pain – and, without too many scares, he was now two matches from the final.

The 2010 French Open quarter-finals completely flipped the script, shocking those who had thought a Nadal–Federer final was a near certainty. Both Federer and Djokovic crashed out, at the hands of Soderling and Jurgen Melzer respectively, as the door opened wide for Rafa to power through and assert his authority.

Nadal found himself in a major battle of his own, however, as fellow Spaniard Nicolas Almagro threatened to pull off another upset. The first two sets went to tie-breaks but, on each occasion, Rafa raised his game and executed better on the key points. After clinching the second tie-break 7-3, Nadal finally dented some of Almagro's resolve and powered to a 6-4 scoreline to seal the victory. Given the surprises elsewhere in the draw, he was delighted to have overcome the obstacles and booked his spot in the last four. The fact that his opponent would be Melzer, the No. 22 seed, rather than Djokovic was an obvious advantage – and a rematch against Soderling, who had eliminated Rafa dramatically in 2009, loomed large for the final.

Melzer was no match for Nadal, as many had anticipated. Pre-match, Rafa had reasoned that, 'if he's in the semi-finals, it is because he's the best of his draw' – but there was a clear gulf between the two players. The first two sets were heavily one-sided as Rafa wasted little time in making his mark. It would have been easy to start thinking about the final – and, perhaps he did, because the third set went to a tie-break as Melzer finally showed why he had made it this far at Roland Garros. Again, though, Nadal proved to be too strong in a tie-break situation and was soon able to celebrate a 6-2, 6-3, 7-6 win and yet another French Open final.

With arms raised, complete with green-and-white sweat-bands, the Spaniard soaked in the applause. He also knew that a victory in the final would see him leapfrog Federer and reclaim the No. 1 ranking.

The Nadal–Soderling showdown was probably not the dream final for French Open organisers but it certainly had its subplots. Rafa's quest to avenge the previous year's shock loss gave the match more intrigue, as did some of the mild verbal sparring from then. Nadal sought to play down any issues between the pair, explaining: 'I think he was very shy in the beginning. But he has improved his personality over the past year. I think he says "hello" more often now.'

Still, there was a definite sense that there could be more hostility than in any Nadal–Federer final. If Rafa needed any additional motivation (and he rarely does), he had the frustration and pain of the 2009 defeat to draw upon. The French Open was supposed to be his tournament and Soderling had prevented him from getting a fifth straight title.

Nadal made the Swede pay in the 2010 final, laying the

ghosts of 2009 to rest with some sublime tennis. From the very start, Soderling struggled to survive in long, punishing rallies, succumbing to the temptation to go for winners, which invariably led to errors. Rafa took the first set 6-4 in professional fashion, then let loose in a one-sided second set that the Spaniard clinched 6-2. With his body and mind clearly in peak condition, Nadal wrapped up a straight sets victory and savoured this memorable moment. He was the five-time French Open champion.

'I lost last year because I was not well prepared, and I had very low morale last year, as well. But this time, I'm back,' he announced triumphantly. Not only was he back, he would also soon officially be the world No. 1 again too.

Given the fears about the extent of his knee injury and whether the tennis world would ever see a fully fit Nadal again, the Spaniard had bounced back remarkably in the space of a few months. The disappointment Down Under was forgotten, replaced by pride in Paris.

Nadal's proven prowess across all surfaces meant that there could be no let-down with the grass court season ahead and a chance to send a reminder of his ability to go toe-to-toe with any opponent at Wimbledon. Injury had cruelly prevented Rafa from appearing at SW19 in 2009, despite desperate efforts to recover in time, and he once again found himself eager to make up for missed opportunities. He was in his prime and every tournament, especially the Slams, represented a chance to add to his trophy haul.

After wrapping up the French Open celebrations, a quick grass court tune-up at Queen's was the first port of call for Nadal. Finding his feet was a little trickier than he might have imagined (his last meaningful grass court match was at Wimbledon two years earlier) and, after registering a couple of victories, he fell to compatriot Feliciano Lopez in the quarter-finals. The loss provided a few extra days of rest and a chance to prepare his body for the tests to come.

As the opening round of Wimbledon began, Nadal savoured the special feeling of being back at the All England Club. Federer was still the favourite for any grass court event but Rafa had proven in 2008 that the gap between the two was extremely small.

However, the early rounds provided a timely reminder that he could not afford to let his level of play drop. After a straightforward three-set win over Japan's Kei Nishikori, Rafa was given a wake-up call in round two against Robin Haase, who took the Spaniard to five sets in an enthralling David vs. Goliath clash. While Rafa cantered through the fourth and fifth sets, he kicked himself for falling behind and requiring the rearguard action. Haase had exposed some encouraging signs for the rest of the pack, particularly in a dominant 6-3 third set. Nadal preferred to praise the Dutchman's performance rather than admit to any complacency on his part.

If the second round brought a scare, the third round brought injury concerns and controversy. Nadal squared off against Philipp Petzschner, the No. 33 seed from Germany who had survived two five-set matches to set up the biggest test of his career. Petzschner again showed his appetite for marathon matches, bouncing back from losing the first set by capturing the next two. Again, Rafa was forced to go the distance – and again he found some quality tennis to get back on track. Defying knee and elbow injuries that required treatment, he took charge of the match and secured a 6-4, 4-6, 6-7, 6-2, 6-3 win.

Nadal played down the injury concerns but did concede that his knees were still not 100 per cent following the enforced absence earlier in the year. Petzschner was unimpressed with the injury timeouts that Rafa called for, even raising the possibility that it was purely a tactic.

The other big storyline was the official warning that the Spaniard received after the umpire felt that he was receiving coaching from Toni during the match. Rafa was dismayed by the decision. 'I told the umpire we're going to talk to the supervisor later, and I will,' Nadal fumed. 'Toni wasn't giving me any tips, only supporting me. When he gave me the warning, Toni was saying "positive".'

Ultimately, the incident led to a £2,000 fine but Nadal quickly switched his focus to his fourth round clash with Paul-Henri Mathieu, who had beaten Youzhny, the No. 13 seed, in round two. Eager to end the run of five-set matches that were sapping his energy levels, Rafa made short work of the Frenchman, winning in straight sets 6-4, 6-2, 6-2. Having reaped the benefits of a day off and a chance for more treatment on his knees, he looked fresher and more focused.

A quarter-final against Soderling awaited, with a new chapter to be written in this new rivalry. Nadal had monitored the Swede's progress and admitted that he would need some luck to counter Soderling's serve and groundstrokes. The early signs were not good as Rafa was totally outplayed in the opening set, coming dangerously close to losing it 6-0. But he rebounded impressively to capture the second set and, as his resolve grew, Soderling's forehand fell apart. The third set tie-break proved to be the decisive moment – and, once Nadal clinched it, Soderling offered little resistance in the fourth set.

Nadal might not have resembled the man who outgunned Federer in the classic final two years earlier, but his chances of a second Wimbledon crown were boosted by the Swiss player's surprise quarter-final exit at the hands of Berdych. Only a semi-final against Murray stood between Rafa and another SW19 final.

Rafa is hardly the type to enjoy the task of defeating a home favourite, but he was ready for the challenge and the unusual scenario of a stadium largely cheering against him. He knew that bringing an aggressive game plan and serving well would be critical. His comeback from injury in Australia had been a spectacular success thus far but, to beat Murray, Nadal would need to conjure up a performance worthy of a No. 1 seed. Both players began boldly and it quickly became clear that capitalising on half chances would be the difference. Murray had a glimmer of an opening on Nadal's serve in the eighth game but could not cash in; presented with a similar chance in the ninth game, Rafa was ruthless. A slick forehand winner brought up break point and an error from the Scot sealed his fate. Nadal held serve to clinch the first set.

Murray quickly revived the home crowd with some fine hitting in the second set, but he just could not get the break on Nadal's serve. Rafa consistently found himself on the back foot, defending desperately to emerge from several deuces on his own service. Whenever he needed a big serve or an impossible winner, the Spaniard found a way to make it happen. When he thwarted Murray's relentless attack to force a second set tie-break, there was a sense that he had soaked up the Scot's best tennis and was ready to counter.

The tie-break was as tight as the match had been thus far but Nadal continued to demonstrate why he was the world No. 1, pulling himself out of some major holes. He fell behind 2-0, quickly recovered to 2-2, then shrugged off a double fault at 5-5 with a calm volley. A stroke of luck with a net cord put Rafa within striking distance and he clinched the second set with an angled forehand.

As hope drained from the home crowd, Nadal recovered from a sloppy service game to start the third set, hauling himself back to 4-4. From there, it was all Rafa, thumping forehands into both corners and leaving Murray no choice but to launch desperate attempts at winners. He finished off a gritty, professional victory to clinch another Wimbledon final appearance.

'It was a very, very good match for me,' Nadal told *BBC Sport*. 'To beat Andy you have to play your best tennis, it's always a big challenge and it was an amazing victory for me against one of the toughest opponents in the world.'

The wait for another British Wimbledon champion would go on, but Nadal had his sights on Berdych, who had beaten Djokovic in three sets in the other semi-final.

When Nadal was forced to walk away from the Australian Open in January, the possibility of two Grand Slam final appearances was a distant dream. It was unclear if he would ever return to an elite level. Now, he was the heavy favourite to add the Wimbledon title to his French Open success.

The experience gained in his previous Wimbledon final appearances gave Nadal a big advantage against Berdych, who had enjoyed a fairy-tale run but had poured a lot of energy into his victories over Federer and Djokovic. As expected, it was Rafa who settled quickest. With the Czech No. 12 seed looking understandably nervous on such a big stage, and a disruptive wind blowing across Centre Court, Nadal took control of the rallies. With the score at 3-3 after the first six games, Rafa sensed his opportunity and blew Berdych off the court, winning the next three games to seal the first set.

The conditions caused errors from both players in the second set but, when the crucial moments arrived, Nadal was able to bail himself out of danger or make the all-important extra shot. He pounced in the 11th game as Berdych faltered, making two costly forehand errors to gift Rafa the break. Moments later, the Spaniard had a two-set lead.

He was riding such a wave of momentum that it would have taken an other-worldly effort for the Czech to deny him. The third set followed a similar pattern, with Berdych playing well but failing to find an opening. Nadal again waited patiently for his opportunity, then, with the set moving towards a tie-break, he unleashed a string of brutal forehands to move to the brink of his second Wimbledon title.

Berdych had no response as Nadal wrapped up the 6-3, 7-5, 6-4 victory. Rafa had not ever truly hit top gear but that mattered little as he pumped his fists and took in the ovation on Centre Court. 'It's more than a dream for me,' Nadal said. 'After a difficult year for me, missing the tournament last year, this year I came back and to have this trophy in my hands is more than a dream.' He also applauded the Wimbledon crowd for their respect during his semi-final when he was facing the home favourite, Murray.

After all the doubts earlier in the year, the topic of conversation was altogether different now, with speculation over just how many Grand Slams Nadal could win over the course of his career. This was number eight and he was still only 24 years of age.

The unrelenting ATP tour moved swiftly on to the hard court season, forcing Nadal and his team to limit the Wimbledon celebrations. The Spaniard played both singles and doubles at the Rogers Cup, falling to Murray in the semi-finals of the singles and crashing out in the opening round of the doubles despite joining forces (surprisingly) with Djokovic. His bid for a title in Cincinnati also fell short with a loss to Marcos Baghdatis. Still, Rafa had some useful hard court match practice under his belt without overexerting himself and would continue to ride the adrenaline wave that had carried him through the French Open and Wimbledon.

After his recent Grand Slam heroics, Nadal was the favourite to add the US Open to his 2010 haul. But, of course, the usual suspects were all snapping at his heels. Rafa had never won three Grand Slams in the same year and, more significantly, the US Open was the one Grand Slam that had thus far eluded his grasp. In seven appearances, he had reached two semi-finals but had been beaten on both occasions. Completing his set of Grand Slams would put him in exclusive company, alongside the likes of Federer, Agassi, Rod Laver and Roy Emerson. By achieving this, he would secure a prominent place in the history books and an enduring legacy.

His journey at Flushing Meadows began against Teymuraz Gabashvili, who quickly stretched Nadal with his solid serving.

Rafa had to survive two tie-breaks to secure a 7-6, 7-6, 6-3 victory and it took him until the seventh game of the third set to finally break Gabashvili's serve. The Spaniard's own serve held up well against the No. 93 seed and he clung to that major positive from the first round. He and his team had focused on slightly reworking his serve ahead of the tournament and he hoped it would be a key ingredient along the road to a first title in New York. 'My serve worked well and hopefully I can continue like this', he said. 'It's not my best shot but I always try hard to keep improving. I know if I want to have chances to win here, this year or any year, I need to serve really well and that's one thing I am focusing on.'

Nadal made quicker work of Denis Istomin in round two, despite a tense second set tie-break in which he trailed 5-1 before rallying, and then built momentum with a comprehensive third round win over Gilles Simon. His serve continued to be the main talking point. 'A few days ago I started to feel very well with my serve and the first two matches I have not lost my serve, which is very good for the confidence', he explained.

Rafa ran into a familiar foe in Feliciano Lopez in round four, brushing aside his fellow Spaniard for another straight sets win. While the No. 1 ranking had put a target on Nadal's back, he was handling the pressure with ease, following the same rituals that had been part of his preparation since his early years. In an ominous warning to his rivals, the Spaniard made it clear that he had not hit top gear yet. 'To get this far two things have to be working really well: the concentration and the serve', Nadal said. 'I am playing well but I am not at my highest level yet.'

With the quarter-finals looming large, Nadal's pursuit of the career Grand Slam was the prominent storyline. It was still hard to believe that there was so much concern over his future in the sport just six months earlier. Another all-Spanish affair awaited Rafa, with Verdasco up next after outlasting Ferrer in a marathon fourth round match. All the signs looked good, given Nadal's 10-0 record against Verdasco and the sublime form he had shown in the past two rounds.

And this match followed a familiar pattern. Though Rafa struggled early on and lost his serve for the first time in the tournament, he recovered impressively to clinch the first set 7-5. From there, it was all Nadal as he took control of the rallies and motored to a comfortable three-set victory. He was one step away from the final – but was determined not to let the opportunity slip away. 'It's a very, very nice feeling to be in the semi-finals for the third time in a row in one of the most important tournaments in the world – for me probably the most important right now,' he admitted.

While Federer and Djokovic did battle in the other semi-final, Nadal's route to a first US Open final proved to be far more straightforward. The No. 12 seed Youzhny stood in his way but it quickly became apparent that he could not hurt Nadal. The 6-2 opening set established the tone and Rafa's complete performance offered the Russian no reason for optimism. With Youzhny trapped on the back foot, Nadal punished him time and time again, defeating him mentally as much as physically. The match lasted little more than two hours, buying Rafa valuable time ahead of his date with destiny. Djokovic emerged from a titanic five-setter with Federer, denying fans a mouth-watering Nadal–Federer bout but setting up a potential epic nonetheless.

'Now I am going to play for the first final in the biggest centre court in the world,' Nadal reflected after the semi-final win. 'I have tried for a lot of years.'

The history books awaited Nadal. A victory at Flushing Meadows would make him the seventh man ever to complete the set of Grand Slams and the first player since 1969 to capture the French Open, Wimbledon and the US Open in the same year. All eyes would be on Nadal as he attempted to take the next step in his incredible season. He could take comfort from his record thus far at the 2010 US Open: he had not lost a set and had dropped serve only twice.

Djokovic's rise had been somewhat under the radar given the excellence of Nadal and Federer. The Serb had all the tools to challenge for the No. 1 seed but had struggled to put all the pieces together consistently. That was beginning to change – and his semi-final victory over Federer proved that he had the belief and temperament to beat the best. The Serb had won his past three matches against Nadal, all on hard courts.

A nagging rain delay added to the tension in New York, with both players admitting their frustration. In truth, Rafa was not surprised. He understood that any tournament where there was no option of closing the roof carried a risk of extra time sitting in the locker room waiting for the weather to improve.

Though a first US Open final brought some nerves, Nadal had mastered the art of bottling up any fears pre-match and preventing them from impacting his play. He flew out of the blocks against Djokovic, breaking the Serb's serve in the first game and settling into a punishing rhythm with his groundstrokes.

Though Djokovic steadied himself and broke back in the fourth game, Rafa always seemed on top in the opening set. He thundered shots from the back of the court, chased down balls that looked like certain winners and built such frustration for Djokovic that the Serb smashed his racquet on the court after Nadal's second break of the set.

Rafa clinched the opening set 6-4 but knew this was not going to be a procession like rounds three and four of the tournament. Djokovic was too good not to hit back aggressively – and the Serb did just that in the second set as his confidence grew. The No. 3 seed grabbed the upper hand early on with a 3-1 lead as Nadal's serve faltered for the first time at the tournament.

But the Spaniard continued to dig deep, relying on those childhood teachings of fighting for every point. He snatched back the break and levelled at 4-4 to temporarily stifle the Djokovic comeback. Then came the rain. If anything, it may have come at a good time for the Serb, given Rafa's momentum, but neither player welcomed the delay. The players headed to the locker room for close to two hours.

After a quick warm-up, the final was back underway. But it was Djokovic who rediscovered his rhythm quickest, holding serve for a 6-5 lead and then earning the set-clinching break. The Serb's defence along the baseline was rivalling Rafa's – and the match looked destined to go late into the New York night.

Djokovic was moving more freely as the third set began, showing no signs of the five-set war with Federer just days earlier. Nadal, by contrast, was clinging on. He held serve at 1-1 but knew he needed to find another gear to withstand the Serb's onslaught.

And the Spaniard did just that – not with any match-altering tactics but with extra grit and grind. He extended the rallies, forced Djokovic to make extra shots and gradually manoeuvred the Serb into errors. Nadal seized the advantage with a break in game three and that would prove to be the difference as his serve withstood the pressure, including a nervy tenth game in which Djokovic reached 30-30. The Nadal camp were on their feet, the crowd was alive – and Rafa was one set away from history.

Nadal continued to be the aggressor in the fourth set, sensing that this was the moment to strike. He did not want the danger of a winner-takes-all fifth set. Again it was the third game where Rafa made his breakthrough. He had taken just 4 of 22 break points up to then, but grabbed a fifth one as the Serb fired long. Just to prove that he was in the driving seat, he held to love for a 3-1 lead.

That simple service game seemed to drain Djokovic, wiping out the last grains of hope. Or maybe it was just Rafa jumping on every chance to hammer winners. The Serb found himself in a 0-40 hole and surrendered his serve for the second straight time. To his credit, Djokovic bounced back and threatened a break of his own but there was no denying Nadal now. He could almost taste the career Grand Slam but he refused to let the moment affect his play.

He was forced to wait a little longer after Djokovic finally got another game on the scoreboard but, presented with the chance to serve for his first US Open title, Nadal would not be denied, even after Djokovic crept back to 30-30. A fortunate net cord brought up match point and then a Djokovic error clinched Nadal's place in history. He fell to his knees in ecstatic celebration even as the scale of his accomplishment began to sink in. Not so long ago, he was deemed a clay court specialist, now he had completed his set of Grand Slams – at just 24 years of age. Given the level of competition and the injury concerns, the achievement was all the more remarkable.

Just as the Nadal–Federer rivalry is built on healthy respect, the post-match actions and speeches reflected how highly Rafa and Djokovic thought of each other. 'I'd like to congratulate Rafa and his team for an amazing tournament,' the Serb said. 'Right now he's the best player in the world and he absolutely deserves this title, well done again.'

'This is more than I ever dreamed – it is unbelievable to have this US Open trophy,' Nadal beamed. 'I played my best match in the US Open at the most important moment, so I am very, very happy for that, for sure. To win in here I think is the more difficult tournament for me to play, more difficult conditions to adapt, to adjust my game on this court, for the balls, for the court, for everything.'

Of course, this victory also revived the 'greatest ever' conversation. While Rafa preferred to sidestep such topics, his case had certainly gathered momentum over the past few months. And there was likely to be much more to come.

While there were still a number of tournaments ahead in 2010, Nadal had thrown everything into his Grand Slam run. A let-down over the final few months of the season was to be expected, but it never really materialised. Somehow, Rafa found the energy to continue his relentless playing style, winning in Japan and reaching the final at the ATP World Tour Finals in London, where he lost to Federer.

As the dust settled on 2010, Nadal could look back on one

of the most memorable, gutsy years of his career – a year that had begun with injury disappointment in Australia but ended with three Grand Slams to his name. He was in high spirits as he headed off for a deserved break with family and friends.

CHAPTER 9

THREE'S A CROWD

Nadal understandably entered the New Year full of confidence after an unforgettable 2010 season. The question now was whether he would have the good health and motivation to continue to conquer the tennis world. Age was gradually catching up with Federer, though the Swiss player remained a serious threat, but Djokovic had shown signs the previous year that he was ready to challenge the Nadal–Federer supremacy. With Murray also eager to win his first Grand Slam, the men's game had never had such a talented quartet of challengers.

But Rafa was in no mood to give an inch to the rest of the pack. He began 2011 by beating Federer to clinch glory in Abu Dhabi, then added the doubles title in Doha. As the Australian Open approached, Nadal was well aware of what victory would mean: he would be the reigning champion for all four Grand Slams. He was entering the tournament as the No. 1 seed and the favourite to lift the trophy for a second time.

The early rounds presented little to unsettle Rafa unduly. He swept past Marcos Daniel in round one, taking a 6-0, 5-0 lead before the Brazilian was forced to retire from the match, then breezing past Ryan Sweeting in a 6-2, 6-1, 6-1 win. He had barely broken sweat in either contest.

Australian Bernard Tomic, spurred on by home support, fared rather better but was still unable to take a set from the world No. 1 as Rafa wrapped up a 6-2, 7-5, 6-3 win. After charming the Australian crowd by predicting that Tomic had a promising future in the game, Nadal turned his attention to his own game and the endless quest for improvement and perfection. 'I have to play a little better if I want to go to the quarter-finals, because I expect a tough match with Cilic,' he said. 'I need to play closer to the lines. I'm playing too straight, in my opinion.'

He need not have worried. Nadal thumped Cilic 6-2, 6-4, 6-3 in round four and it was hard to imagine many gentler starts for the Spaniard at a Grand Slam. But then the injury jinx struck, frustrating Rafa at the Australian Open yet again. In fairness, compatriot Ferrer put together a fine performance to eliminate Nadal in straight sets but Rafa was limited by a hamstring injury – suffered early in the match – that prevented him from playing with his usual mobility and aggression. His body language confirmed that this had been a painful, emotional loss.

'I don't have to tell you what I felt on the court, but it is obvious I did not feel at my best,' he explained after the game. 'I had a problem with the match at the very beginning, and after that, the match was almost over.' Ferrer acknowledged that his victory felt hollower given that Rafa was dealing with an injury.

The quest to hold all four Grand Slams was over. Nadal had lost at a Grand Slam tournament for the first time since the Australian Open a year earlier. That made it back-to-back years that injury had derailed Rafa in the quarter-finals of the event. The good news was that the hamstring injury would probably be a quick fix rather than the type of lengthy layoff that a recurrence of his knee injuries might have caused.

There was some consolation in early February as Nadal was named Laureus Sportsman of the Year in recognition of his stunning performances in 2010. Being selected ahead of the leading stars of other sports, many of which Rafa followed closely, was a big honour and a timely reminder of his standing within the sports world.

Nadal was soon back on the court, this time representing Spain in the first round of the 2011 Davis Cup against Belgium. He clinched victories in both his matches as the Spanish team earned a comprehensive win. It was important for Rafa to get more playing time under his belt ahead of the clay court season and he responded to that challenge by reaching the finals of the BNP Paribas Open and the Sony Ericsson Open. On both occasions, he lost to Djokovic, the Australian Open champion who had begun 2011 in blistering form, but Rafa was finding his rhythm again.

As the clay court season kicked off, the talk was no longer focused solely on Nadal vs. Federer. Djokovic's emergence could not be ignored and he looked the biggest threat to Rafa's No. 1 ranking and his strong grasp on the French Open crown.

For now, though, Rafa was still the undisputed King of Clay and he wasted no time in making his presence felt. A dominant effort in Monte Carlo saw Nadal crowned champion once again, losing just one set along the way. This triumph stretched his record to seven straight titles there – and set a record for consecutive titles at an ATP event. He then added his sixth Barcelona Open title, beating Ferrer in the final.

But his budding rivalry with Djokovic added extra layers as the two men squared off in back-to-back finals in Madrid and Rome, with the Serb winning both matches. With Roland Garros just around the corner, Nadal had shown a few possible chinks in his armour, while Djokovic had proved that he was a serious challenger for the French Open. The Serb had beaten Nadal in their last four matches, seemingly finding the recipe to neutralise Rafa's relentless style. An unbeaten run of 39 matches put Djokovic on the cusp of history.

'I am not disappointed with my performance, my level', Nadal explained in Rome. 'He is doing amazing things. He is very tough mentally and physically, every week. He played very well but this week was very positive for me. I finished better than I started, which is not what happened in Madrid.'

It was another reminder of how quickly things can change in tennis – and in the sports world as a whole. Nadal's hat-trick of Grand Slams in 2010 had elevated him above the pack, yet just months later Djokovic was the unstoppable force captivating the fans.

While Rafa was generous with his praise for Djokovic, the level of competition drove him to a new level as he prepared for the French Open. The journey towards a sixth title at Roland Garros began against American John Isner, who stretched Nadal further than anyone anticipated. After Rafa grabbed the first set 6-4, it looked like one-way traffic ahead but Isner's serve kept him in contention in the second and third sets, forcing back-to-back tie-breaks. The American took control of both and powered into a shock lead. Nadal would need to go the distance to turn the match around. To his credit, he quickly righted the ship and battled through to a 6-4, 6-7, 6-7, 6-2, 6-4 victory – but Rafa had shown vulnerability and the rest of the draw took encouragement from Isner's strong play. Worse still, Nadal had spent four hours on the court and, given that his knees were always a concern, this was less than ideal.

The upside, as Isner pointed out, was that Nadal had played some sublime back-to-the-wall tennis. 'What it came down to is the way he played in the fourth and fifth sets,' the American said. 'I haven't seen tennis like that ever. That's why he's No. 1 in the world and one of the greatest players ever.'

Brought to life by that early scare, Rafa marched into the quarter-finals without dropping another set. Compatriot Pablo Andújar fought hard in round two, even forcing a third set tie-break, but Nadal's third round opponent Antonio Veic was swept off the court in a 6-1, 6-3, 6-0 defeat. But there were still question marks over the Spaniard's status as tournament favourite – his serve had looked shaky at times and he had only provided glimpses of his typical clay court form.

But he was alive and kicking in his bid to equal Borg's record of six French Open crowns. Despite the frustrating mistakes, Nadal remained confident that the pieces would fall into place by the time the biggest challenges came his way in the latter rounds. He shrugged off Ljubicic in straight sets to reach the last eight, limiting his time on court and allowing more time for rest and treatment.

The quarter-finals brought Nadal face-to-face with his old nemesis Soderling in a repeat of the tournament's 2010 final. The Swede was still the one loss on Rafa's Roland Garros record and the world No. 1 seemed to feed off those memories as he put together his best performance thus far. He looked fresher and more focused, making a mockery of his comments days earlier that he was not playing well enough to lift the trophy.

It took until the third set for Soderling to truly test Rafa, who took the first set 6-4, then dismantled the Swede 6-1 in the second. This was the performance that Nadal, his team and his fans had been waiting for – the King of Clay was gradually returning to championship form.

'I just had the feeling I was running better, covering the court quicker and what's satisfied me most was the improvement in my game,' he explained. 'There's nothing secret about the improvement, nothing magic. Only try to do your best and enjoy it. I've overcome a tough situation and I'm in the semi-finals without having played my best.'

Tournament organisers' wishes had been granted – the top four players in the world would contest the two semi-finals. For Nadal, it was Murray who stood between him and another French Open final, in what was remarkably the pair's first meeting on clay. In testing winds, and on his 25th birthday, Rafa provided another reminder of his clay court supremacy, soaking up a fine display from Murray and counterpunching his way to a 6-4, 7-5, 6-4 win. Sure, it was a straight sets scoreline but it had been a battle for the Spaniard, with

Murray correct in his assessment that he 'had played well for the most part'. In the end, it boiled down to Rafa's composure and quality on the decisive points, particularly in protecting his own serve.

After acknowledging that he had raised his game for the most important moments of the match, Nadal was able to enjoy a triple celebration – it was his birthday, he had reached the French Open final and he would hold onto his No. 1 ranking for a little longer after Djokovic's loss to Federer in the other semi-final.

That Federer would be Nadal's opponent in the 2011 French Open final was a surprise given Djokovic's momentum. But the Swiss player was performing beautifully and was no doubt desperate to finally defeat Rafa at Roland Garros. Time and again, the Spaniard had humbled Federer on clay.

With the 'greatest of all time' debate rumbling on, Federer's track record against Nadal was under scrutiny. Rafa had won 16 of their 24 matches prior to the French Open final, an overwhelming advantage that really hurt the Swiss player's case. This would be yet another intriguing chapter to add to one of the most gripping rivalries of all time. It was also the first occasion that two players had squared off in four finals at the same Grand Slam event.

The chance to equal Borg's record of six French Open wins was a hot topic but Rafa insisted that this was a secondary target. 'For me, seriously, I don't think about that,' he explained. '[I have] a lot of respect for the great Bjorn but I am focused on trying to play well. For me, it's much more important to win Roland Garros than equal Bjorn.

'If you compare now to one week ago, it is completely

different. Seriously, being in the final of Roland Garros you can't have problems, you cannot have doubts. I had to forget about the anxiety or the fears I had something like two weeks ago, and now I have gained more confidence. There's nothing new against Roger, I know what's going to happen. I know he's going to play aggressive, for sure. I have to try to play long, to play consistent all the time, and try to be aggressive when I have the chance.'

As the two players walked out onto the court, Nadal was ready. After several average displays earlier in the tournament, he was peaking at the right time and facing a player he knew how to handle on clay.

In truth, the outcome was decided in the first set. Federer raced into a 3-0 lead, with a focus on attacking Nadal's second serve, and Rafa's shaky start played into the Swiss player's hands. And the signs looked bleak for the world No. 1 when, with Federer leading 5-2, he required treatment on his left foot.

But, while others might have begun turning their thoughts to the second set, Nadal had not given up on the first set. Though Federer was cruising, the Spaniard still felt he had a chance. And he was right – in one of the most remarkable stretches of their rivalry, Rafa rattled off five straight games to steal the first set from under the Swiss's nose. To play that well and come away empty handed left Federer wearing an expression of pure disbelief.

To his credit, Federer fought back from a break down twice in the second set to force a tie-break, denying Nadal even after the Spaniard had broken for a 5-4 lead just before a brief rain delay. But Rafa had seemingly saved his best for the tie-break, thumping two forehand winners then inducing errors from the Swiss to grab a 4-0 lead. Moments later, Nadal was celebrating a two-set lead, having weathered some of the best tennis that Federer had ever produced at Roland Garros.

However, the Swiss dug deep for one more assault on the title. Nadal edged in front in the third set, breaking for a 4-2 advantage, but Federer quickly responded to his now-or-never predicament with a sublime patch of tennis. Subduing Rafa with some stunning drop shots, he broke back and seized the momentum. After a second break in the 11th game, Federer did not waste the opportunity and, with the crowd roaring him on, he clinched the set.

With the vast majority of the crowd at Roland Garros seemingly cheering for Federer, Nadal suddenly found himself in an intimidating cauldron of noise against a man desperate to remind the tennis world that he still belonged in the conversation with Nadal and Djokovic.

Rafa's response was emphatic. After fighting off three break points in the first game of the fourth set, Nadal flipped the switch, settling into pure warrior mode. The rallies were no longer oozing with quality; instead, it was scrappy, gritty tennis – right in the Spaniard's wheelhouse. As Federer tired, Rafa kept fighting and secured a crucial break in the fourth game while maintaining control of his own serve. A second break gave him a 5-1 lead and finally brought Federer's resistance to an end. Nadal raced to the finish line with some of the finest winners of the match, then cried tears of joy as Federer fired long to give the Spaniard his sixth French Open title.

In stretching his record to 45-1 at Roland Garros, Rafa leapt further into the history books. While he soaked up the applause and was literally apologetic towards the beaten finalist, Federer took a rather different approach.

'It's always me who's going to dictate play and decide how the outcome is going to be,' Federer said. 'If I play well, I will most likely win; if I'm not playing so well, that's when he wins.' The pain of the defeat was still fresh – but surely the Swiss did not believe that?

Federer's surprising post-match comments were indicative of the mental strain of yet another loss to Rafa. He had brought his A-game and it was just not enough to sink the Spaniard. Having dominated the sport for so many years, perhaps the Swiss was struggling to come to terms with his fall to the No. 3 seed.

As usual, Nadal had little time to savour the moment before preparing for Wimbledon. He had managed to cling onto his clay court supremacy but his body was beginning to show signs of more wear and tear, a hangover from his hat-trick of 2010 Grand Slam wins.

All the while, Djokovic loomed large. The Serb had been the unstoppable force of the tennis world in 2011 and would soon take over as world No. 1. He had always had the talent to match Nadal and Federer but now he had put the whole package together – focus, temperament, consistency.

Rafa used the momentum from Paris to kick-start his bid for a third Wimbledon title, completing straight sets wins over Americans Michael Russell and Ryan Sweeting before beating Gilles Muller 7-6, 7-6, 6-0 in round three.

That set up a clash with Del Potro in round four, which was likely to provide a much sterner test. But, in a resilient four-set victory for Rafa, the big story proved to be Nadal's left foot, which he injured in the opening set. Somehow, he blocked out the pain to complete the match in front of Prince William and Kate, who were in the audience – but he admitted that he had been close to throwing in the towel.

'I felt really bad for half of the first set,' he explained. 'With the score at 6-5, I [suddenly] felt terrible. I thought I had broken my foot. It happened at the deuce point that gave me set point. I thought I might have to retire.

'I pushed hard with the forehand defending shot and crossed. I felt something crushed in the back of the foot. The pain stayed with me for all the match. But it didn't hurt so much with the tape. To run to the forehand was very, very tough for me.'

He nervously awaited the results of an MRI scan to confirm whether or not his Wimbledon title defence was over. Sadly, Rafa was all too familiar with the injury waiting game and the usual doubts crept in. A quarter-final showdown with Mardy Fish was his reward for beating Del Potro and he just crossed his fingers that injury would not cruelly intervene.

The good news was shared early the next day, via Nadal's Facebook page. The Spaniard wrote: 'Good morning everybody. Yesterday after the match I went to take an MRI at a London hospital. During the match I thought I had something serious but as the match went through the pain got better and thankfully the tests don't show an injury. Today I will practise at 4.30 pm and I'll play tomorrow. Thanks all for the support.' The quarter-final was on; his title defence could continue.

Despite the MRI results, Rafa was eager to limit his court time where possible. He used a strong start to gain the upper hand against Fish, winning the first two sets by a 6-3 margin. Though the American hit back to win the third set, Nadal moved in for the kill in set number four and sealed a spot in the last four. While his foot was still troubling him, he insisted that the Wimbledon crown was too important to walk away from.

'It is not fine but this is Wimbledon, it's an emergency,' he said. 'It's my last big tournament for a month-and-a-half so I'm not worried. We've done tests and they didn't show anything important. I have pain in the foot, I cannot run in perfect condition, but the anaesthetic means I can't feel pain for five hours.'

And so, Nadal had overcome his opponents and his injury woes to reach the last four – where the home favourite Murray awaited him once again. Rafa prepared to be public enemy number one again but he knew the drill by now and understood the atmosphere that would greet the two players. On the other side of the draw, Djokovic was playing well and would face Tsonga in the last four after the Frenchman produced a remarkable comeback from two sets down to beat Federer.

By the time Nadal and Murray stepped onto the court, Djokovic had booked his place in the final and, in doing so, had guaranteed that he would leapfrog Nadal in the rankings and take over the No. 1 seed. It was hardly good news but Rafa kept his focus on the task at hand. As expected, Murray flew out of the blocks, willed on by the home crowd as he attempted to become the first British man to reach a Wimbledon final since 1938.

The first set stayed with serve through the first 11 games,

with Murray looking composed and Nadal being forced to work for every point, even on his own serve. Up 6-5, the Scot finally got the break as Rafa twice went long and then sliced the decisive break point into the net. Centre Court roared its approval and the noise level was cranked up to another level.

Nadal quickly regrouped. There was still a long way to go and Murray was unlikely to sustain the barrage of winners that he had produced in the opening set. The turning point in the match came in the fourth game of the second set, with Murray ahead 2-1 and poised to break serve again. At 15-30, the Scot wasted a golden opportunity to bring up two break points but missed the simplest of shots at the net. In the blink of an eye, Rafa then wrapped up the game. It was a single point, a single rally – but, against Nadal, every opportunity needed to be cashed in.

The reprieve provided the wake-up call that Rafa needed. Eager to reap the benefits, he finally settled into a rhythm and turned the match on its head with a magnificent 30-minute spell in which he won seven straight games. From the dangerous predicament of trailing 2-1, he rattled off the next five games and snatched the second set 6-2. He then grabbed a 2-0 advantage in the third set as he sucked the life out of the home crowd.

Murray briefly stemmed the bleeding but, by now, Rafa was on a roll. He broke again for a 5-2 lead as he pulled the Scot from side to side and delivered an array of forehand and backhand winners. Once Nadal clinched the third set, there was no doubt about the outcome – Rafa knew, the Centre Court crowd knew and, in all likelihood, Murray knew too. The Scot was not playing badly but he had run into one of the best hours of tennis that Nadal had played in the tournament. That said, there was a noticeable difference in body language between the two players when faced with adversity in this match – whereas Nadal dug deep and quickly put mistakes behind him, Murray let his emotions get the better of him, with shoulders sagging and a constant frown.

The fourth set was quickly under Nadal's control and he refused to make the kind of mistakes that would provide Murray with hope of a comeback. Halfway through the set, a telling statistic confirmed where the match had been won and lost – Murray had hit more winners (37) than Nadal (35), but, while the Spaniard had made 7 unforced errors, the Scot's tally was a whopping 33. As soon as an extended rally developed, Murray tended to be the first to falter.

Rafa raised his arms and looked to the heavens as he celebrated earning another trip to the Wimbledon final – and the neutrals celebrated the prospect of a Nadal–Djokovic final. 'I think I played very well to win against Andy,' Nadal said post-match. 'Only playing my best tennis would I have any chance, and I played today my best tennis. Always it's an honour to play against him, he's a great champion, and to beat him the only way is to play really aggressive and play fantastic shots, and probably I did that today.'

'I was playing very high-risk tennis for most of the match – maybe I got the balance wrong,' said Murray. 'But you need to try to find a way. Each time you play against one of the best you need to play differently.' Once again, Nadal's brilliance had forced an opponent to make drastic tactical decisions.

And so the game's two powerhouses would meet in the 2011 Wimbledon final. Despite Nadal's success at Roland

Garros, this had unquestionably been Djokovic's year. The Serb's remarkable unbeaten run earlier in 2011 confirmed his rise to an elite level and he had now climbed above both Federer and Rafa in the rankings. His confidence was sky high.

The final proved to be a step too far for Rafa as the exertions of the fortnight at SW19 and the foot problems finally caught up with him. He ran into an on-song Djokovic, who had won all four of his previous matches against the Spaniard in 2011 and clearly sensed this was his moment. The Serb edged a tight first set, grabbing the only break in the tenth game as Nadal's focus wavered on the key points. Fresh off that disappointment, Rafa stumbled into the second set and was blown off the court by some sublime shot-making from Djokovic, who attacked relentlessly to secure a double break and win the set 6-1.

Rafa knew that the only way back was to take some risks in an attempt to regain control. In the third set, he flipped the script from the second set; now he was the one hammering winners in every direction while Djokovic contributed the errors. Nadal motored on to seize the set 6-1 and keep his dreams of another Wimbledon title alive.

But not for long as Djokovic regrouped in what was turning into a rather erratic final. Nadal showed his resilience to recover from an early break and pull level at 3-3, only to see the Serb find another gear and move in for the kill with another break in the eighth game. It was the final nail in the coffin – Djokovic held his nerve and completed a fine victory.

'I lost because I am playing against the best player of the moment, the best player of the world tomorrow, and I am the second,' Nadal modestly explained. 'When you play against these players and they are playing unbelievably, the normal thing is to lose. That's what has happened the last few times. When I was 100 per cent to play, I lost against him five times. The rest of the year I won almost every match, so I'm doing things very well, but probably not against him.'

Djokovic admitted that facing Nadal had brought out the best in him. 'When you're playing the best player in the world, Rafael Nadal, who has won two out of the last three Wimbledons and he has always been winning the big matches against me in the Grand Slams, I had to be on the top of my game, I had to play my best,' the Serb said. 'I think I played probably my best match on the grass courts ever.'

Falling short in the Wimbledon final was a painful blow for Rafa to bounce back from. While the agony was not quite at the level of the 2007 defeat that prompted uncontrollable tears in the shower, it was hard not to replay the key moments and harbour regrets. He elected to take a brief spell away from the game to fully recover from his foot injury, increasing his chances of a deep run at the US Open. But he looked rusty in his return to action, suffering surprise losses at the Rogers Cup and the Cincinnati Masters. It was hardly ideal preparation for a Grand Slam but Nadal was convinced he could raise his game on the big stage. His chances in Cincinnati were not helped by a bizarre incident in which the Spaniard burned his fingers on a hotplate at a restaurant and thereafter struggled both with his grip and with throwing up the ball to serve. Meanwhile, Djokovic still had just a single loss on his 2011 record.

Nadal's bid to defend his US Open title began in convincing fashion with solid victories over Andrey Golubev and Nicolas Mahut, who was forced to retire from his second round match with Rafa leading two sets to love. After an anxious first set tie-break, he then saw off Nalbandian in straight sets to reach the fourth round. Nadal was fighting hard and producing patches of unstoppable tennis – but he knew that he would need to reach another level to survive the latter rounds of the tournament.

In the next round, he was too strong for Muller, though Rafa's slow starts were becoming a trend as he faced another first set tie-break; this time after initially trailing 4-0. Once he had cleared that obstacle, he flew through the next two sets for the loss of just three games.

An in-form Roddick now stood between Nadal and another US Open semi-final – and, with all eyes on that match, the Spaniard took the chance to remind the rest of the pack that he had lost none of his trademark intensity and power. Rafa came out swinging, determined to put his run of sluggish starts behind him, and it was immediately clear that Roddick would be unable to withstand the barrage. Nadal dominated with an array of forehand winners, leaving the American to reflect that he had witnessed Rafa's best performance of the summer. With the home crowd stunned into silence, Nadal was ruthless in clinching a 6-2, 6-1, 6-3 victory. He had not dropped a set thus far at the tournament and a thrilling day of semi-final action lay ahead as Rafa faced Murray while Djokovic and Federer renewed their rivalry.

The Scot believed it would be 'a close, close matchup' but Rafa had other ideas as he breezed through large periods of the semi-final and found plenty of opportunities to pick off Murray's serve. Nadal holds an impressive record when he wins the first set of a Grand Slam match and, after he grabbed the opening set 6-4, the Scot's prospects looked bleak. When he fell into a two-set hole, those prospects all but disappeared. Murray finally seized chances on Nadal's serve in the third set but it was too late by this point and Rafa booked his place in the final with a convincing fourth set, winning it 6-2.

Murray was left to reflect on what might have been. 'I've got to improve,' he said. 'It's disappointing to get so close. I've lost to Rafa a few times this year. I need to work on my game and get physically stronger.

'I was disappointed with the first two sets but the third and fourth were better. I know the right tactics for playing against Rafa but I didn't implement them in the first two sets. It's very easy from the side to suggest what I should be doing out there – you should see some of his passing shots. There's many things I could have done a bit better but I didn't. He's probably the greatest player who has played tennis.'

Reaching another Grand Slam final was pleasing for Rafa but only a victory over Djokovic would relieve some of the Wimbledon heartache. Unfortunately, the Serb had had Nadal's number all year, counterpunching expertly where so many others wilted against Rafa's punishing style of play.

Djokovic entered the final having lost just 2 of his 65 matches in 2011 – a simply staggering run. The top of the men's game had never been stronger, with the quality of play arguably at a higher standard than elite level competition of any other sport.

For Nadal to win, he would need to play aggressively. While Rafa typically had the upper hand in lengthy rallies against

Federer, it was a different story when facing Djokovic. The Serb hammered home that point with 55 winners in the final. Nadal made the type of start he had dreamt of, racing into a 2-0 lead in the first set, before everything fell apart as Djokovic produced a compelling half hour of attacking tennis to rattle off six straight games.

Rafa tried to regroup but Djokovic continued to have the answers. The Spaniard recovered impressively to break back at 4-4, only to see his opponent snatch back control and serve out for the set. The Serb just could do no wrong. Time and again, punishing rallies ended with Djokovic delivering the finishing blow.

While Nadal dug deep to win the third set tie-break, it only roused Djokovic to unleash more unstoppable hitting. The Serb clinched victory – and the US Open title – with a 6-1 demolition in the fourth set.

Inevitably, the spotlight was firmly on Djokovic's remarkable season, during which he had broken up the Nadal and Federer stranglehold and asserted himself as a dominant force. After the US Open, John McEnroe reflected on the Serb's achievements, explaining: 'He bewildered Nadal. I've never seen Nadal look as if he doesn't know what to do and, even on clay in Rome, Djokovic made him look like that. Wimbledon was where he separated himself and took himself to a whole new level. Djokovic is having the greatest year in the history of our sport.' It was a big claim but the numbers backed it up.

Rafa dusted himself down and prepared for the final tournaments of the year. A welcome break was not far away but he refused to let his focus slip. While Djokovic deserved the headlines, Nadal had been in contention throughout the year, with victory at Roland Garros plus the finals at Wimbledon and Flushing Meadows. All was not lost.

Nadal's 2011 season ended with a whimper, as he lost in the final of the Japan Open Tennis Championships, then suffered an early exit in Shanghai at the hands of Florian Mayer. The Spaniard was also below par at the ATP World Tour Finals, where losses to Federer and Tsonga quickly ended Rafa's hopes. Given that he had battled his way to three Grand Slam finals, it was understandable that, by now, there was simply nothing left in the tank. As he headed home to enjoy time with his friends and family, he vowed to use the disappointment of the key defeats to Djokovic to turn the tide in 2012.

CHAPTER 10

A YEAR OF AGONY

By this point, aged 25, it would have been easy for Nadal to coast. He had won all four Grand Slam titles, he had set countless records on clay and he had amassed a fortune in prize money. But his thirst for competition was unquenched, with Toni on hand to ensure that Rafa never lost his focus. The disappointment of his 2011 losses to Djokovic just provided extra motivation.

The 2012 season came around in the blink of an eye, leaving Nadal with those familiar mixed feelings: the sadness of leaving Mallorca and the excitement of continuing the pursuit for more silverware. The Spaniard's year began at the Qatar Open, where he suffered a semi-final defeat to Monfils. He was clearly still finding his rhythm. But he had a solid track record of saving his best for the Grand Slams and he headed for the Australian Open in good spirits, with positive memories from 2009 to fall back on.

After a solid week of practice, Nadal felt acclimatised and ready to take on Djokovic, Federer and the rest of the pack. However, he suffered a setback just prior to his first round match against American Alex Kuznetsov. A seemingly innocuous movement of sitting down in a chair led to Rafa feeling a crack in his knee and then a wave of pain. Suddenly, his participation in the tournament was in jeopardy.

Fortunately, rapid diagnosis and treatment did the trick, as Nadal explained after breezing past Kuznetsov, having raced to a 6-1 scoreline in the second and third sets. 'I had to go to the hospital for an MRI and yesterday evening I was not 100 per cent sure I would play but I had a lot of treatment and the MRI was positive,' the Spaniard said. 'I am really happy that today I was ready to play.'

Rafa still needed taping on his right knee to complete the match and, though he had powered to a quick win, there were now big question marks over his chances of reaching the final. But he looked more comfortable in the next round, easing past Tommy Haas in straight sets and insisting that he had played without pain during the match. A 6-2, 6-4, 6-2 victory over Lukas Lacko then booked Nadal's place in the fourth round as he landed 81 per cent of his first serves and made few mistakes.

Up next was an all-Spanish clash against Feliciano Lopez – a man who Nadal had dominated over the years. This match just continued that trend as Lopez's game plan played into Rafa's hands. Long baseline rallies would always favour Nadal, whereas Lopez looked more at home with a serve-volley approach. As soon as the contest became a slugfest, it was one-way traffic. With scorching temperatures hitting

Melbourne, Rafa was delighted to wrap up the win in straight sets, 6-4, 6-4, 6-2.

Rafa fully expected a bigger challenge in the quarter-finals – and he got it in the shape of Berdych, who promptly prevailed in a first set tie-break to give Nadal a timely jolt. Where Lopez had been tentative, the Czech was going to lay it all on the line. Given the energy-sapping conditions, Rafa was well aware of how damaging a two-set deficit would be – but Berdych's rocket forehand continued to find the mark. Nadal needed every bit of his trademark defence to survive the second set and level matters in another tie-break.

Winning the second set settled the Spaniard and the rest of the match largely unfolded on his terms. He was able to secure the crucial breaks in the third and fourth sets and his serve – and knee – held steady. Rafa had channelled his visible first set frustrations into a composed, clinical finish to the match. As he completed the 6-7, 7-6, 6-4, 6-3 victory, all thoughts turned to another potential classic against Federer in the last four. The Swiss had brushed aside Del Potro with ease and was playing with a real swagger.

Nadal was quick to shoot down any suggestions that the match would be the Spaniard's warm-up for a final against Djokovic. After all, as he explained, Federer had 16 Grand Slams under his belt and would be out for revenge after some painful losses to Rafa in recent years. Reaching the final was far from a done deal – and Nadal knew it.

However, there was no question that the Spaniard had a mental edge over Federer. The string of demoralising losses to Nadal on clay had taken their toll, as had the defeats in the 2008 Wimbledon final and the 2009 Australian Open final.

Rafa's knee problems were under control and he felt confident that he could outlast his great rival.

But it was Federer who jumped in front, establishing a 3-0 lead and making a mockery of the predictions that suggested he had no chance of prevailing. Nadal hit back to force a tie-break but the Swiss recovered his poise and clinched the first set. Rafa refused to panic, knowing that he could up the intensity and wear Federer down. And he did so in the second set as the Swiss failed to match the quality of his earlier play. Nadal grabbed two breaks of serve, the second of which came after a brief stoppage for Australia Day fireworks, and clinched a dominant set 6-2.

Federer shrugged off the disappointment of seeing his advantage wiped out but his play continued to be littered with unforced errors (63 in total). Rafa's court coverage was forcing the Swiss to aggressively attempt winners and that strategy brought mixed results. Both players made inroads on the other's serve but the third set headed for a tie-break – and this time Nadal grabbed the upper hand. Federer showed his resilience by saving five set points before Rafa finally landed the knockout blow to move one set away from a place in the final.

Winning the final two sets always seemed beyond Federer, even though he had been on a fine run of results. Nadal focused on giving nothing away cheaply and waited patiently for his chance to strike. It finally arrived in the ninth game of the fourth set as Federer stuttered and opened the door for break points. Rafa seized the opportunity, moved 5-4 up and then held his serve to set up the final against Djokovic that had been the talk of Melbourne throughout the fortnight. After the injury uncertainty and the emotions that went hand-in-hand with that scare at the beginning of the tournament, a place in the final was a huge accomplishment.

'Sunday afternoon, 24 hours to play my first match, I was in my room crying because I believed I didn't have the chance to play in Melbourne; he admitted. 'So it was a very, very tough situation for me, those hours. Two weeks later I am here in the finals, so it is a dream for me because I had very bad expectations 24 hours before the first match, and now two weeks later I am playing well. I am in the final!'

As he rushed to ready himself for the final, he knew he had a mountain to climb to beat Djokovic. Many felt that the Serb had proven to be a more accomplished hard court player than Nadal and the speed of the courts seemed to favour the world No. 1. One of the critical differences for Rafa in matches against Djokovic was that he had finally met his match in terms of stamina and endurance. Both players could trade shots from the baseline for hours and believed that, whatever the match situation, there was always a chance for a comeback. For instance, to reach the final, Djokovic had bounced back from a two sets to one deficit against Murray.

In front of a noisy, passionate crowd, Nadal produced the fast start that he needed – with Djokovic still riding high on his momentous 2011 season, Rafa could not afford to lag behind. The Spaniard had fallen into a rut against the Serb, losing their last six finals. After a gritty opening to the first set, Nadal grabbed the decisive break for a 6-5 lead and held his nerve on serve to move ahead.

Djokovic responded immediately with some breathtaking shot-making in the second and third sets, using a punishing first serve to dictate the rallies. Rafa let too many mistakes creep into his play as he scrambled to keep each point alive. The Serb won the second set 6-4, breaking early, relinquishing the advantage and then taking it back in the tenth game. All square.

As the tide turned in the Serb's favour, the memories of his recent dominance over Nadal came flooding back. The third set was all Djokovic as Rafa struggled with his serve and, in the blink of an eye, the Spaniard's margin for error was gone. He had to win the last two sets.

Predictably, this did not faze Rafa. Nadal stuck to his game plan and scrapped his way to a fourth set tie-break, in which he remained the steadier player on the big points. He won the breaker 7-5 and, as the match hit the five-hour mark, a pivotal fifth set beckoned. Rafa could not have given more on this occasion, pushing Djokovic to the limit and continuing to chase every ball, but the Serb would not be denied. Djokovic edged in front and held on to win the decisive set 7-5 and snatch the trophy from under Nadal's nose.

When Djokovic clinched victory after 5 hours and 53 minutes of pulsating action, the final was already in the history books for the longest Grand Slam final ever played. It was another epic to add to Rafa's collection – only this time, he had finished on the wrong end of the scoreline.

It was a crushing loss, both physically and mentally, but he mustered the strength to reflect positively on his fortnight in Melbourne, which had begun and ended painfully. Nonetheless, he had played with great courage and had pushed Djokovic all the way. In the end, the Serb had been just too strong, sending Rafa and his team back to the drawing board to craft the strategy that would help Nadal overcome this talented obstacle. For all Djokovic's fine performances in 2011, this was arguably the signature win that announced his position as the leading light in the men's game, ahead of Rafa and ahead of Federer.

As was so often the case, the clay court season was the perfect medicine for Nadal. The lingering heartache from the Australian Open would eventually subside, in part because Rafa was busy stuffing his trophy cabinet with more titles. The warm-up tour events ahead of the French Open also provided Rafa with a chance to halt his losing run against Djokovic. He outlasted the Serb in Monte Carlo to lift the trophy for the eighth consecutive year, then beat Ferrer to win the Barcelona Open. After a disappointing early exit in Madrid, he reached another final against Djokovic in Rome, battling his way to a narrow victory over the Serb.

Redressing the balance of power in his new rivalry with Djokovic was a huge achievement and a key psychological step ahead of Roland Garros. Nadal would be the favourite to defend his title – but the smart money said that another final against the Serb lay ahead. This time, Rafa would be arriving with the upper hand.

The journey towards a seventh French Open crown got off to the smoothest of starts as Nadal cruised through the opening rounds without breaking sweat. While Djokovic had the No. 1 ranking, it was Rafa who grabbed all the attention with his ruthless hitting, particularly in the first four rounds as he left his opponents totally demoralised. Italian Simone Bolelli was the first victim, winning just five games on his way to a crushing straight sets loss.

Istomin fared even worse in round two, picking up only four games. Nadal was everywhere, thumping winners and conceding nothing defensively. The third set, which Rafa clinched 6-0, sent a clear message to the other contenders. His third round 6-1, 6-3, 6-4 drubbing of Eduardo Schwank was equally impressive.

Round four saw Rafa at his most clinical, humbling the No. 13 seed Juan Monaco with a blistering performance that left the Argentine packing his bags after a mere 1 hour and 46 minutes of action. It was an ominous sign for Djokovic, Federer and Murray, who had all faced some nervy moments already at the tournament. Nadal reeled off 17 straight games against Monaco to finish off the match and gain some valuable rest.

Without undue effort, Rafa was into the last eight and felt he was peaking at the right time. Compatriot Almagro finally gave Nadal a scare, forcing a first set tie-break, but was unable to capitalise. Rafa was just too strong on the key points and, once this opening had been and gone, Almagro was overwhelmed by the defending champion's power, succumbing 7-6, 6-2, 6-3. While a semi-final against Murray had looked the likeliest scenario, the Scot was outgunned by Ferrer, putting Rafa face-to-face with another of his friends.

Ferrer has proved to be a tricky opponent at times for Nadal over the years and has handed him a few painful losses. But on this occasion, on this surface, Nadal would not be denied. Ferrer's bright start quickly faded away and he was powerless to stop the onslaught.

It was over in no time, with Nadal securing a 6-2, 6-2, 6-1 win. 'Today was my best match of the tournament, against the best player I've faced here so far,' he explained. 'It is a very important victory for me – to win with this result against one of the best players of the moment, and the world.'

There was little time for reflection with yet another French Open final to prepare for – it would be his seventh final at

Roland Garros and Rafa was fully aware that he was creating history on a regular basis with his continued clay court dominance. Again, it was Djokovic who stood in Nadal's path.

Knowing that Djokovic would probably have more nerves early in the match, Nadal concentrated on making an aggressive start. The Spaniard got the tactics just right and Djokovic, despite all his improvements in 2011, could not keep up with the pace of the rallies. Rafa earned a decisive break in each of the first two sets to gain a firm advantage, serving solidly and displaying his usual court coverage. Winners that the Serb had been nailing throughout the fortnight were no longer unreturnable as Nadal scrambled to salvage rally after rally.

Djokovic hinted at a comeback by clinching the third set 6-2 but it was not enough to rattle the champion. Even as the rain forced the final to continue the next day, Rafa kept his cool. After all, he was playing for more than just the trophy this year. He bounced back from that disappointment to take the fourth set 7-5 and once again lift the French Open trophy.

Rafa had ruled the roost at Roland Garros for the seventh time in eight years, moving past Borg's record of six French Open crowns. After clinching the final point on a Djokovic double fault, emotion swept over Nadal and the tears flowed. His injury heartache had reminded him to enjoy every minute of his tennis career, and winning Grand Slams made all the hard work pay off. He constantly reminded himself how short an athlete's career could be – and his injury-enforced absences had put things into perspective.

As he basked briefly in his moment of glory in Paris, Rafa felt back on top of the tennis world, even if the rankings told a slightly different story. What he did not know was that this promising season was about to be cruelly derailed, putting his tennis future in doubt and preventing him from chasing the goals he had set out for 2012.

The signs were there at Wimbledon as Nadal tumbled out of the tournament in the second round against Czech underdog Lukas Rosol. He had travelled to SW19 with good intentions and high hopes of another deep run – but he had no response to the counterpunching from Rosol, who was able to execute his game plan more effectively, preventing Rafa from settling into the type of rhythm that had been so successful in Paris.

The loss went down as one of the biggest shocks in tournament history as Rosol defied his No. 100 ranking. While the Czech had played the match of his life, Nadal also felt defeated by the match officials after several close-cut calls. 'The bad thing of this is anything that I will say now will sound against me,' Rafa said. 'So it is not the right moment for me to say what happened out there because it's going to sound an excuse, and I never want to put an excuse after a match like today. But the umpire said a few things that weren't right.'

As the fallout from the defeat began to subside, Nadal's eagerness to return to action had to be addressed. This year, there was the added drama of the 2012 Olympics in London, prior to the US Open. However, Nadal would play no part in either event as he fell victim to the injury curse once again, with lingering knee pain needing attention. Knee problems were nothing new for Rafa but this latest tendinitis was excruciating, making it impossible to play his usual punishing style. Further tests confirmed a partial tear of the patella tendon in his left knee as well as painful inflammation.

Missing the Olympics, in particular, was a crushing blow,

denying him the chance to defend his title. Rafa had relished the chance to represent Spain in Beijing in 2008 and had played with skill and passion en route to the gold. Now, he would be forced to watch the London Olympics from afar.

'I do not find myself in a condition to compete,' he said. 'It is one of the saddest moments of my career. I have to think about my colleagues. I cannot be selfish and I have to think of the good of Spanish sport, especially Spanish tennis, and let a teammate who is better prepared to compete. I've waited until the final moment of my preparation and my training, but I cannot do it.'

At the time, it was unclear just how long Nadal would be sidelined. Despite committing wholeheartedly to the routine of rest that was imposed upon him, Rafa struggled to shrug off the knee pain. He was forced to sit out the start of the hard court season and suddenly his participation in the US Open was in jeopardy as rest continued to be prescribed as the best medicine for his knees. As time ran out, he was forced to drop out of the Grand Slam.

'I am very sad to announce that I am still not ready to play and have to withdraw from this year's US Open in NYC,' Rafa explained in a statement. 'I am sorry since I always found great crowds and great support, but I have to continue with my recuperation and preparation to be ready to play in the right conditions. I want to say hi and thanks to all the fans in particular to the New Yorkers. I'll miss you all this year at the Open!'

Nadal's absence certainly helped his rivals push ahead, both in the rankings and at the major tournaments. Murray beat Federer to win gold at the Olympics in front of his home fans, then went on to clinch the US Open, his first Grand Slam triumph. Unable to aid his own points tally, Nadal slipped to the No. 4 seed. But his rivals were certainly sympathetic to his predicament, including his great rival Federer.

'I wrote him and he told me it wasn't looking good at all. I kind of knew,' the Swiss said. 'But obviously when it's official it's disappointing for tennis, there's no doubt about it. I would love to have him in the draw. In particular, 12 days before the Open you figure he might still have time to fix what he has to fix to get ready.

'That's what is sort of scary. There is obviously the whole debate going on if he is going to come back for this year. I hope he will. He's definitely got some more weeks off now because of it. I hope in hindsight this is a very smart decision by him. But it's obviously a big blow and disappointing news for the tennis world.'

All in all, it was one of the toughest summers of Rafa's career, with fresh doubts creeping in as to whether he would make a full recovery and be capable of performing at the elite level required to take on Djokovic, Federer and Murray.

As 2012 neared its conclusion, Rafa began plotting his return to the tour, though it was a difficult decision after a lengthy period away from the day-to-day grind. 'I have my doubts – it's normal, we are talking about a knee, so of course I am afraid to see how it is going to respond,' Nadal admitted. 'But I can only trust my doctors and believe in myself and that everything will be all right.'

'I would like to return in January,' he later told Spanish radio. 'I don't expect to return and win the Australian Open, I have to be realistic.'

In the end, he would have to wait a little longer.

CHAPTER 11

ON TOP OF THE WORLD AGAIN

Seeing the calendar turn to 2013 was a blessing for Rafa after the painful, frustrating end to 2012. He sought to put the injury nightmare behind him and focus on returning to the court. But it quickly became apparent that the early events of the year would come too soon in Nadal's recovery, including the Australian Open, where injury had derailed him time and again. The Spaniard officially ruled himself out of the Grand Slam and sought out a new target – returning to dominate the clay court season.

Returning from a seven-month spell away from the tour was a major challenge for Nadal. It would take time to rediscover his form and rhythm, yet his style of play did not leave room for a gentle reintroduction. As January came and went, and Nadal was still sidelined, doubts about his future in the game continued to grow. Would he be able to return? And would he ever rediscover the form that had made him the world No. 1? Nadal admits that even his own team had their concerns over whether he could make a full recovery.

In February, Rafa began to provide answers. He returned to action in a minor event in Chile, which presented the ideal chance to test his fitness without swarms of attention. The results were encouraging – he reached the final of the singles and doubles and, though he lost both finals, his knees came through this first examination. He then won tournaments in Sao Paulo and Acapulco as he began to regain his usual rhythm and movement.

Facing all the big guns at Indian Wells provided a sterner test. Entering the tournament as the fifth seed was an unusual feeling for Rafa but he was simply delighted to be back in action. It did not take long for Nadal to remind his rivals that, while his ranking might have slipped, he was still a force to be reckoned with.

The Spaniard sped through the opening rounds then won a fourth round battle with Gulbis 4-6, 6-4, 7-5. That victory set up a quarter-final against Federer and a chance to make a real statement. Rafa seized it with both hands, continuing his dominance over the Swiss in a 6-4, 6-2 win.

Federer was struggling with a back injury but Nadal's performance confirmed that he had lost none of his unique pugnacious attributes. 'Two weeks ago I didn't know if I can be here, and tomorrow I will be in semi-finals here,' he explained post-match. 'But it is a big surprise for me to have these results. I was able to practise just a little before the comeback. Important thing is be healthy. And if that happens and I'm able to practise as much as I can, as much as I want, probably that the comeback will be a little bit less difficult, no?'

Rafa then outlasted Berdych in two gritty sets in the semi-final and came back from a set down to beat Del Potro in the final. It capped a fine spell of tennis and ensured that Nadal was on a roll heading into the clay court season, where he hoped to really prove that he was back.

Rafa travelled to Monte Carlo full of confidence and put together a fine run to reach the final for the ninth straight year. But he could not make it nine straight titles as Djokovic broke the Spaniard's stranglehold on the trophy. Nadal entered the final having won 46 straight matches at the tournament but the Serb used a strong first set to turn the match in his favour.

Nadal refused to be discouraged. He was still enjoying the honeymoon period of his return to action and more opportunities for silverware were just around the corner. He continued his momentum with notable victories in Barcelona and Madrid before heading to Rome for another tournament that he had dominated in recent years. He reached the final for the eighth straight year and lifted the trophy for the sixth time, clinching an emphatic 6-1, 6-3 victory over Federer in the final. This fairy-tale return from his seven-month layoff was surprising even Rafa.

The Swiss took the defeat in his stride and provided a telling assessment of why Nadal's style of play was so challenging for opponents. 'He plays so well from deep and you should try to play more serve and volley, but he makes it difficult,' Federer said. 'You can't dictate play, so you take more chances. I had more time to get set in rallies against other players this week – against Rafa you don't get that time.'

As for Nadal, this was all a bonus. 'If anyone had told me

[that] when I came back I would win six titles, I would have told them they were crazy, he admitted. 'It has exceeded my wildest dreams.'

It set the stage perfectly for the French Open, with Nadal hoping to crown his comeback with an eighth title at Roland Garros. But it quickly became clear that there would be no procession to the final as Rafa dropped the opening set in his first two matches. German Daniel Brands threatened to pull off a colossal upset in round one, winning the first set 6-4 then earning a second set tie-break. Nadal dug deep to win the tie-break and eventually regained control of the contest, securing key breaks of serve to complete a 4-6, 7-6, 6-4, 6-3 victory. The Spaniard looked a relieved man as he left the court and later admitted that winning the second set tie-break was 'just like some oxygen – I could finally breathe'.

Another slow start allowed Slovakian Martin Klizan to gain an early advantage but Nadal was solid in the next three sets to ensure safe passage into the third round, where he saw off Fabio Fognini in three hard-fought sets. This was not Rafa at his best but he was doing just enough to keep that eighth French Open title in sight.

Nadal responded well in the next two rounds, producing the type of dominant tennis that the crowd at Roland Garros had become accustomed to witnessing. He breezed past No. 13 seed Kei Nishikori 6-4, 6-1, 6-3, then made quick work of Wawrinka, who won just six games in his straight sets loss. Suddenly, Rafa's march towards the final had an air of inevitability about it. A semi-final against Djokovic awaited.

But Djokovic had proven that he could match Nadal on clay,

with the recent victory in Monte Carlo and other impressive wins over the past few years. The Serb was the No. 1 seed and, if anyone was going to deny Rafa at Roland Garros, it was him. What followed was arguably the greatest match ever played on clay.

The scorching temperatures in Paris seemed to favour Nadal, but Djokovic had the arsenal to not only stay in rallies but also dominate them. Both players sniffed breaks early in the opening set yet it was Rafa who struck the first blow, cashing in on a Djokovic slip to break serve in the seventh game. A fine cross-court backhand drew gasps from the crowd and then Rafa converted his third break point as the Serb fired long.

Nadal consolidated the break with a love service game and, though Djokovic closed the gap to 5-4, the Spaniard would serve for the first set. His game plan was working well, preventing the world's best returner from imposing himself. Rafa knew he had to take every opportunity and kept his nerve to seal the first set as Djokovic dragged a return wide.

After such a flawless set of clean hitting, it was hard to imagine anything slowing Nadal on his path to the final. When Rafa jumped into a 3-2 lead in the second set with another break, Djokovic looked like his frustrations might get the better of him. But he channelled the anger into his play, breaking straight back and swinging the momentum once more in his favour. He held serve for 4-3, then broke Nadal's serve again with a classy forehand winner. With four straight games, the world No. 1 had turned the match on its head.

With every passing rally, this semi-final had more of a feel of a final. Rafa returned to his chair and brushed off the disappointment. It had become a best of three sets final and he still fancied his chances of outlasting anyone on clay.

Nadal was forced to battle again in his opening service game of the third set as the two players exchanged clubbing groundstrokes from the back of the court. But holding serve and stopping the rot gave Rafa a second wind. Suddenly, it was the Serb who was on the back foot. Nadal's backhand was hitting the mark; Djokovic's was faltering. Rafa broke for a 2-0 lead, produced a dominant hold, then broke for a second time. In the blink of an eye, the seven-time French Open champion had flown into a 5-0 lead before the world No. 1 finally got on the board in the sixth game. It only delayed the inevitable, as Nadal wrapped up the third set 6-1.

The fourth set turned this contest into a classic, with unpredictable twists and turns keeping the crowd on the edge of their seats. Outstanding serving set a quick pace but Rafa landed a critical blow with a break in the seventh game after wild Djokovic forehands on the decisive points. But the Serb was not finished – it was time to take chances and he did so, with a thumping backhand winner and a perfectly placed return to break back and level at 4-4.

Both players steadied their serves, managing a hold each to maintain parity at 5-5, before the drama rose to a new level. Nadal upped the ante and found an opening in the 11th game as Djokovic struggled to handle the Spaniard's movement and spinning forehands. When the Serb fired a forehand out to gift Rafa the break, the match was seemingly over.

But never count Djokovic out. Just as Nadal looked poised to saunter into the final, the Serb hit back. Fighting to earn a break point and then landing a stunning forehand winner,

Djokovic forced a tie-break and ensured that this incredible match continued.

Rafa was as shocked as the crowd. Djokovic pounced on the opportunity, won the first two points of the tie-break and never let go. An overhead smash gave the Serb a 6-3 advantage – and he levelled the match after a Nadal error. The Spaniard had been so close to victory. Now he had to regroup.

But Djokovic smelled blood. He broke Nadal in the opening game of the fifth set, matching the Spaniard shot for shot but consistently finding a well-placed winner. Rafa looked to hit back in the next game, collecting a break point only for Djokovic's backhand to ride to the rescue.

Nadal stayed in contention with a gutsy hold but he still trailed. More fabulous tennis followed in the fourth game as Djokovic moved into a 3-1 lead. The clock was ticking for Rafa, especially when he found himself at 30-30 and had to scrap through multiple deuces in his next service game, but a backhand winner helped him escape. Moments later, Djokovic kept his nose in front, moving ahead 4-2 with a clinical hold.

It was kitchen-sink time for Nadal – he had to throw everything he had at Djokovic to keep his French Open dreams alive. He was already hitting the ball hard but he raised the intensity further in the seventh game to clinch an important hold, then prepared himself to chase a break.

A frantic eighth game ebbed and flowed but eventually turned in Rafa's favour. Djokovic fought off two break points but Nadal, sensing his moment had arrived, crafted a third and levelled the set after the Serb netted a forehand. It was all square again.

Given the pressure and the high stakes, both players were

performing at an incredible level and refusing to give an inch. Mentally and physically, they had been stretched to the limit, yet the quality of play remained admirably high. The remarkable shot-making continued as the score ticked from 4-4 to 5-5 to 6-6 to 7-7. Just like that famous fifth set at Wimbledon in 2008, the next break would be sudden death.

Rafa held his nerve, limiting Djokovic to a single point on his serve, grabbing an 8-7 advantage and forcing the world No. 1 to serve to stay in the match. But Djokovic lost his rhythm at the worst possible moment as his forehand strayed and Nadal uncorked a delicious forehand winner. Suddenly, Rafa had three break points – and three match points.

The Serb had nothing left. With the match on the line, he fired a forehand long to seal his fate. Nadal had reached yet another French Open final. Amid all the years of dominance in Paris, this had been his sternest test – an epic bout that belonged alongside the all-time greats. After a whopping 4 hours and 37 minutes in the sapping heat, there had been little to separate these two titans – but Rafa did just enough to squeeze through, making Djokovic wait to complete his career Grand Slam.

'This court is the most special one on the tour,' Nadal explained. 'Novak's a fighter. When I was serving for the match in the fourth, I was serving against the wind so I knew that was going to be a very tough game. I was ready for the fight. In Australia in 2012, it was a similar match and he won, today it's me.'

It was easy to forget that this was not the final. Ferrer awaited Rafa in that contest and it was now a race against time for his team to get his body ready for another potential battle of attrition. As it turned out, Nadal would have a far easier time in the final, sweeping past Ferrer in straight sets 6-3, 6-2, 6-3. He had his hands on another French Open title, improving his own record-setting mark to eight and becoming the first player to ever win the same Grand Slam eight times. After all the emotion of his semi-final marathon, the victory in the final and his comeback from injury as a whole (43 wins from 45 matches), this was a perfect moment to reflect on his staggering efforts.

'Some weeks I didn't feel well but the last couple of weeks my knee started to feel better,' he told the media post-match. 'And the knee came through tough matches in Rome against Ernests Gulbis, David Ferrer. The knee [came through] a very tough battle against Novak Djokovic the other day. Yesterday I didn't have a terrible feeling, so that's very positive news.

'So far the season has been good for me. I played nine tournaments and I can only say thank you to life. In an athlete's life there are ups and downs. I'm not going too high up or too low down. My perspectives are normal. Winning 17 grand slam titles? I'm not even thinking about it. The next tournament is Wimbledon, fine.'

As for Ferrer, he was in awe. 'He has everything,' the Spaniard gushed. 'Mentally, he's the best I have ever seen. He can play aggressively, has soft hands at the net, physically he is unbelievable. He played five sets two days ago and today he can play like that.'

Rafa's reward for winning in Paris? Dropping to the No. 5 seed due to Ferrer's fine performances in 2013. But the Spaniard continued to focus on his tennis, knowing that he was a leading contender at any tournament, regardless of the seeding.

Wimbledon beckoned next for Nadal as he sought to keep the momentum going. But rushing from the French Open drama to SW19 proved too much for Rafa on this occasion. He had pulled off the feat numerous times over the years, including 2006, 2007 and 2008 when he raced from Roland Garros glory and surged to the Wimbledon final. But his 2013 bid ended at the first hurdle as he was involved in another big upset.

Nadal faced unseeded Belgian Steve Darcis in the first round but came unstuck in two tie-breaks on the way to an eyebrow-raising straight sets exit. More worryingly, Rafa was a step slow as his injury issues returned to haunt him. Limping valiantly, he refused to throw in the towel but it was clear that he was unable to play at his usual level. 'It's not a tragedy – it's sport' was Nadal's post-match assessment, though it was painful to follow up last year's shock exit at the hands of Rosol with this disappointment.

The Spaniard quickly turned the page and focused on getting into peak physical shape for the hard court season. It paid dividends, with important wins in Montreal (beating Djokovic in the semi-final) and Cincinnati. It was the ideal preparation for the US Open where Nadal hoped to replicate his 2010 success. Having completed his career Grand Slam, earning multiple titles at each Grand Slam was the next challenge. He had already done that at the French Open and Wimbledon but he had won the Australian Open and US Open just once.

He carried his form from Montreal and Cincinnati into the early rounds, dispatching Ryan Harrison and Rogerio Dutra da Silva with ease. Croatian Ivan Dodig fared little better in a 6-

4, 6-3, 6-3 third round loss. With 56 wins from 59 matches in 2013, Nadal was arguably putting together the best season of his career and the idea of someone winning three sets against the Spaniard was looking far-fetched.

'Here we are after six months back playing again in a great position,' he explained. 'I am trying to play more aggressively, it's true, but that's because I am playing well. If I'm not playing well, I have to be more defensive.'

After a wobble in the first set of his fourth round clash with Kohlschreiber, in which he dropped the tie-break, Rafa rallied to punish the German the rest of the way, including an emphatic 6-1 scoreline in the fourth set. In the quarter-final, he had more brilliance up his sleeve, thumping compatriot Robredo 6-0, 6-2, 6-2. Robredo had beaten Federer in impressive fashion in the fourth round – denying the tennis world a first ever Nadal–Federer match at Flushing Meadows – but he had no answer to Rafa's unstoppable hitting. Nadal explained that the opening set was the first set of the year in which he felt 100 per cent.

Gasquet was the surprise opponent in the last four, after beating Ferrer in a five-set battle. Heading into a match against Nadal after that kind of marathon match was hardly ideal and it certainly counted against the Frenchman. Rafa was a man on a mission, having not lost his serve thus far in the tournament (in 67 service games), and he clinched the first set via an early break. But he was pushed to the limit in the second set as Gasquet broke Nadal for the first time during the fortnight and forced a tie-break with some gritty shot-making.

Rafa showed no mercy in the tie-break, though, losing just

one point. That setback killed off Gasquet's charge and Nadal stamped his ticket for the final by cruising through the third set. 'Last year I didn't have the chance to play on this court,' said Nadal. 'To have the chance to play in the final on Monday is just a dream for me. It has been two amazing weeks.'

And so, tennis fans could look forward to another instalment of the Nadal–Djokovic rivalry. By now, Rafa knew what to expect when squaring off with Djokovic, a player who was a mirror image of himself in some respects and capable of matching Nadal in long rallies.

While the Serb called Rafa the best player in the world for 2013, Djokovic was still the world No. 1 and, whereas Nadal always held a slight edge on clay, the hard court perhaps slightly favoured Djokovic. Dressed all in grey, Rafa made a fast start, earning a break in the third game with a thumping forehand winner and continuing to keep his nose in front during long, bruising rallies. Rafa broke again in the seventh game as his dogged defence began to frustrate Djokovic and the Spaniard quickly sealed the set with an easy hold.

Thus far, Nadal had been relatively untroubled on his own serve but that would change in the second set. The Spaniard escaped from two break points in his first service game but the Serb got a dramatic break in the sixth game as he outlasted Rafa in a staggering 54-shot rally. Nadal quickly made amends by breaking back, only for Djokovic to break again and hold on to clinch the set 6–3.

While both players were producing magical shots in seemingly never-ending rallies, the momentum was now with Djokovic. The match had the feel of another five-set epic. The Serb broke Rafa in the first game of the third set, held serve and then earned another break point as Nadal found himself on the ropes. But he was often at his best when backed into a corner and forced to play with an air of desperation – as he proved here by preventing Djokovic from moving further ahead and preparing for his own moment to pounce. It came in the sixth game as Nadal upped the pressure and benefitted from a string of unforced errors. Toni roared his approval as Rafa went on the offensive.

With the match teetering one way then the other, the final two games of the third set played a large part in determining the outcome. At 4-4, Djokovic moved 40-0 ahead on Nadal's serve but the Spaniard refused to panic – a fine passing shot saved one break point, a Djokovic error wiped out another and a timely ace pulled Rafa back to deuce. Tense rallies ensued before Nadal wrapped up the game with an overhead. He had dodged a major bullet – and he knew it.

And Rafa's ability to extend rallies was the key to him clinching the third set, as Djokovic dropped his serve at a critical moment to hand the third set – one that he had been in control of – to Nadal. It had been one of the most gripping sets of tennis that the pair had played and the Spaniard had needed every ounce of resilience to endure Djokovic's early onslaught.

Now he was a set away from a second US Open title. And he was in a hurry to cross the finish line. While the Serb may have been dwelling on missed opportunities in the third set, Nadal earned a quick break for a 3-0 lead. Even as Djokovic unleashed ferocious attempted winners, Rafa was returning the ball with interest – and no shortage of devilish spin. The Serb got back on track in his second service game but it was too little, too late. Nadal refused to falter on serve, then seized a double break as Djokovic missed makeable shots in his bid to shorten the rallies. The Serb had racked up 52 unforced errors and the end was nigh.

Rafa did not hesitate. His serving had been phenomenal throughout the fortnight and he held firm to clinch the US Open title with a 6-2, 3-6, 6-4, 6-1 victory. His fairy-tale comeback had a new chapter – 22 consecutive hard court victories, including a pulsating and heroic win over the world No. 1, who had lost two unforgettable battles with Nadal in 2013.

The plaudits poured in for the Spaniard's efforts since returning from injury. Given that time away from the game, it would have been entirely natural for Nadal to require six months or more before recovering his swagger. Instead, it had taken him a matter of weeks. His haul of two Grand Slams and a string of tour victories made 2013 one of the most special years of Rafa's career.

'All of my team knows how much this match today means to me,' he explained. 'Playing against Novak is always a very special feeling and nobody brings my game to the limit like he does.

'Every time I play Novak we have amazing points, amazing rallies. Today there were lot of moments when I felt I played amazing tennis, but at the end of the second and start of the third Novak was on fire. I tried to wait for the opportunities.

'I am 100 per cent sure this was the most emotional season of my career. I only remember in those moments all of the people who were with me in the tough moments – the fans, family and my team. Their support gave me positive energy to be back on the tour.'

With both Nadal and Djokovic still some way from their

30th birthdays, the tennis world could look forward to plenty more classic duels. The Serb had had Rafa's number in 2011, beating the Spaniard in a string of finals, but Nadal had clearly held the edge in the big matches in 2013.

The US Open triumph had taken a lot out of Rafa. He managed to fight on and help Spain clinch a Davis Cup World Group Playoff spot, winning in the singles and doubles, before heading to the China Open, where he lost to Djokovic in the final but did enough to ensure he would take over as the world No. 1 for the first time since 2011. It spoke volumes for the quality of tennis he had played over the course of the season.

After losing in the semi-finals in Shanghai, Rafa reached the final of the 2013 ATP World Tour Finals in London, where he again lost out to Djokovic. It brought down the curtain on a whirlwind, memorable season for Nadal – one in which he had put himself firmly back on top of the tennis mountain and re-established himself as the man to beat.

CHAPTER 12

THE ROAD AHEAD

Despite having 13 Grand Slam titles to his name, Rafa wanted more in 2014. He continued where he had left off in 2013 by winning the Qatar ExxonMobil Open in Doha and arrived at the Australian Open full of confidence.

Djokovic was the three-time defending champion but Nadal was fully focused on adding a second Australian Open title to his list of Grand Slams and becoming the first player to win each Grand Slam twice. He barely broke sweat in the first three rounds, losing just eighteen games across the three victories. His fourth round clash with Nishikori provided a sterner test, including two tie-breaks, but Nadal stood firm to win 7-6, 7-5, 7-6.

A stunning quarter-final round saw Murray, Ferrer and, more notably, Djokovic dumped out of the tournament. Meanwhile, Rafa had to dig deep to beat talented Bulgarian Grigor Dimitrov in four sets. Had the Bulgarian cashed in a routine chance on set point in the third set, the outcome could have been entirely different – and Nadal knew he had been fortunate.

'I was so lucky', said Nadal. 'Especially on one set point, he missed an easy one. The fourth set was for me and I'm very happy for that. I love this tournament. I'm very happy to be in the semi-finals after missing it last year.'

Nadal was troubled during the match by a large blister on his left hand that limited his groundstrokes and impeded his serve. With tape to protect the blister, he was able to battle on and would need to treat it carefully ahead of a mouth-watering semi-final against Federer.

The Swiss was enjoying a fine run in Melbourne but had fallen short against Rafa time and again in recent years. Nadal's game plan had left Federer stumped and even a number of different coaches could not help him to plot a successful counter strategy. The opening set would be crucial for the Swiss, who needed to keep the match – and the rallies – short.

A tight opening set went to a tie-break. Rafa had decent openings in the seventh and ninth games but did not dwell on the missed opportunities. Instead, he dominated the tie-break and, though Federer pegged him back at 5-4, Nadal produced the knockout blows to snatch the first set.

From there, the Spaniard never seemed like surrendering the advantage. A single break was enough to clinch the second set and, with Federer on the ropes, Nadal broke his serve at will in the third set to seal the victory. It was another indication that while the Nadal–Djokovic rivalry continued to wow fans, the Nadal–Federer rivalry was no longer the even battle that it had been four or five years earlier – Rafa simply had the Swiss player's number. Some of Federer's comments post-match, related to Nadal's grunting during points, suggested that the Spaniard was very much in his head.

Wawrinka – conqueror of Djokovic – had suprised many with his run to the final, making Rafa the overwhelming favourite to lift the trophy, given that this would be the Swiss player's first Grand Slam final. But, just as Nadal was powering into peak form, the Melbourne injury jinx struck again.

He strode out confidently for the final but during the warm-up he began to feel pain in his back, which got progressively worse once the match was underway. He did not have his usual mobility and Wawrinka simply hit him off the court on the way to a two-set lead. Clearly in agony, Rafa received treatment to try to ease the pain and refused to retire from the match, once again showing his remarkable fighting spirit as he held back his emotion. Somehow, he summoned the strength of mind to set aside the injury and win the third set 6-3, raising the possibility of an unthinkable comeback. But this was Wawrinka's moment and he recovered his poise to seal his first Grand Slam title.

Nadal was understandably tearful and disconsolate after seeing injury derail him yet again in Melbourne. He had little to say on the injury post-match as he struggled to deal with the cruel blow. 'It is a tournament that I really had some troubles physically in my career and is something that is painful for me,' he said. He preferred to give Wawrinka his moment in the spotlight.

Despite his understandable anger over the costly injury, the calendar was only just turning to February and there would be plenty more chances for Nadal to make his mark in 2014. The first priority was to go through the necessary rest and rehab – and then the clay court season would soon be looming on the horizon, providing Rafa with a chance to continue his domination on that surface.

By now, it feels as though Nadal has been on the scene for decades. Yet he is arguably entering his prime in his late twenties. And, despite all the Grand Slam titles and accolades, his desire to keep winning remains as strong as ever. He has already written himself into the history books - the big remaining question is whether he can strengthen his claim to being the greatest player of all time. If injuries do not rear their ugly head again, all the signs point to the Spaniard surpassing Federer's Grand Slam titles record and staying at the very top of the men's game.

While his on-court accomplishments are widely known, his humility and character off the court makes for an equally impressive story.

Perhaps the most interesting part of Nadal's rise to fame has been his success in remaining a grounded, well-liked individual. His popularity comes from his willingness to give up his time to talk with fans and the press as well as the general impression that he is a man with good values. Rafa will no doubt continue to do his family proud with his all-round attitude. Jeremy Bates, when working for the LTA, was bowled over by the Spaniard's modesty. Bates said: 'He has such a humble approach to the game. He does his own paperwork, books his own flights and arranges his own practice courts. He doesn't expect anyone to do things for him – it's just the way he was brought up.

'Three years ago, he had just won the French Open and he was coming over to get ready for Wimbledon. I got a call from the Nadal camp arranging practice courts and I expected it would be a coach or even his uncle Toni. The phone rang and when I answered a voice said "Hi, it's Rafael Nadal". He wanted to fix up some practice. I'll tell you what, there are hardly any players in the world who would have made that call. He is amazing – a superstar.'

Rafa also seems likely to keep up his commitments to his various sponsors. Since taking the tennis world by storm, his team have been inundated with offers from companies desperate to use Nadal's name and face for their product. Everyone wants to be associated with champions and it came as little surprise to see brands lining up for Rafa's services.

Nike remain a key sponsor and go to great lengths to make sure their client is happy with all his kit and equipment. The company have benefited massively from Rafa's triumphs in recent years and, with Federer also signed to the brand, tennis is a huge money-maker for Nike – having two of the world's best players on the books is certainly good for business. Morgan Shaw, a spokesperson for Nike, told the media: 'Nadal continues to be the cutting edge for fashion in tennis. We will continue to try new and exciting things on Nadal, as well as Federer in a more conservative way.'

Rafa's look was certainly different and the capris and vest – now replaced by the short-sleeved top – had proved a big hit with youngsters. He was cool in their eyes and it helped generate interest in tennis, not to mention merchandising profits for Nike. With every success, and especially after capturing Wimbledon and then an Olympic gold medal, the Spaniard has become a bigger face for the brand and has taken over the mantle from the likes of footballer Ronaldinho. Nike, like so many others, have their fingers crossed that Nadal stays injury free.

Nadal has signed other deals too which bring in more income and demand some of his attention during the season. Back in 2006 he made an agreement with Versaly Entertainment, a leading mobile media and entertainment company, for mobile phone wallpapers, ringtones, text messages and videos. Also during 2006, Rafa signed with Kia Motors, the Korean car maker, as a global ambassador. The role involved making appearances in advertising campaigns aired all over the world and supporting a variety of Kia schemes and motor shows. After sealing the deal, Nadal told the media: 'I am delighted to have this opportunity to represent a world class automaker such as Kia. I will do my best to promote the Kia brand across all of its key global markets by continuing to improve my play on the court.' More recently, he clinched a deal with PokerStars and has starred in a couple of commercials. He has also partnered with Babolat for many years for his racquets and tennis bags.

The offers are bound to keep pouring in as Rafa's career pushes on. Not only does Nadal win, but he wins in style. This makes him a very hot property. He is well aware of the dangers of taking on too many marketing distractions and his team are there to check he does not lose focus. He is already busy with advertising commitments for tour events as organisers know the importance of having Rafa's face on the posters. Sports shop windows also often display a photo of Nadal in action, catching the attention of eager customers. And every time he arrives at a tournament, he knows there are certain jobs that must be done such as conducting press conferences and TV interviews and ensuring that all his equipment is ready.

On the other hand, Nadal rarely finds such tasks a chore and he enjoys the chances to meet and chat to his fans at such sponsorship commitments. It is simply a case of finding an acceptable balance that does not interfere with his job on the court. Charity work will also figure in his plans, particularly putting time into his foundation.

Uncle Toni has been a great coach for Rafa to work with over the years, offering all the right advice and support off the court while still pushing his nephew to the limit. Possibly, he will follow that career path when he hangs up his racquet. Again, this is still a long way off but he loves the sport and, by then, will know all the tips for getting to and staying at the top. Of course, the big hope among tennis fans is that Nadal will bow out of tennis when he is ready to do so and not when injury dictates he must.

But the Spaniard has not shirked the topic and has been refreshingly honest about the possibility that his devotion to the sport might curtail his career. He told *TIME* magazine: 'I started playing very young, and if my career ends short, then it would be because I started playing younger than almost anyone else. My tennis is aggressive, though I wouldn't say that it's more physical than technical. I rely more on technique than physique, but being physical is always a help to me.'

Jeremy Bates is just one personality within the sport who predicted that Nadal's time at the top could be cut short by injury. Prior to the 2009 Australian Open, he said: 'How long can he keep it up? His style of play is so emotional, so committed.' Bates also pointed to Jim Courier and Lleyton

Hewitt as examples of players who reached the number one spot through sheer hard work and then fell away somewhat because they simply could not keep churning out gruelling victories.

The biggest joy that Nadal will get from finishing his playing career will be the opportunity to return to a quieter, more relaxed way of life with all his family. In some respects, he is a very private person. He and his girlfriend Maria Francisca Perello – nicknamed Xisca – have been together for many years yet she is rarely in the headlines. She prefers to avoid the media and the possibility of distracting Nadal, leaving Rafa to focus on his tennis. But she is never out of touch with her boyfriend's progress. The *Daily Mail* informed the British public of the relationship in June 2008, with many previously unaware that Nadal was a taken man. Xisca, like Rafa, is from Manacor and studied business in Palma. They are a good match – both are shy, unassuming and generous – and she does not go out of her way to seek publicity, defying some people's stereotype of WAG behaviour.

The *Mail*'s Angella Johnson quoted Toni Nadal as saying: 'I guess a lot of girls will be upset to know the truth. My nephew always maintained he was single. It was a well-kept secret but actually his girlfriend is waiting for him in Majorca.'

Mallorca seems to be the most obvious place for him to live when he retires and he will be able to spend more time with Xisca. He has already revealed – in his *TimesOnline* blog – that he would like to have two or three children in the future. And Nadal will certainly have financial security when he walks away from the game.

It will all come as quite a shock when he stops having to live out of suitcase and is not in a different part of the world each fortnight. He claims that he handles jet lag well but all the flying clearly takes its toll on all the players. And he rarely has the chance to explore the cities in which he is playing due to his consistently solid displays on the court. However, he has established some favourite restaurants around the globe, including Cambio de Tercio in London and Restaurante Napolitano in Paris. The tour has been wonderful for Rafa so far in so many ways and will no doubt continue to bring him high points. But there will be certain aspects of life as a top tennis player that he will not miss too much when he eventually calls a halt to his career.

When Nadal unwinds, he likes to take his mind off the ups and downs of the tour and relax. In the years ahead, he will have more time to savour his favourite films and shows. He enjoys watching DVDs, particularly *Prison Break* and *Lost*. In this sense, he is a typical young man. He is hooked on the same programmes as anyone else his age – he just has less free time to sit down and watch them. The gripping US thrillers make a welcome change from all the hours of footage that Rafa watches before facing each opponent.

The box-sets of these US shows travel in Rafa's bags on tour and come out of their cases at every opportunity. With the pressure and media attention, it is vitally important for him to have something to take his mind off the challenges ahead. He is also a big Playstation fan and, like so many youngsters, is often found taking on the best in the world on Pro Evolution Soccer. Playing on the Playstation is an essential part of Nadal's preparation for tournaments.

Rafa always stresses the point that he is just a normal guy.

Such an insistence makes him all the more likeable to neutrals but it is not just a publicity stunt. This is genuinely how Nadal is. He will watch DVDs just like the next person, he follows others sports closely and he also finds time to listen to music – his favourite artists include Bryan Adams and Bon Jovi as well as Spanish singer David Brisbal; and there will be nothing to keep him from watching important football matches when he retires from tennis. His interest in football goes deep. While Real Mallorca and Real Madrid are of course his favourites, he has also revealed his admiration for stars such as Cristiano Ronaldo, Thierry Henry and Frank Lampard. It is refreshing to hear him talk about fellow global stars with such awe, as though he is merely a sports fan.

Having decided on a career as a professional tennis player so early on, Nadal had never really weighed up many other options. Of course, he had to make the tricky choice between pursuing football or tennis, but he didn't ever make strides towards a different profession and so there is no obvious avenue that he will be eager to go back to explore that he was unable to in his youth. However, this could be a positive thing for the Spaniard. It gives him a totally free choice over which direction he goes in after tennis. There is no end of options.

One thing that is for sure, though, is that while Nadal will be greatly missed when he eventually retires from the sport, he will leave the game of tennis in a far greater position than when he entered it. His epic finals with Federer and Djokovic have illuminated the men's game and his domination on clay will surely not be seen again for many years. He has unquestionably captured the hearts of fans in numerous different ways. Injury is the one opponent that Nadal has struggled to shake off since breaking onto the scene and, so long as he stays healthy, he will have built a rock solid case for being the greatest player of all time.

THE TOP TEN – RAFA'S BIGGEST HITS

Rafael Nadal's career to date has been full of big performances and has brought trophy after trophy. These successes have come on a range of surfaces too. Clay is clearly still his preferred surface – and where he truly rules the roost – but the Spaniard has also thrilled crowds with some epic displays on grass and on hard court. It is no easy task to pick out his career highlights but here are the top ten Nadal matches:

10) Davis Cup final 2004, v USA (Roddick), W

Nadal forced his way into the Spanish team for the Davis Cup final and was a surprise selection for a singles clash against Andy Roddick. It was a daunting challenge for a young player but Rafa was sensational. He bagged a stylish 6-7, 6-2, 7-6, 6-2 victory and really showed the way for his team-mates. He was everywhere on the court, pinging unstoppable forehands and dominating on his serve. Roddick was stunned. It was an early indication of Nadal's bright future. The American would have expected to motor on to victory after bagging the first set but Rafa was brimming with self-belief and, with age on his side, he flourished as Roddick faded.

Nadal has always loved representing his country and here he thrived on the pressure rather than wilting. It was a special day for him and was the beginning of his fine Davis Cup record.

9) Wimbledon second round 2006, v Robert Kendrick, W
This match could have been the one that convinced Rafa that he could fight successfully on grass just like on clay. His spirit in storming back from a disappointing start was impressive, as was his unflappable demeanour in the face of intense pressure. Nobody gave Kendrick the slightest hope of pulling off an upset yet the American brought his A-game to the contest and began blowing Nadal off the court with some perfect groundstrokes that subdued the Spaniard's all-action style.

This was one of Nadal's most mentally challenging contests. The rain did not help matters either as he found himself constantly adjusting from one situation to another. Kendrick played out of his skin, taking a two-set lead, and it looked as though Rafa's dreams of winning Wimbledon would be over for 2006. Nothing was coming off for him. But the Spaniard showed his maturity and confidence by fighting his way back into a match that some players might have given up on. He had to take some risks along the way yet this did little to deter him. Nadal bagged the third set then levelled dramatically as Kendrick began to look out of his depth.

And Rafa cashed in on his clear momentum in the fifth and final set. The 6-7, 3-6, 7-6, 7-5, 6-4 victory owed much to Nadal's character and ability to produce his best tennis when the chips were down.

8) French Open final 2005, v Mariano Puerta, W

Nadal's clash with Puerta was his first Grand Slam final appearance. He was still coming to terms with life on the tour but Rafa had great self belief. Puerta might not have been the most intimidating opponent – however he had arrived in the final on merit and demanded respect. The Spaniard would have been forgiven for exhibiting plenty of nerves on such a huge occasion in his fledgling career. Yet he appeared to handle it brilliantly. He started with a little wobble but recovered expertly and simply had too much quality in the end for Puerta, clinching a 6-7, 6-3, 6-1, 7-5 victory and falling to the ground in celebration. Rafa had worked hard to be fully prepared for the event and now he was reaping the rewards as he lifted the trophy amid raucous applause from the fans. This win gave him the belief that he could win big matches. It kick-started his fabulous record at Roland Garros and fired him even further into the public eye. Nadal was not seeking media attention but after this win he got it whether he liked it or not. He was being billed as a fearless matador who was ready to conquer the world of tennis.

7) Olympic final 2008, Beijing, v Fernando Gonzalez, W

This is ranked in the top five more for the glamour of the occasion than the performance. Nadal has certainly played many better matches than this but his gutsy efforts at the

2008 Beijing Olympics won him the greatest of prizes. He will be able to look back with pride at his gold medal success for the rest of his life. Gonzalez troubled him at times but once Rafa had recovered from a stutter in the second set he was always on top. He simply closed the door on the Chilean. With such a massive global audience gripped to the action, Nadal put on a convincing show. He was already set to take over the world number one spot after the Olympics and this 6-3, 7-6, 6-3 triumph further enhanced his status.

He was on cloud nine after winning in Paris and Wimbledon and it was so long since he had lost a meaningful match that he was fully focused yet always quietly confident. Nadal had hoped to be fit for the 2004 Olympics in Athens but injury had stepped in to deprive him of the chance. Now, though, he had cashed in and he was heading home with the gold. The event was squeezed into the tight TV schedule but made compulsive viewing. He just tried to enjoy the moment, knowing that it was unlikely he would ever have a four-month spell to match this 2008 hot streak.

6) Wimbledon final 2007, v Roger Federer, L

Nadal's surging run to the final in 2006 had taken most tennis fans by surprise but there was something far more inevitable about his success a year later. He and Federer seemed to be on a predestined collision course and, to the delight of neutrals, the pair ended up in the final again. Rafa was admittedly still finding his way on grass but, despite giving up a lot to Federer in experience on the surface, he produced a phenomenal performance on one of the biggest occasions of his career. There was more belief in this effort too. The previous year, it had been a struggle and maybe the Spaniard did not truly believe he could win three sets against the champion. It was a different story in 2007 as Nadal trailed twice yet found a way to stay in contention and force a fifth set. Federer clinched the opening set in ominous fashion but it was quickly clear that Rafa would not be swept away. The Spaniard hit back ferociously, bagging the all-important break and levelling the match. The Swiss was unflustered and went back ahead. Nadal again answered the champion, hitting harder and running faster to take the match the full distance in front of a captivated Wimbledon audience.

As the match entered a fifth set it was impossible to suggest where the momentum lay or to pick a winner. It had been that tight. Nadal had several golden opportunities to take charge of the match – moments that would haunt him over the coming months – but could not convert them. And Federer punished him, ruthlessly claiming a 7-6, 4-6, 7-6, 2-6, 6-2 victory. It had been an amazing rollercoaster ride for both players – yet incredibly they managed to go one better the following year. Nadal had put in a superb display and went away knowing he was close to ending the Swiss' SW19 dominance.

5) US Open final, 2013, v Novak Djokovic, W

Nadal had made his mark at the US Open in 2010, completing his career Grand Slam, but the 2013 tournament represented a chance to make another statement in his return from injury. He was on a remarkable run, after wins at the Rogers Cup and Cincinnati.

Djokovic and Nadal were both in peak condition and this

contest contained countless lengthy rallies as both brought their A game. Rafa took control of the match by winning the opening set but was pegged back a Djokovic purple patch in the second set. As the match entered best-of-three territory, the Serb was in control but Nadal demonstrated again that he can endure tough patches and bounce back stronger. He turned the third set on its head, winning it 6-4, then powered to a 6-1 scoreline in the fourth set to seal the victory. It was a major statement - Nadal was back and as unstoppable as ever.

4) US Open final 2010, v Novak Djokovic, W

Heading into the second half of the 2010 season, the only trophy missing from Rafa's cabinet was the US Open crown. Time and again, he had arrived at the tournament exhausted after successful runs at Roland Garros and Wimbledon – but this time he was a man on a mission. A place in the history books awaited, with the chance to become the seventh man to complete a Career Grand Slam.

Rafa and his team worked hard to tweak his serve ahead of the tournament, with a sense that he would need to serve faster and more aggressively, and it paid dividends as he reached the final for the first time. Djokovic stood in Nadal's way but the Serb was yet to establish himself in the way that he would in 2011, making Rafa the clear favourite. Of course, naturally, there were nerves for the Spaniard with so much at stake but he started boldly, winning the first set, before Djokovic hit back to level after the players dealt with a frustrating rain delay. The Serb had battled through a five-set semi-final against Federer yet looked fresh as he pushed Nadal to the limit. But the Spaniard sensed that this was his moment, taking control of the third set and then powering through a dominant fourth set to claim the trophy 6-4, 5-7, 6-4, 6-2.

Cue emotional celebrations and the gradual realisation that he had finally conquered Flushing Meadows. At the age of just 24, Nadal had proven himself to be a master of all surfaces, completing his Career Grand Slam with a real flourish.

3) Australian Open final 2009, v Roger Federer, W

This heroic victory saw Nadal add hard court glory to his stunning resume and eat away further at Federer's self-belief. The Swiss' supremacy on the hard surface was a thing of the past now. Having outlasted Fernando Verdasco in a five-set semi-final - a performance that narrowly misses out on a place in this list - Nadal arrived in the final facing an in-form, fresher Federer. But the Spaniard used spurts in the first and third sets to take a two-one lead as he put a thigh injury to one side to keep pace with the Swiss. Rafa kept fans all over the world glued to their TVs with an all-action performance packed with thumping winners. And when it came down to a decisive fifth set, it was all Nadal. He believed in himself, he found the killer shots, he held himself together. Federer, meanwhile, unravelled in the face of yet more relentless Rafa hitting. As the Swiss fired long, Nadal could celebrate a sixth Grand Slam with a 7-5, 3-6, 7-6, 3-6, 6-2 victory.

It had been another epic encounter between two tennis players playing on a different planet from the rest of the field but Nadal's warrior-like display had given him the edge on the day and it provided a dream start to 2009.

2) French Open semi-final 2013, v Novak Djokovic

With Djokovic and Nadal continuing to be head and shoulders above the rest of the pack, their rivalry rose to the level of the Nadal-Federer rivalry. This clash at the French Open was a classic.

Rafa remained the best clay court player on the tour but Djokovic was gaining fast and had recorded a key victory in the build-up to Roland Garros. The momentum swung back and forth all afternoon, with Nadal winning the first and third sets but being pegged back on both occasions. Long, gruelling rallies thrilled the French crowd as Rafa fought to shrug off an opponent who was just as confident exchanging bombs from the back of the court.

Though Nadal had looked to be on the path to victory after winning the third set 6-1, Djokovic refused to wilt and forced a deciding fifth set. As the epic rumbled on and on, the Spaniard finally landed the knockout blow, clinching the decisive set 9-7 in what many called the greatest match ever played on clay. Despite the after effects of this marathon, Nadal marched on to lift the trophy for an eighth time.

1) Wimbledon final 2008 v Roger Federer, W

This was the day that Nadal shook up the tennis world and grabbed his first Grand Slam success away from Roland Garros. Not only was it arguably the best tennis match ever played but it was also the first concrete proof that Rafa was the best player in the world. He showed all his qualities on the big stage. He blazed into a two-set lead with some stunning shot-making then exhibited all his mental toughness to get over the line, despite being pegged back to two sets all. It was a great match played by two outstanding players.

Unlike the two previous years, Nadal got out to a fast start. It was a tight contest but Rafa stepped up and hit the big shots that earned him a two-set lead. Suddenly, he needed just one set out of three to knock Federer off his SW19 perch. The Swiss hit back as the match was hindered by several rain delays. Nadal refused to be bullied, though, and held his nerve on serve to force a third set tie-break. After some thrilling exchanges – which presented Rafa with a couple of great openings – Federer emerged as the victor, keeping his title chances alive.

Nadal battled on and, despite losing another tense tie-break, retained his belief that this could be his year. The only way that Federer seemed to be able to take a set was through a tie-break and there would be no fifth set breaker. It had come down to a deciding set and the Spaniard was ready for battle. Unsurprisingly, neither player let their standards drop. Eventually, after a titanic, unforgettable dogfight, Rafa emerged as the champion, winning the final set 9-7 as darkness closed in. Cue huge celebrations.

It was the final of all finals and one that would be discussed for years and years to come. And Nadal had come out on top. Sadly, though, it also marked the major high point before the injury curse kicked in and left the Spaniard fighting to stay healthy and save his career.